別冊 問題

大学入試 全レベル問題集

英語長文

4 私大上位レベル

三訂版

JN047123

Obunsha

大学入試　全レベル問題集　英語長文　レベル４［三訂版］ 別冊（問題編）

目 次

英文 1（東京理科大学）……………………………………… 2
〔全文通し〕◀)) 01

英文 2（中央大学）…………………………………………… 6
〔全文通し〕◀)) 05

英文 3（南山大学）…………………………………………… 8
〔全文通し〕◀)) 10

英文 4（茨城大学）…………………………………………… 10
〔全文通し〕◀)) 14

英文 5（大阪歯科大学）……………………………………… 14
〔全文通し〕◀)) 21

英文 6（青山学院大学）……………………………………… 18
〔全文通し〕◀)) 26

英文 7（立教大学）…………………………………………… 22
〔全文通し〕◀)) 37

英文 8（成蹊大学）…………………………………………… 26
〔全文通し〕◀)) 44

英文 9（法政大学）…………………………………………… 32
〔全文通し〕◀)) 53

英文 10（東京理科大学）……………………………………… 37
〔全文通し〕◀)) 65

英文 11（明治大学）…………………………………………… 44
〔全文通し〕◀)) 72

英文 12（津田塾大学）………………………………………… 50
〔全文通し〕◀)) 85

編集部より

問題を解くときには英文音声は必要ありませんが，復習の際にはぜひ音声を利用して英文の通し聞きを繰り返しおこなってください。語彙やイントネーションの定着に，音声を介したインプットは非常に効果的です。

次の英文を読んで，あとの問いに答えなさい。

　　The Modern Olympic Games were first held in Athens in 1896.　Although the games have had to overcome many difficulties, including wars and (1)boycotts, for the most part, they have been held every four years. In recent years, more countries have shown an interest in holding the Games as <u>there is an understanding that doing so could help attract tourists and generate income.</u>

　　Prospective host cities look to the many expected economic benefits and indeed many studies have shown some distinct economic advantages in staging the games. (**ア**) tourism development there are many other economic spin-offs such as (2)<u>infrastructure</u> development that have attracted the attention of many cities.　However, potential host communities need to pose the question of whether, in fact, these economic benefits are pragmatic and, (**イ**), the extent to which such benefits actually offset the costs.

　　Many of the economic studies on the Olympics have emphasized the long-term benefits such as newly constructed event facilities and infrastructure, urban revival, enhanced international reputation and increased tourism, (**ウ**) improved public welfare, additional employment, local business opportunities and corporate relocation.　In contrast, there are some potential negative impacts that need to be considered, for example the high construction costs of public sports infrastructure and all the needed supporting investments which can place a heavy burden on the government (3)<u>budget</u>.　Other problems include temporary crowding problems and property rental increases.　Nonetheless most host cities think the Games are a good bet.

問1 下線部(1)～(3)の単語の定義を完成させるために(　　　)に適切な語(句)を下の①～④から１つ選びなさい。

(1) boycott

A boycott is a (　　　) to buy, use, or participate in something as a protest or a punishment.

① contract　　② mission　　③ permission　④ refusal

(2) infrastructure

Infrastructure is the (　　　), such as transportation and power supplies, which a country or organization needs to function properly.

① demand for goods　　　② estimated cost
③ inflation rate　　　　　④ underlying foundation

(3) budget

A budget is the (　　　) available for a particular purpose.

① amount of money　　　② benefits
③ energy　　　　　　　　④ savings

問2 空所(ア)～(ウ)に入る適切な語句を下の①～④から１つ選びなさい。

(ア) ① By and by　　　　② On the other hand
③ In addition to　　④ Consequently

(イ) ① neither　　　　　② if people are
③ if they are　　　④ nor are they

(ウ)　① as well as　　　　② as many as

　　　③ as good as　　　　④ as long as

問3　二重下線部を日本語に訳しなさい。

_____

_____

問4　本文の内容と一致する文を2つ選びなさい。

① Many countries have felt that profits from the Games are likely to exceed costs and therefore want to host them.

② Many prospective host cities need to attract the attention of other cities to create infrastructure development.

③ The economic benefits prospective host cities expect from the Games have always proved to be an illusion.

④ Many economic studies have shown the benefits from hosting the Games will likely increase negative impacts.

⑤ Governments need to spend a lot of money to build facilities, roads and buildings which can cause many financial difficulties for cities.

⑥ An enhanced international reputation and improved public welfare will deprive the Olympic Games of the merits.

次の英文を読んで，あとの問いに答えなさい。

　　Mainstream free-market theory assumes that you are contributing to the society and the world in the best possible manner if you just concentrate on getting the most for yourself. (ア)When believers in this theory see gloomy news on television, they should wonder whether the pursuit of profit is a cure-all, but, instead, they blame all the bad things on market failures. They have trained their minds to believe that well-functioning markets simply cannot produce unpleasant results.

　　I think things are going wrong not because of market failures. The problem is much deeper than that. Mainstream free-market theory fails to capture the essence of what it is to be human.

　　In the conventional theory of business, we've created a one-dimensional human being to play the role of business leader. We've insulated him from the rest of life, the religious, emotional, political, and social. He is dedicated to one mission only — maximize profit. He is supported by other one-dimensional human beings who give him their investment money to achieve that mission. To quote Oscar Wilde, they know the price of everything and the value of nothing.

　　Our economic theory has created a one-dimensional world inhabited by those who devote themselves to the game of free-market competition, in which victory is measured purely by profit. And (イ)since we are persuaded by this theory that making money is the best way to bring happiness to humankind, we enthusiastically imitate the theory, striving to transform ourselves into one-dimensional human beings. Instead of theory imitating reality, we force reality to imitate theory.

問 下線部(ア)と(イ)を日本語に訳しなさい。

(ア)

(イ)

次の英文を読んで，あとの問いに答えなさい。

　　Being left-handed gives me some insights into what it is like to be a minority. That is because we lefties are （　ア　） against every day. Oh, it is not for serious things: we are not （　イ　） housing, jobs, medical care, or seats on a bus. However, we do （　ウ　） anti-lefty bias in ways right-handed people probably never realize. Did you know, for example, that shirt buttons and trouser zippers are （　エ　） for right-handed people? Most kitchen tools, as well — can openers, ladles and sauce pans, and various knives and peelers — are ineffective, awkward, or impossible to use （　オ　） the left hand. Every day in school we must put up with such things as desks, pencil sharpeners, scissors, cutters, and three-ring binders, all which （　カ　） the right-handed person. Musical instruments and sports equipment, too, are made for right-handed people. We must either learn to play right-handed or spend extra money to get things specially made for us — （　キ　） they are even available. Then there is the mechanical world. Vending machines, with the controls to the right, are a minor （　ク　）, but power tools can be dangerous for us.

　　Occasionally, however, there are a few advantages to being left-handed. In sports, particularly one-on-one situations such as tennis or boxing, we often have the advantage. That is because we are （　ケ　） to facing right-handed opponents, and so are our opponents. So, our left-handedness （　コ　） to confuse them. In baseball, as well, a left-handed batter is already one step closer to first base than a righty, which can make the （　サ　） between being safe or out on a close play.

　　So, would I want to be right-handed? The answer is simple: No! Left-handedness is part of my （　シ　）, myself. I would sooner cut off my right arm than be (ス) to right-handedness. Left-handedness is such an integral part of me that I could not imagine living (セ).

問 文章が完成するように，空所(ア)〜(セ)のそれぞれについて，①〜④のうちから最も適当なものを1つ選びなさい。

(ア) ① discriminated ② disciplined
    ③ disputed ④ distinguished

(イ) ① turned down ② rejected ③ denied ④ eliminated

(ウ) ① try ② associate ③ experience ④ contact

(エ) ① designed ② invented ③ aimed ④ ordered

(オ) ① by ② for ③ to ④ with

(カ) ① choose ② favor ③ prefer ④ support

(キ) ① if ② however ③ while ④ as

(ク) ① disturbance ② inconvenience
    ③ mistake ④ fault

(ケ) ① adapted ② achieved ③ accustomed ④ adjusted

(コ) ① tends ② tenses ③ treats ④ tries

(サ) ① distance ② difference ③ distinction ④ division

(シ) ① identity ② imagination
    ③ importance ④ independence

(ス) ① adapted ② converted ③ exchanged ④ transferred

(セ) ① whatever ② without ③ somehow ④ otherwise

(ア) ☐ (イ) ☐ (ウ) ☐ (エ) ☐ (オ) ☐

(カ) ☐ (キ) ☐ (ク) ☐ (ケ) ☐ (コ) ☐

(サ) ☐ (シ) ☐ (ス) ☐ (セ) ☐

次の英文を読んで，あとの問いに答えなさい。

The truth is, many of our daily actions and behaviors add greenhouse gases to the atmosphere, and (ア)it's not entirely our fault. Many of the technologies, institutions, and ways of living that we embrace today were designed and created before we understood what the consequences would be.

But in December 2007 at the annual United Nations Framework Convention on Climate Change in Bali, 200 of the world's leading climate scientists issued a major call to arms*. (イ)These scientists declared that we have only a small window* of time in which to reduce worldwide greenhouse gas emissions in order to prevent some of the drastic impacts of global warming.

In the next 10 to 15 years, they said, (ウ)emissions must begin to decline each year rather than grow — and by 2050, emissions must be *half* what they were in 1990. If we don't accomplish this, the scientists wrote, *many millions of people will be at risk from extreme events such as heat waves, drought, floods and storms, our coasts and cities will be threatened by rising sea levels, and many ecosystems, plants and animal species will be in serious danger of extinction.*

That's a lot to digest. But rather than being overwhelmed, let's start with what you can do today. One person can make a huge difference. (エ)Making changes in the way in which we live is key not only to our health and happiness — but to our survival as well.

Not too long ago, I decided to figure out just how much I personally was contributing to global warming by calculating my carbon footprint. The measure of our impact is often called a carbon footprint because carbon dioxide is the most common greenhouse gas.

Considering that I live in an eco-friendly apartment building, recycle, walk to work, and no longer own a car, I assumed my impact on the planet would be relatively low. It turns out that because I fly so often, my carbon footprint is much higher than I thought. Doing (オ)<u>this one simple exercise</u> quickly showed me changes I could make to lower my carbon footprint and inspired me to do more.

[注 *]　call to arms : an appeal to undertake a particular course of action
　　　　window : a period of time

問1 下線部(ア)の内容を日本語で具体的に説明しなさい。

_____

_____

_____

問2 下線部(イ)を日本語に訳しなさい。

_____

_____

_____

_____

問3 下線部(ウ)のようにしなければならない理由を日本語ですべて述べなさい。

_____

_____

_____

_____

問4 下線部(エ)を日本語に訳しなさい。

_____

_____

_____

問5 下線部(オ)の内容を日本語で具体的に説明しなさい。

_____

_____

_____

次の英文を読んで，あとの問いに答えなさい。

There are several issues raised by the technological revolution. The first is the merging* of technology providers. A single company can now provide access to television shows, telephone service, cell phone service, and the Internet. On the one hand, as communication media merge, more and more options become available to the home user at lower and lower prices. On the other hand, fewer companies own more of all media (radio, TV, newspapers, magazines). Some worry that this trend will eventually limit the variety of programs and points of view offered. For example, Clear Channel is a company that owns a large number of radio stations throughout the country. (ア)The owner has strong political views, and he has on occasion refused to play music of musicians who publicly criticized the president.

Another challenge is the effect of all this technology on children. Some worry that American children and young people are spending too much time watching television, using their computers, and playing video games. Clearly, they are not getting enough exercise, and the lack of physical activity has led to serious problems of childhood obesity and a sharp rise in the number of children with type 2 diabetes*.

Others worry more about the quality of what children are watching on TV and what they are seeing on the Internet. (イ)Americans face a constant dilemma — how to balance the right to free speech with the need to protect children and maintain standards of decency*. Because Americans place such a high value on individual freedom, particularly freedom of speech, they have traditionally been very hesitant to censor*, or even restrict, the flow of information by any means of communication. True censorship* occurs when the government sets the standard; Most Americans would prefer that the entertainment industry regulate itself, and the movie industry does have a rating system for films. Now that many American children have access to the Internet, there is a debate over whether and how to regulate it. For example, there have been arguments over whether public libraries should deny Internet users access to certain websites.

Finally, there is a concern about the growing "digital divide," the gap between Americans who own computers and those who do not. People who have more education and are higher on the socioeconomic scale are likely to spend less time watching television and more time on their computers. Many of those on the other side of the digital divide, those who do not own computers, live in poverty, and some belong to minority populations.

[注＊]　merging：合併

　　　　type 2 diabetes：２型糖尿病

　　　　decency：品位

　　　　censor：検閲する

　　　　censorship：検閲

問1 下線部(ア)を和訳しなさい。

問2 下線部(イ)を和訳しなさい。

問3 アメリカの子供たちの間で肥満や2型糖尿病が増えている原因を，本文にそって簡潔に説明しなさい。

問4 デジタル・ディバイド ("digital divide") とはどのようなものか，本文にそって簡潔に説明しなさい。

次の英文を読んで，あとの問いに答えなさい。

A study has revealed the surprising extent to which we rely on modern media. According to Ofcom*, the media regulator, the average Briton spends more than seven hours a day — or almost half their waking hours — watching television, texting, sending e-mails and reading newspapers. We are sending four times as many texts a day as in 2004 and spending almost a quarter of our time on the Internet on social-networking sites, the study found.

In total, an average person's digital day includes 173 minutes spent watching television, 62 minutes listening to the radio, 34 minutes reading e-mails, 31 minutes reading newspapers and 28 minutes making calls.

Buoyed by the success of shows such as *The X Factor* and *Britain's Got Talent**, we are watching more TV than at any time since 1992. Another study found that the average viewer tuned in for three hours and 45 minutes a day last year.

"Live evening TV still remains the main entertainment event of the day," said James Thickett, Ofcom's director of research. "Although mobile and computer use is up, families still like coming together into the living room to watch Simon Cowell* on big high-definition screens."

TV has also been boosted by strong growth in the use of digital video recorders — 37 per cent of households now own one — and the introduction of high definition.

"High definition has enhanced the viewing experience," Mr. Thickett said. "Even though investment in TV has fallen, the effect has been outweighed by high definition and digital video recorders."

More than five million homes now have access to HD* channels.

Helped by increasing numbers of mobile phone contracts that include "unlimited texting", consumers sent record numbers of texts last year. More than 100 billion messages were sent, equal to 1,700 for every person in Britain — a figure that is more than triple the number sent six years ago.

The study also offered a glimpse into a new Internet-enabled future, as it surveyed people aged 16 to 24. Unlike older generations, they spent more than half of their "media time" on computers and mobile phones, shunning television. They consumed less media output overall, at six hours and 35 minutes a day, but they multi-tasked more effectively — with two thirds of that time spent using more than one device.

If spread out, the total time spent by those aged 16 to 24 consuming media was just under ten hours. "We were really surprised at how many different types of media a teenager could use at once," Mr. Thickett said. "They'll use a computer and a mobile phone, or tweet when they're watching television."

[注＊]　Ofcom（通称オフコム）：英国における電気通信・放送等の規律・監督を行う規制機関

The X Factor ∕ Britain's Got Talent：どちらも英国の音楽オーディション番組

Simon Cowell：音楽オーディション番組の審査員で知られる音楽プロデューサー

HD：High Definition の略。テレビ等における高解像度（高精細・高画質）のこと

本文の内容に合致するように，(1)〜(5)の各設問に対する答えとして最も適当なものを①〜④の中からそれぞれ1つずつ選びなさい。

(1) According to the article, what would the correct ranking of time allocation (from the least amount to the most) for an "average Briton" be?

① telephone; newspapers; e-mail; radio; television

② television; e-mail; newspapers; radio; telephone

③ television; newspapers; e-mail; telephone; radio

④ telephone; e-mail; television; radio; newspapers

(2) According to the article, digital video recorders have resulted in an increase in what?

① multitasking   ② e-mail traffic

③ television viewing   ④ texting

(3) According to statistics used in the article, six years ago, Britons texted approximately how often per year?

① 560 times   ② 760 times   ③ 960 times   ④ 1,260 times

(4) According to the article, younger people engage in what kind of media-related behaviour?

① They illegally download their media content from the Internet.

② They text while driving — thus creating accidents.

③ They use TV and mobile phones far more than computers.

④ They use their mobile phones while watching TV.

(5) According to the article, the future trend in media consumption seems to point to what kind of model?

① One where TV is the centre of attention.

② One where various devices are employed simultaneously.

③ One where texting is charged on a per-message basis.

④ One where newspapers and radio play an ever-increasing role.

次の英文を読んで，あとの問いに答えなさい。

　　Well known for its annual floods, Bangladesh may seem the last place in the world to worry about a drying up of the rivers that flow from the Himalayas.　But the country is as much at risk from drought as it is from flooding.　Already farmers who used to grow rice have turned to farming shrimp because the water in their fields has turned so salty nothing will grow there. Bangladesh is the front line of global warming, with rivers drying up, and increasingly unusual weather conditions that include out-of-season tornadoes and tides that have stopped changing.　The entire country is one huge delta*, formed by the Ganges, Brahmaputra and Meghna rivers.　Flooding may seem to be Bangladesh's greatest enemy, but in fact the rivers are its lifeline. They are the main source of fresh water for a country where agriculture represents 21 per cent of the economy.　And environmentalists fear that if the Himalayan glaciers melt, the rivers' flow will decrease drastically.

　　Most people tend to think the main risk in Bangladesh is a (ア)catastrophic flood from rising sea levels.　But the country has a defense against that: a series of seawalls along the coast which should be able to (イ)withstand predicted rises in the sea level. There is no defense against drought.

　　Professor Ainun Nishat, one of the country's leading climate experts, says it is the melting of the Himalayan glaciers that worries him most — more than rising sea levels or changing local weather patterns.　"At the moment, we're probably seeing a slight increase in the river flow because of the glaciers melting," he says.　"But what happens in two to five years when the glaciers are gone?"　The northwest faced an unprecedented drought last year, after the annual rains failed completely.　Farmers had to

(ウ)resort to pumping ground water to survive, but they fear the ground water will dry up if the rains fail again.

In the southwest, trees in the famous Sundarbans National Park, home to the world's largest remaining population of wild tigers, are dying out — and falling river levels may be one reason. Bangladeshi scientists believe the trees are dying because of rises in salt levels in the mangrove swamps*. That could be because rising sea levels are flooding the swamps, but it could also be that the river flow has decreased in recent years.

So far, the reduction in flow is purely due to dam projects upstream in India. But experts fear the loss of fresh water would be far more drastic if the Himalayan glaciers melt and the rivers start to dry up. Already Bangladesh is fighting a losing battle against rising salt levels. Its farmers can only produce 8 tons of rice per hectare, compared with 17 tons in China.

Faced with potentially disastrous effects on agriculture, the country has come up with a (エ)strain of rice that grows in salty water. "We are fighting climate change on the front line," Professor Nishat told *The Independent* earlier this year. "But the battle has to be integrated across all countries." Bangladesh has good reason to feel angered over global warming. Its annual carbon emissions* total only 0.172 tons per person, compared to 21 tons in the US. If the rivers dry up, it would leave Bangladesh completely at the mercy of the rains.

[注＊]　delta：河口の三角州

　　　　mangrove swamps：マングローブの生える沼地

　　　　carbon emissions：排出される二酸化炭素

問1 次の①～⑦から本文の内容と一致するものを2つ選びなさい。

① Environmentalists fear that the melting glaciers in the Himalayas are causing floods in the deltas of Bangladesh.

② Farmers who had previously been growing rice are now raising shrimp in the salty water.

③ Flooding represents a greater risk to Bangladesh farmers than drought.

④ Last year, an unusually large amount of rainfall melted glaciers in the northwest of Bangladesh.

⑤ Ainun Nishat is encouraged by the increase in river flows from glacier melting.

⑥ The dams built in India are the main cause of the reduction in river flows in Bangladesh.

⑦ Climate change has had such an effect on agriculture in Bangladesh that new types of salt-resistant mangroves have been developed.

問2 文中の下線部(ア)～(エ)の意味に最も近い語(句)を,それぞれ①～④から1つずつ選びなさい。

(ア) ① continuous ② regular ③ terrible ④ worldwide
(イ) ① endure ② overcome ③ reach ④ understand
(ウ) ① dig away ② keep from ③ rely on ④ tend to
(エ) ① difficulty ② sound ③ type ④ worry

(ア)　　　(イ)　　　(ウ)　　　(エ)

次の英文を読んで，あとの問いに答えなさい。

The promise of self-driving cars can be attractive. Imagine taking a nap or watching a movie in a comfortable armchair while being shuttled safely home after a long day at work. But (ア) many over-optimistic images of the future, it is a bit of an illusion.

Automated cars may indeed make commuting more pleasurable while preventing accidents and saving many lives — someday. But (イ)a recent fatal crash suggests that some of these cars are not ready for the busy American roads: a lot of sensors and software turned this car into a high-tech vehicle you might see in a science fiction movie. In fact, (ウ)the technology that powers these vehicles could introduce new risks that few people appreciate. For example, when a computer controlling the car does not hit the brakes to avoid a car crash, the person in the driver's seat — many automated cars on the road today still require someone to be there in case of an emergency — may also fail to intervene because the driver trusts the car too much to pay close attention to the road. That is what appears to have happened in the crash.

"Technology does not eliminate error, but it (エ)the nature of errors that are made, and it (オ) new kinds of errors," said Chesley Sullenberger, the former US Airways pilot who landed a plane in the Hudson River in 2009 after its engines were struck by birds. He now sits on a Department of Transportation advisory committee on automation. "We have to realize that it's not a solution for everything."

What concerns him and other safety experts is that industry executives and government officials are rushing to put self-driving cars on the road without appropriate safeguards and under the (力) that the technology will reduce crashes and fatalities.

Even as officials (ぇ)place a big bet that autonomous cars will solve many of our safety problems, American roads are becoming less safe. More than 37,000 people were killed in 2016, up 5.6 percent from 2015. The death toll is estimated to be more than 40,000 in 2017.

Experts who are skeptical about the unstoppable march of technology say fatalities are rising because public officials have become so fond of the shiny new thing that they have taken their eyes off problems they could be solving today. In the federal government and most states, there appears to be little interest in making policies with proven track records of saving lives now, (ク)as opposed to some time in the distant future.

Other industrialized countries have made great progress in reducing traffic crashes over the last two decades. Road fatality rates in Canada, France, Germany and Sweden, for example, are now less than half the rate in the United States. And no, these countries don't have loads of self-driving cars. (ケ)They have reduced accidents in the old-fashioned way. Some of them have worked to slow down traffic; speed is a leading killer. They have made changes to roads so pedestrians will not have to pay much attention to cars. European regulators have encouraged the use of seatbelts by putting visual reminders even in the back seat. Germany requires much more rigorous driver education and testing than most American states do.

Mr. Sullenberger is worried that the rush to develop automated cars will lead to many unforeseen problems. "Even though there is a sense of urgency to prevent human-caused accidents, (コ)."

問 1 空所(ア)に入れるのに最も適切な語を次の①〜④の中から 1 つ選びなさい。

① as ② like ③ unlike ④ without

問 2 下線部(イ)の事故についてこれまでに判明したことはなにか。最も適切なものを次の①〜④の中から 1 つ選びなさい。

①人が乗っていない自動運転車両が起こした。

②道路を見ていなかった運転手に責任がある。

③コンピュータの誤作動によって引き起こされた。

④ その原因はまだ特定するまでには至っていない。

問 3 下線部(ウ)の意味に最も近いものを次の①〜④の中から 1 つ選びなさい。

① Few people express concerns about dangers introduced by the technology behind self-driving cars.

② Few people apprehend the new technology used in these modern, powerful vehicles.

③ The technology used in these new cars may cause accidents that are difficult to predict.

④ The technology applied to these modern cars is so powerful that they are unappreciated.

問4 空所(エ)と(オ)に入れるのに最も適切なものの組み合わせを次の①〜④の中から1つ選びなさい。

① (エ)introduces　　(オ)introduces

② (エ)introduces　　(オ)changes

③ (エ)changes　　(オ)changes

④ (エ)changes　　(オ)introduces

問5 空所(カ)に入れるのに最も適切なものを次の①〜④の中から1つ選びなさい。

① established theory

② concealed assumption

③ unproven hypothesis

④ misguided circumstances

問6 下線部(キ)の意味に最も近いものを次の①〜④の中から1つ選びなさい。

① are confident　　② are suspicious

③ do realize　　④ do not understand

下線部（ク）の書き換えとして最も適切なものを次の①〜④の中から１つ
選びなさい。

① although federal and state lawmakers have spent time
preparing bills to save lives in the future

② because experts have warned that there will be more serious
concerns about future risks

③ when public officials should oppose an increase in the future
death rate

④ but they nevertheless expect a bright future with no fatal
accidents

問8 下線部（ケ）にあるようなこととして，その直後の部分で実例が４つ挙げ
られているが，実はこのうち１つは例としてふさわしくないものに書き
換えられている。それはどれか。次の①〜④の中から１つ選びなさい。

① Some of them have worked to slow down traffic.

② They have made changes to roads so pedestrians will not have
to pay much attention to cars.

③ European regulators have encouraged the use of seatbelts by
putting visual reminders even in the back seat.

④ Germany requires much more rigorous driver education and
testing than most American states do.

問9 空所(コ)に入れるのに最も適切なものを次の①〜④の中から 1 つ選びなさい。

① the government is not working fast enough to fix these problems, nor is the industry

② the auto industry needs to make money, not in the future but now

③ self-driving cars should neither be banned, nor regulated, because of it

④ we need to do it in a responsible way, not the fastest way

問10 この記事のタイトルとして最も適切なものを次の①〜④の中から 1 つ選びなさい。

① Time for Automated Vehicles? Think First

② Making American Roads Safe Again

③ The Potential and Promise of Self-driving Cars

④ Old Versus New Ways of Traffic Control

次の英文を読んで，あとの問いに答えなさい。

In a first-of-its-kind study, some scientists compared four different items of polyester* clothing (including one blended with cotton) and how many fibers were released when they were being worn and washed.

The results showed that up to 4,000 fibers per gram of fabric could be released during a conventional wash, while up to 400 fibers per gram of fabric could be released by items of clothing during just 20 minutes of normal activity.

Scaled up, the results indicate that one person could release almost 300 million polyester （　**ア**　） per year to the environment by washing their clothes, and more than 900 million to the air by simply wearing the （　**イ**　）.

In addition, there were significant differences depending on how the garments were made; the researchers conclude that clothing design and manufacturers have a major role to play in preventing （　**ウ**　） from being emitted to the environment.

The research, published in the journal Environmental Science and Technology, was conducted by scientists at the Institute for Polymers, Composites and Biomaterials of the National Research Council of Italy (IPCB-CNR) and the University of Plymouth. It builds on their previous studies which showed large quantities of fibers are released during the laundry process.

Dr. Francesca De Falco, Research Fellow at IPCB-CNR said: "Recently, more evidence has been accumulating on the presence of synthetic microfibers not only in the water, but also in the air. That is why we decided to design this set of experiments to study microfiber released by garments to both environments. This is a type of pollution that should be mainly tackled at its source, the fabric itself, but we investigated the influence of different textiles on the release. Results have shown that tightly woven textiles can release fewer microfibers to both air and water."

The study compared four different garments, which were washed at 40℃ with any released fibers being collected. It showed that anywhere between 700 and 4,000 individual fibers could be released per gram of fabric during a single wash.

The researchers also created a (1)dedicated clean laboratory used by multiple volunteers wearing each of the four garments separately and then performing a sequence of movements simulating a mix of (2)real life activities. Any fibers emitted by the garments were then collected, with up to 400 being released per gram of fabric in just 20 minutes. The garment loosely woven with cotton and polyester showed the greatest release during both washing and wearing, with a tightly woven polyester one releasing the least quantity of microfibers.

However, based on the overall results, the researchers say that previous studies of microplastic pollution have actually (エ) the disadvantage of synthetic textiles since they did not take into account the quantities released directly into the air.

Professor Richard Thompson, Head of the University of Plymouth's International Marine Litter Research Unit, was a senior author on the current study and gave evidence to both the British Government's Sustainability of the Fashion Industry inquiry and a recent OECD* Forum in the garment and footwear sector.

He added: "The key story here is that the emission of fibers while wearing clothes is likely of a similar amount as that from washing them. That constitutes a non-neglectable* and previously unquantified* direct release to the environment. The results also show textile design can strongly influence both release to the (オ) and release due to laundering; that is a crucial message highlighting the importance of sustainable design for the fashion industry. Indeed many of the current issues associated with the environmental impacts of plastic items stem from a lack of comprehensive thinking at the design stage."

［注＊］　polyester：ポリエステル（化学繊維，合成繊維の一種）

　　　　OECD：経済協力開発機構

　　　　non-neglectable：無視できない

　　　　　＜neglect：無視する

　　　　unquantified：計量されていない，数量化されていない

　　　　　＜quantify：量を計る，数量で表す

問1 空所(ア)～(ウ)に入るものとして最も適切な組み合わせを，次の①～⑥より1つ選びなさい。

① ア garments　　イ garments　　ウ microfibers

② ア garments　　イ microfibers　　ウ garments

③ ア microfibers　　イ garments　　ウ garments

④ ア microfibers　　イ microfibers　　ウ garments

⑤ ア microfibers　　イ garments　　ウ microfibers

⑥ ア garments　　イ microfibers　　ウ microfibers

問2 下線部(1) dedicated の本文中の意味に最も近いものを，次の①～⑤より1つ選びなさい。

①寄付された　　②献身的な　　③贈呈された　　④純粋な　　⑤専用の

問3 下線部(2) real の本文中の意味に最も近いものを，次の①～⑤より1つ選びなさい。

① valuable　　② innovative　　③ ordinary　　④ unimaginable

⑤ vivid

問4 空所(エ)に入る最も適切なものを，次の①～⑤より1つ選びなさい。

① excluded　　② implied　　③ measured

④ overestimated　　⑤ underestimated

問5 空所(オ)に入る最も適切なものを，次の①～⑤より１つ選びなさい。

① air ② body ③ earth ④ mouth ⑤ water

問6 本文の内容と一致するものを，次の①～④より１つ選びなさい。

① 昔の洗濯機に比べて，最新式の洗濯機の方が，繊維を放出する量が10分の１なので，環境への害がより少ない。

② 合成繊維による大気汚染についての従来の知見が，今回の実験でさらに確認された。

③ 今回の実験結果によれば，織り方が密なポリエステルよりも，織り方が粗い綿・ポリエステル混合の方が，着用時に多くの繊維を放出する。

④ 環境保持のためには，洗濯時の繊維の放出量よりも着用時の繊維の放出量に注意すべきである。

Read the passage below and answer the questions.

The literary genre that is most directly related to science and technology is of course science fiction (SF). Fans of science fiction love reading the many detailed descriptions of science and technology, and the many, often precise, predictions about the future. Science fiction is also interesting because it shows society's attitudes towards technological development as well. Science fiction is not only a projection into the future, or into outer space, but it is also a reflection of ①contemporary society's cultural values towards technology.

Those values have been quite varied over the past two centuries. For example, the novels of Jules Verne in the second half of the nineteenth century expressed an optimistic view of technological progress. However, other writers have taken a more pessimistic view of technological progress. This can be seen in many of the SF movies from the later decades of the twentieth century, in which technological development is often shown as something (ア). The relationship between technology and culture is clearly quite complex. Science fiction has shown technological progress in both a negative and positive light. Stories about technological progress often swing between (イ), between celebration and warning. Furthermore, these two totally opposite attitudes are also mixed together in works of science fiction.

Works of science fiction have been influenced by many other literary traditions. For example, Francis Bacon's *New Atlantis*, published in 1627, was a work of both fantasy and science fiction. The story describes an ideal society in the future that was founded ②on the principles of science. The citizens of this imagined society enjoy the benefits of technological inventions including telephones and flying machines. It is a vision of discovery and knowledge. Creators of science fiction have also been (ウ) by traditional storytelling techniques. Many works of SF follow storylines that are typical of ancient myths and legends. For example, the movie *Star Wars* follows a traditional "hero's journey" storyline, a pattern ③(**1** ancient   **2** found   **3** in   **4** many   **5** myths). Another good example of ancient stories influencing science fiction is the Jewish legend of the *Golem*. The *Golem* is a clay figure that magically comes to life. This idea of objects ④(**1** came   **2** come   **3** coming   **4** has come) to life is quite similar to the many human-like robot characters that often appear in science fiction books and movies.

Science fiction emerged as a literary genre in the nineteenth century when writers began creating stories of wonder or horror in the context of science and technology. In SF, amazing things happen not by (エ), as in traditional narratives, but because of science. Typically, they are amazing stories, set in the future or some parallel world. Writers create stories, making predictions about the future based on scientific and technological concepts. Science fiction is a genre that expresses itself through the language of science.

Mary Shelley's character Dr. Frankenstein is a man of both ancient and modern science. Through a series of experiments, he discovers the secrets of life, and manages to create life itself. His creature is a technological ⑤copy of humanity, created in a laboratory. Shelley's story, written in 1818, is thus a journey of scientific discovery. The experiments described in the novel were based on the technologies of the early nineteenth century, and in particular the developing technology of electricity. The story is based on the idea that life itself might somehow be created using electricity. Yet Shelley's work is a reaction against technology. It shows technology in a negative light. Dr. Frankenstein's creation is a horrible monster rather than a perfect model of technology. It is a monster of science that ends up doing terrible things,

(6)ultimately killing its own creator.

The story of Frankenstein shows the dark side of technological progress. It shows its dangers. It is a classic story that carries with it a warning. Frankenstein's monster represents technology that (オ), that destroys its human creator. There are many variations on this basic pattern, particularly in the film versions of *Frankenstein*. At times the scientist is warm-hearted, and we can see his human side. At (カ) times, he is a man driven crazy by his own search for personal power and greatness. His great experiment is cursed by both bad luck and his search for power. While Frankenstein's monster is a caring and emotional creature who only wants to live and share his life with others, it is also capable of great destruction. However, its violence is generally directed against its creator. This is an often-seen pattern. The monster is the result of a scientific project that has gone horribly wrong and it punishes the man who pushed the science too far. Shelley's story is still relevant today, because it expresses a fear, as strong today as it was in Shelley's time, that human beings cannot always control the consequence of scientific development.

問1 From the choices below, choose the word to complete the definition of the underlined part ① in the passage.

contemporary: belonging to the (　　) time as something or somebody else

① next 　　　　② whole 　　　　③ same 　　　　④ only

問2 From the choices below, choose the phrase that best fits into the space (ア) in the passage.

① to guarantee 　　　　② to be feared

③ to promote 　　　　④ to be pleased

問3 From the choices below, choose the phrase that best fits into the space (イ) in the passage.

① fiction and cinema 　　　　② reflection and attitude

③ future and outer space 　　　　④ hope and despair

問4 From the choices below, choose the phrase that best matches the meaning of the underlined part ② in the passage.

① thanks to the improvement of science

② according to established rules or practices of science

③ for the sake of the acceleration of scientific advancement

④ at the cost of the latest scientific value

問5 From the choices below, choose the word that best fits into the space (ウ) in the passage.

① described　② imagined　③ influenced　④ included

問6 Arrange the words in the underlined part ③ in the passage so that it matches the following meaning:「古代の神話の多くに見られる」. Mark the 2nd and 5th words.

2nd ☐　5th ☐

問7 From the choices in the underlined part ④ in the passage, choose the word or phrase that best fits into the part.

問8 From the choices below, choose the word or phrase that best fits into the space (エ) in the passage.

① robots　　　　　　② magic
③ series of experiments　④ technological inventions

問9 From the choices below, choose the word that best matches the meaning of the underlined part ⑤ in the passage.

① electrician　② magician　③ double　④ printer

問10 From the choices below, choose the word that best matches the meaning of the underlined part ⑥ in the passage.

① deliberately　　　　② virtually

③ eventually　　　　　④ inevitably

問11 From the choices below, choose the phrase that best fits into the space (オ) in the passage.

① resembles ancient myths　② runs out of control

③ gives in to humanity　　　④ enters some parallel world

問12 From the choices below, choose the word that best fits into the space (カ) in the passage.

① another　　② other　　③ others　　④ none

問13 The following words all appear in the passage. For each group of words, choose the one whose primary stress is placed differently from the others.

A ① decade　　　　② manage　　　③ pattern　　　④ relate

B ① horrible　　　② imagine　　　③ invention　　④ reflection

C ① development　② technology　③ particular　④ scientific

A 　　　　　B 　　　　　C

問14 From the choices below, choose the two statements that most closely match the passage.

① Francis Bacon's *New Atlantis* describes the people in the 16th century whose lifestyle is inseparable from the benefits of science and technology.

② In terms of the attitudes towards technological progress, there is a difference between the novels of Jules Verne and many SF movies in the 1980s.

③ Jules Verne, Francis Bacon and Mary Shelley are all science fiction writers whose works have influenced ancient myths and legends.

④ Some readers love reading SF all the more for its complicated scientific descriptions of technology and predictions about the time yet to come.

⑤ The storylines of many SF works including *Star Wars* have nothing in common with ancient myths and legends.

⑥ The story of Frankenstein is a tragedy in the sense that Dr. Frankenstein had to kill himself to warn people of the destructive power of technology.

次の英文を読んで，あとの問いに答えなさい。

　　If you were to walk along the streets of your neighborhood with your face up and an open expression, how many of those who passed you would smile, or greet you in some way?

　　Smiling is a universal human practice, although readiness to smile at strangers varies according to culture. In Australia, where being open and friendly to strangers is not unusual, the city of Port Phillip, an area covering some of the bayside suburbs of Melbourne, has been using volunteers to find out how often people smile at those who pass them in the street. It then put up signs that look like speed limits, but tell pedestrians that they are in, for example, a "10 Smiles Per Hour Zone."

　　Frivolous* nonsense? A waste of taxpayers' money? Mayor Janet Bolitho says that putting up the signs is an attempt to encourage people to smile or say "G'day"— the standard Australian greeting — to both neighbors and strangers as they stroll down the street. Smiling, she adds, encourages people to feel more connected with each other and safer, so it reduces fear of crime — an important element in the quality of life of many neighborhoods.

　　In a related effort to get its residents to know each other, the city government also facilitates street parties. It leaves the details to the locals, but offers organizational advice, lends out barbecues and sun umbrellas, and covers the public liability insurance*. Many people who have lived in the same street for many years meet each other for the first time at a street party.

　　All of this is part of a larger program that attempts to measure changes in the city's quality of life, so that the city council can know whether it is taking the community in a desirable direction. The council wants Port Phillip to be a sustainable community, not merely in an environmental sense, but also in terms of social equity, economic viability, and cultural vitality.

Port Phillip is serious about being a good global citizen. Instead of seeing private car ownership as a sign of prosperity, the city hails a *declining* number of cars — and rising use of public transport — as a sign of progress in reducing greenhouse gas emissions while encouraging a healthier lifestyle in which people are more inclined to walk or ride a bike. The city is also seeking designs for new buildings that are more energy efficient.

Some local governments see their role as being to provide basic services like collecting the trash and maintaining the roads — and of course, collecting the taxes to pay for this. Others promote the area's economy, by encouraging industry to move to the area, thus increasing jobs and the local tax base. The Port Phillip city government takes a broader and longer-term view. It wants those who live in the community after the present generation has gone to have the same opportunities for a good quality of life as today's residents have. To protect that quality of life, it has to be able to measure all the varied aspects that contribute to it — and friendliness is one of them.

For many governments, both national and local, preventing crime is a far higher priority than encouraging friendship and cooperation. But, as Professor Richard Layard of the London School of Economics has argued in his recent book *Happiness: Lessons from a New Science*, promoting friendship is often easy and cheap, and can have big payoffs in making people happier. So why shouldn't that be a focus of public policy?

Very small positive experiences can make people not only feel better about themselves, but also be more helpful to others. In the 1970s, American psychologists Alice Isen and Paula Levin conducted an experiment in which some randomly selected people making a phone call found a ten-cent coin left behind by a previous caller, and others did not. All subjects were then given an opportunity to help a woman pick up a folder of papers she dropped in front of them.

Isen and Levin claimed that of the 16 who found a coin, 14 helped the woman, while of the 25 who did not find a coin, only one helped her. A further study found a similar difference in willingness to mail an addressed letter that had been left behind in the phone booth: those who found the coin were more likely to mail the letter.

Although later research has cast doubt on the existence of such dramatic differences, there is little doubt that being in a good mood makes people feel better about themselves and more likely to help others. Psychologists refer to it as the "glow of goodwill." Why shouldn't taking small steps that may produce such a glow be part of the role of government?

Here is one measure of success: over the past year and a half, the proportion of people who smile at you in Port Phillip has risen, from 8 percent to 10 percent.

(出典：Peter Singer, "No Smile Limit," *Ethics in the Real World: 86 Brief Essays on Things That Matter*, The Text Publishing Company, 2016)

[注＊]　frivolous：くだらない

　　　　liability insurance：賠償責任保険

（1）　問1〜4の質問に対する答えとして，最も適切なものをそれぞれ1つ選びなさい。

問1 In the second paragraph, what does the author mean when he states that smiling is a universal human practice?

① Humans are not naturally good at smiling.

② Humans learn how to smile properly.

③ Our universe requires smiling humans.

④ Smiling is something that all humans do.

問2 Why does the city government facilitate street parties in Port Phillip?

① To give people a chance to interact with their neighbors.

② To improve neighborhood organizational advice.

③ To provide food to people in its neighborhoods.

④ To teach people how to be happy at neighborhood parties.

問3 Based on the article, which of the following would the Port Phillip city government likely prefer its residents do?

① Stay home if they cannot travel to street parties by using public transport.

② View private car ownership as something to be avoided if possible.

③ Inform the city government about the details of their street parties.

④ Stop walking or riding bicycles to buildings that are not energy efficient.

問4 According to the article, which of the following affects neighborhood quality of life?

① How long the street parties last.

② How much volunteers are paid with taxpayer money.

③ How often greeting standards like "G'day" are used.

④ How safe residents feel living there.

(2) 本文の内容に即して，問5〜8の英文を完成させるのに最も適切なものをそれぞれ1つ選びなさい。

問5 If you walk with your face up and have an open expression in Port Phillip, then you will probably be thought of as being

① sensitive and shocked to meet new people.

② decisive and determined to be judged by people.

③ approachable and approving of others.

④ recognizable and ready to debate with strangers.

問6 It is understood that the Port Phillip police cannot give fines or arrest pedestrians for not smiling in a "10 Smiles Per Hour Zone" because

① it is simply impossible for anyone to smile that much in an hour.

② it is too difficult for the police to confirm if all pedestrians are actually smiling.

③ the police are not allowed to attend any neighborhood street parties.

④ those pedestrians would not be breaking any laws.

問7 In the research conducted by Isen and Levin, the finding of money in a phone booth is meant to represent

① a positive experience.　② a random selection.

③ an act of theft.　④ an opportunity for friendship.

問8 The Port Phillip city government's program to change the city's quality of life is likely working because people there

① glow brightly with goodwill.

② have been found to smile more now than they did previously.

③ calculate their yearly success rates of smiles.

④ are more willing than ever to mail addressed letters whenever coins are found.

次の英文を読んで，あとの問いに答えなさい。

　　Many languages in the world are gradually **[(a) die]**, but at least one has recently been born, created by children living in a remote village in northern Australia.　A linguist* called Dr. O'Shannessy has been studying the young people's speech in that area for more than a decade and has recently concluded that they speak neither a dialect nor the mixture of languages called a creole*, but a new language with unique grammatical rules.

　　This new language, known as Light Warlpiri, is spoken only by people under 35 in a village of about 700 people in Australia, called Lajamanu.　In all, about 350 people speak the language as their native tongue.　Mary Laughren, another linguist, values Dr. O'Shannessy's research because "many of the first speakers of this language are still alive," and because "she has been able to record and document a 'new' language in the very early period of its existence."

　　Everyone in the village also speaks "strong" Warlpiri, an aboriginal* language unrelated to English and shared with about 4,000 people in several Australian villages.　Many also speak Kriol, an English-based creole developed in the late 19th century and widely spoken in northern Australia among aboriginal people with many different native languages.　The villagers are happy to have their children learn English for use in the wider world, but they are also eager to preserve "strong" Warlpiri as the language of their culture.

　　The village's remoteness may have something to do with the creation of a new way of speaking.　Lajamanu is about 550 miles south of Darwin, and the nearest commercial center is Katherine, about 340 miles north.　An airplane lands on the village's dirt landing field twice a week carrying mail from Katherine, and once a week a truck brings food and supplies that are sold in the village's only store. Oil and solar energy supply electricity.

Lajamanu was established by the Australian government in 1948, without the consent of the people who would inhabit it. The native affairs branch of the federal government, concerned about an excess of people and a lack of rain in one area, removed 550 people from there by force to the place where the village is now. At least twice, the group walked all the way back to where they used to live, only to be transported back when they arrived. By the 1970s, villagers had (ア)resigned themselves to their new home, and a new council had been set up as a self-governing community authority.

Dr. O'Shannessy, who started investigating the language in 2002, spends three to eight weeks a year in the village. She speaks and understands both "strong" Warlpiri and Light Warlpiri, but is not fluent in either of them.

People in the village often (イ)engage in what linguists call code-switching, mixing languages together or switching from one to another as they speak. And many words in Light Warlpiri are derived from English or Kriol. But Light Warlpiri is not simply a combination of words from different languages. Peter Bakker, a professor of language development, observes that "These young people have developed something entirely new. Light Warlpiri is clearly a mother tongue."

Dr. O'Shannessy offers this example, spoken by a 4-year-old (an English translation is given below the example):

Nganimpa-ng gen wi-m si-m worm mai aus-ria. (Light Warlpiri)
We also saw worms at my house. (English)

It is easy enough to see several words derived from English. But the -ria ending on aus (house) means "in" or "at," and it comes from "strong" Warlpiri. The -m ending on the verb si (see) indicates that the event is either happening now or has already happened, a "present or past but not future" tense that does not exist in English or "strong" Warlpiri. This is a way of talking so different from either "strong" Warlpiri or Kriol that it constitutes a new language.

The development of the language, Dr. O'Shannessy says, was a two-step process. It began with parents using baby talk with their children in a combination of the three languages. But then the children took that language as their native tongue by adding (ウ)radical changes to the grammar, especially in the use of verb structures that are not present in any of the source languages.

Why a new language developed at this time and in this place is not entirely clear. It was not a case of people needing to communicate when they have no common language, a situation that can give rise to a creole. New languages are discovered from time to time, but until now no one has been there at the beginning to see a language develop from children's speech. Dr. O'Shannessy suggests that subtle forces may be at work. "I think that identity plays a role," she said. "After children created the new system, it became a mark of their identity as being young Warlpiri from the Lajamanu community."

The language is now so well established among young people that there is some question about the 【(b) survive】 of "strong" Warlpiri. "How long the kids will keep their ability to speak two or more languages, I don't know," Dr. O'Shannessy said. "The elders would like to preserve "strong" Warlpiri, but I'm not sure it will happen. Light Warlpiri seems quite strong."

[注＊]　linguist：言語学者

creole：クレオール言語。主にヨーロッパ言語などと現地語との混成語として作られ，その子供たちの世代が母語として話すようになった言語

aboriginal：オーストラリア先住民の

問1 本文の[　　]内の(a)および(b)の語を必要に応じて適切な形に変えて書き
なさい。

(a) _____　　(b) _____

問2 下線を付した (ア)〜(ウ) について，それぞれ最も近い意味の語(句)を①
〜④の中から選び，その番号を書きなさい。

(ア) resigned themselves to
① happily accepted　　　　　② unhappily accepted
③ unwillingly left their jobs for　④ willingly left their jobs for

(イ) engage in
① attract attention with　　② have arguments with
③ jointly anticipate　　　　④ participate in

(ウ) radical
① major　　② realistic　　③ sensitive　　④ unusual

次の 1〜4 について，それぞれ①〜④の中から本文の内容に最もよく合うものを選び，その番号を書きなさい。

1. Why is Dr. O'Shannessy's research on Light Warlpiri significant?

   ① Light Warlpiri is being used widely in northern Australia.

   ② Many people have information about this language.

   ③ New aboriginal languages have not been discovered since 1948.

   ④ She has been able to study this language so soon after its birth.

2. Which of these statements about Light Warlpiri is correct?

   ① Children are not willing to speak the language at home.

   ② Many of its words have their origins in English or Kriol.

   ③ The language is categorized as a kind of Kriol.

   ④ The language is spoken by around 700 people.

3. What makes the grammar of Light Warlpiri different from other locally spoken languages?

   ① It has a "present or past but not future" tense.

   ② It has a simplified grammar as often seen in baby talk.

   ③ It has many words that begin with "si."

   ④ It has no "strong" Warlpiri word endings.

4. Dr. O'Shannessy says that Light Warlpiri is "quite strong" in Lajamanu. Which of the following factors contributes to its strength, according to the passage?

    ① It is based on "baby talk," which children speak to their parents.

    ② Speakers of Light Warlpiri get a sense of identity from speaking it.

    ③ There are now fewer speakers of "strong" Warlpiri than of Light Warlpiri.

    ④ Villagers lack opportunities to speak other languages that they know.

問4 ラジャマヌ (Lajamanu) という共同体で新しいライト・ワルピリ語 (Light Warlpiri) が生まれ，広まりつつある背景には，どのような要因がありますか。本文の内容に即して 80 字程度の日本語で説明しなさい。

_____

_____

_____

_____

_____

_____

問5 下線部を日本語に訳しなさい。

_____

_____

_____

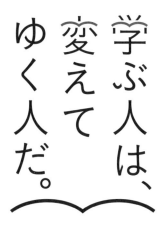

学ぶ人は、
変えて
ゆく人だ。

目の前にある問題はもちろん、

人生の問いや、

社会の課題を自ら見つけ、

挑み続けるために、人は学ぶ。

「学び」で、

少しずつ世界は変えてゆける。

いつでも、どこでも、誰でも、

学ぶことができる世の中へ。

旺文社

大学入試 全レベル問題集

英語長文

駿台予備学校講師 三浦淳一 著

4 私大上位レベル

三訂版

はじめに

　大学受験に向けた英語学習は，書店の学習参考書コーナーに行けばすぐにわかるとおり，とても細分化されています。単語・熟語，文法・語法，構文，英作文，長文読解，リスニング，会話表現，発音・アクセント…

　これを1つずつやっていたら，何年かかっても終わりそうにありません。

　「一石二鳥」という言葉がありますが，短期間で英語の学習を仕上げるには，いわば「一石五鳥」「一石六鳥」の学習をすることです。つまり，1つの学習で複数の効果を得られるような学習をすべきなのです。

　『大学入試 全レベル問題集　英語長文』シリーズは，長文読解の問題集という形をとっていますが，これにとどまらず，語彙力をつけたり，重要な文法事項の確認をしたり，音声を用いた学習により，発音・アクセント，リスニングの力をつけることも目指しています。

　本シリーズはレベル別に6段階で構成されており，必ず自分にピッタリ合った1冊があるはずです。また，現時点の実力と志望校のレベルにギャップがあるなら，1〜2段階レベルを下げて，英語力を基礎から鍛え直すのもおすすめです。受験生はもちろん，高校1・2年生からスタートすることもできます。

　本シリーズは最新の大学入試問題の傾向に対応し，さらに，英語4技能（Reading / Listening / Writing / Speaking）を今後ますます重視する入試制度にも対応しうる，本質的・普遍的な英語力をつけることを目的にしています。

　本シリーズを利用して，皆さんが第一志望の大学に合格することはもちろん，その先，一生の武器となる確固たる英語力を身につけてほしいと願っています。

三浦　淳一

目　次

本シリーズの特長 ……………………………………………………………… 4

志望大学別　入試長文分析と学習アドバイス ………………………… 6

英文を読むための基礎知識 ……………………………………………… 12

英文 1 （東京理科大学）……………………………………………… 14

英文 2 （中央大学）……………………………………………………… 26

英文 3 （南山大学）……………………………………………………… 38

英文 4 （茨城大学）……………………………………………………… 48

英文 5 （大阪歯科大学）……………………………………………… 60

英文 6 （青山学院大学）……………………………………………… 72

英文 7 （立教大学）……………………………………………………… 85

英文 8 （成蹊大学）……………………………………………………… 98

英文 9 （法政大学）…………………………………………………… 115

英文 10 （東京理科大学）…………………………………………… 132

英文 11 （明治大学）…………………………………………………… 152

英文 12 （津田塾大学）……………………………………………… 172

音声について

本書の英文を読み上げた音声を，専用ウェブサイト・スマートフォンアプリで聞くことができます。英文ごとに，2種類の音声を収録しています。全文通し読みの音声と，段落ごとに区切ったややゆっくりめの音声があります。段落ごとに区切った音声は，ディクテーションでご利用ください。◀》 01 のように示しています。

●ウェブサイトで聞く方法

・以下のサイトにアクセスし，パスワードを入力してください。
　https://service.obunsha.co.jp/tokuten/zlr3/
　※すべて半角英数字。検索エンジンの「検索欄」は不可。
　パスワード：zlr3f
・右上の QR コードからもアクセスできます。

●スマートフォンアプリで聞く方法

・音声をスマートフォンアプリ「英語の友」で聞くことができます。「英語の友」で検索するか，右下の QR コードからアクセスしてください。
・パスワードを求められたら，上と同じパスワードを入力してください。

△ご注意ください　◆音声を再生する際の通信料にご注意ください。◆音声は MP3 形式となっています。音声の再生には MP3 を再生できる機器などが別途必要です。デジタルオーディオプレーヤーなどの機器への音声ファイルの転送方法は，各製品の取り扱い説明書などをご覧ください。ご使用機器，音声再生ソフトなどに関する技術的なご質問は，ハードメーカーもしくはソフトメーカーにお問い合わせください。◆スマートフォンやタブレットでは音声をダウンロードできないことがあります。◆本サービスは予告なく終了することがあります。

本シリーズの特長

「大学入試 全レベル問題集 英語長文」シリーズには，以下の特長があります。

1．細かく分かれたレベル設定
本シリーズはレベル別からなる6冊で構成されており，学習者の皆さんそれぞれがベストな1冊を選んで大学入試対策をスタートできるようにしています。各書がレベルに応じた収録英文数と設問構成になっています。

2．語彙力を重視
語彙力は語学学習における基本です。単語がわからなければ英文を読むにも書くにも不自由します。本書ではオールラウンドな語彙力をつけられるよう，幅広いテーマの英文を選びました。各ユニットの最後に，本文の単熟語や英文が復習できる確認問題や，音声を利用した単語のディクテーション問題を設け，語彙力が増強できるよう工夫しています。

3．英文構造の明示
すべての英文の構造を示し（ＳＶＯＣ分析），英文を完全に理解できるようにしました。さらに，本文の和訳例も，あまり意訳をせず，文構造を反映させた直訳に近い日本語にしました。

4．文法事項のわかりやすい解説
近年の入試問題では，難関大学を中心に文法問題の出題が減少しており，「文法問題を解くための文法学習」は，もはや時代遅れです。本書では「英文を正しく読むための文法」を心がけて解説しています。

5．設問の的確な解説
すべての設問に，なるべく短く的確な解説をつけました。特に本文の内容に関する設問は，根拠となる箇所を明示して解説しています。類書と比較しても，わかりやすく論理的な解説にしています。これは，解説を読んで納得してほしいということもありますが，それ以上に，読者の皆さんが自分で問題を解くときにも，このように論理的に考えて，正解を導き出せるようになってほしいからです。

6．音声による学習
付属の音声には本書に掲載した英文の音声が2パターンで収録されています。主にリスニング力UPを目的としたナチュラルに近いスピードのものは，シャドーイング*1やオーバーラッピング*2用です。また1つ1つの単語の発音がわかるようなややゆっくりしたスピードのものは，ディクテーション問題用です。

> *1　シャドーイング・・・すぐ後から音声を追いかけて，同じ内容を口に出す練習方法
> *2　オーバーラッピング・・・流れてくる音声とぴったり重なるように口に出す練習方法

著者紹介：**三浦淳一**（みうら じゅんいち）

早稲田大学文学部卒。現在，駿台予備学校・医学部受験専門予備校 YMS 講師。『全国大学入試問題正解 英語』（旺文社）解答・解説執筆者。『入門　英語長文問題精講 [3訂版]』『医学部の英語』『大学入学共通テスト 英語〔リーディング〕集中講義』（以上，旺文社），『世界一覚えやすい中学英語の基本文例100』（以上，KADOKAWA）ほか著書多数。「N 予備校」「学びエイド」などで映像授業も担当する。

〔協力各氏・各社〕

装丁デザイン：ライトパブリシティ	録音・編集：ユニバ合同会社
本文デザイン：イイタカデザイン	ナレーション：Ann Slater, Guy Perryman, Katie Adler
校　　　　正：大磯巖，笠井嘉雄 (e.editors)，武田裕之，大河恭子，Jason A. Chau	編 集 協 力：株式会社カルチャー・プロ
	編 集 担 当：清水理代

志望校レベルと「全レベル問題集 英語長文」シリーズのレベル対応表

＊ 掲載の大学名は本シリーズを購入していただく際の目安です。また, 大学名は刊行時のものです。

本書のレベル	各レベルの該当大学
① 基礎レベル	高校基礎〜大学受験準備
② 共通テストレベル	共通テストレベル
③ 私大標準レベル	日本大学・東洋大学・駒澤大学・専修大学・京都産業大学・近畿大学・甲南大学・龍谷大学・札幌大学・亜細亜大学・國學院大學・東京電機大学・武蔵大学・神奈川大学・愛知大学・東海大学・名城大学・追手門学院大学・神戸学院大学・広島国際大学・松山大学・福岡大学 他
④ 私大上位レベル	学習院大学・明治大学・青山学院大学・立教大学・中央大学・法政大学・芝浦工業大学・成城大学・成蹊大学・津田塾大学・東京理科大学・日本女子大学・明治学院大学・獨協大学・北里大学・南山大学・関西外国語大学・西南学院大学 他
⑤ 私大最難関レベル	早稲田大学・慶應義塾大学・上智大学・関西大学・関西学院大学・同志社大学・立命館大学 他
⑥ 国公立大レベル	北海道大学・東北大学・東京大学・一橋大学・東京工業大学・名古屋大学・京都大学・大阪大学・神戸大学・広島大学・九州大学 他

本書で使用している記号一覧

Check! ……………… 文法事項の説明
🔊 ……………… 音声番号

SVOC分析

S, V, O, C ……… 主節における文の要素

S, V, O, C ……… 従属節における文の要素

S′, V′, O′, C′ …… 意味上の関係

① ② ③ ………… 並列関係にある要素

〈 　 〉………… 名詞句, 名詞節

〔 　 〕………… 形容詞句, 形容詞節

(　) ………… 副詞句, 副詞節

関代 …………… 関係代名詞

関副 …………… 関係副詞

等接 …………… 等位接続詞

従接 …………… 従属接続詞

疑 ……………… 疑問詞

… so 〜 that … 相関語句

語句リスト

動 ……………… 動詞

名 ……………… 名詞

形 ……………… 形容詞

副 ……………… 副詞

接 ……………… 接続詞

前 ……………… 前置詞

熟 ……………… 熟語

志望大学別 入試長文分析と学習アドバイス

大学名	学習院大学	明治大学	青山学院大学
英文レベル	★2.4　1……2……3……4	★2.5　1……2……3……4	★2.4　1……2……3……4
出題ジャンル	科学・技術2.8%　産業2.8%　自然19.4%　文化30.6%　社会19.4%　日常生活25.0%	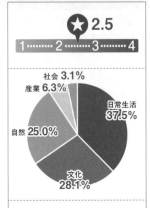社会3.1%　産業6.3%　日常生活37.5%　自然25.0%　文化28.1%	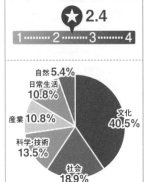自然5.4%　日常生活10.8%　文化40.5%　産業10.8%　科学・技術13.5%　社会18.9%
	長文問題の平均出題大問数　**3.0 問**	長文問題の平均出題大問数　**2.1 問**	長文問題の平均出題大問数　**2.47 問**
	長文1題あたり平均語数　**566 語**	長文1題あたり平均語数　**914 語**	長文1題あたり平均語数　**827 語**
設問形式	☑ 内容一致（選択式） ☐ 内容一致（ T or F ） ☑ 空所補充 ☑ 下線部言い換え ☐ 表題選択 ☑ 下線部和訳 ☐ 記述説明 ☑ その他	☑ 内容一致（選択式） ☐ 内容一致（ T or F ） ☑ 空所補充 ☑ 下線部言い換え ☐ 表題選択 ☑ 下線部和訳 ☑ 記述説明 ☑ その他	☑ 内容一致（選択式） ☑ 内容一致（ T or F ） ☑ 空所補充 ☑ 下線部言い換え ☑ 表題選択 ☑ 下線部和訳 ☑ 記述説明 ☑ その他
三浦先生Check！	空所補充, 内容一致, 指示語など多種多様な出題形式。記述問題が出題され, 字数制限のある和訳問題が特徴的。	下線部言い換えや内容一致を中心とした出題。一部の学部で記述問題も。分量が多いのでスピードが重要。	内容理解を問う問題が中心。一部の学部でグラフなどの資料も。下線部和訳が出るのが特徴。

※T or F：内容真偽判定問題

立教大学	中央大学	法政大学

★2.1
1……2……3……4

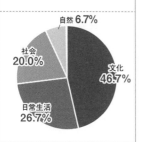

自然 6.7%
社会 20.0%
文化 46.7%
日常生活 26.7%

長文問題の平均出題大問数
3.0 問

長文1題あたり平均語数
820 語

- ☑ 内容一致（選択式）
- ☐ 内容一致（T or F）
- ☑ 空所補充
- ☑ 下線部言い換え
- ☑ 表題選択
- ☑ 下線部和訳
- ☐ 記述説明
- ☑ その他

個別試験での英語は文学部のみ。段落ごとに内容理解を問う問題が中心。まず設問に目を通してから本文を読むのが効率的。

★2.7
1……2……3……4

産業 5.0%
自然 10.0%
社会 10.0%
文化 45.0%
日常生活 30.0%

長文問題の平均出題大問数
2.5 問

長文1題あたり平均語数
768 語

- ☑ 内容一致（選択式）
- ☐ 内容一致（T or F）
- ☑ 空所補充
- ☑ 下線部言い換え
- ☐ 表題選択
- ☑ 下線部和訳
- ☐ 記述説明
- ☑ その他

法学部は特に難易度が高く，和訳の記述量も多い。他の学部は段落ごとに設問を処理していけば効率よく解くことができる。

★2.4
1……2……3……4

科学・技術 11.9%
産業 4.8%
社会 11.9%
文化 38.1%
自然 14.3%
日常生活 19.0%

長文問題の平均出題大問数
3.5 問

長文1題あたり平均語数
668 語

- ☑ 内容一致（選択式）
- ☑ 内容一致（T or F）
- ☑ 空所補充
- ☑ 下線部言い換え
- ☐ 表題選択
- ☐ 下線部和訳
- ☐ 記述説明
- ☑ その他

出題形式は多様だが，基本的に記述問題は出題されない。内容真偽問題では，正確な理解が要求される。

大学名	獨協大学	芝浦工業大学	成城大学
英文レベル※	★2.1　1……2……3……4	★1.8　1……2……3……4	★2.2　1……2……3……4
出題ジャンル	社会 5.1%　産業 7.7%　科学・技術 15.4%　自然 17.9%　文化 23.1%　日常生活 30.8%	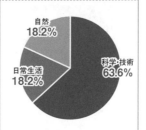自然 18.2%　日常生活 18.2%　科学・技術 63.6%	自然 11.1%　日常生活 11.1%　社会 22.2%　文化 55.6%
	長文問題の平均出題大問数(1) **10.0 問**	長文問題の平均出題大問数 **2.75 問**	長文問題の平均出題大問数 **2.25 問**
	長文1題あたり平均語数 **404 語**	長文1題あたり平均語数 **492 語**	長文1題あたり平均語数 **741 語**
設問形式	☑内容一致（選択式） ☐内容一致（T or F） ☑空所補充 ☐下線部言い換え ☑表題選択 ☐下線部和訳 ☐記述説明 ☑その他	☑内容一致（選択式） ☐内容一致（T or F） ☑空所補充 ☑下線部言い換え ☐表題選択 ☐下線部和訳 ☐記述説明 ☑その他	☑内容一致（選択式） ☐内容一致（T or F） ☑空所補充 ☑下線部言い換え ☐表題選択 ☐下線部和訳 ☑記述説明 ☑その他
三浦先生Check!	短めの英文が数多く出題され，内容一致問題のほか，文を補充する空所補充も。「主題は何か」を問う問題が中心。	長文は長めのものが1問と短いものが数問。内容一致問題，空所補充問題が中心。代名詞の指示内容が問われる。	英文全体より，各部分の理解を問う問題が中心。記述説明問題が複数出題されており，私立大にしては記述量が多め。

※T or F：内容真偽判定問題　(1) 外国語学部英語学科のみ。他学科は7問程度

8

成蹊大学

⭐ 2.0

1⋯⋯2⋯⋯3⋯⋯4

科学・技術 7.3%
産業 7.3%
社会 9.8%
日常生活 17.1%
文化 39.0%
自然 19.5%

長文問題の平均出題大問数
3.4 問

長文1題あたり平均語数
661 語

- ☑ 内容一致（選択式）
- ☐ 内容一致（T or F）
- ☑ 空所補充
- ☑ 下線部言い換え
- ☐ 表題選択
- ☑ 下線部和訳
- ☑ 記述説明
- ☑ その他

日本語の選択肢が多いので，取り組みやすい。理工学部はグラフやイラスト付きの英文が出題され，記述問題も多い。

津田塾大学

⭐ 1.8

1⋯⋯2⋯⋯3⋯⋯4

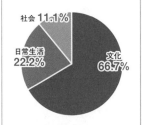

社会 11.1%
日常生活 22.2%
文化 66.7%

長文問題の平均出題大問数
2.25 問

長文1題あたり平均語数
578 語

- ☑ 内容一致（選択式）
- ☐ 内容一致（T or F）
- ☑ 空所補充
- ☑ 下線部言い換え
- ☐ 表題選択
- ☑ 下線部和訳
- ☑ 記述説明
- ☑ その他

空所補充，内容一致問題のほか，和訳や説明問題も出題され，いずれも記述量が多いので，日本語の表現力がポイントになる。

日本女子大学

⭐ 1.9

1⋯⋯2⋯⋯3⋯⋯4

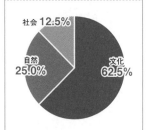

社会 12.5%
自然 25.0%
文化 62.5%

長文問題の平均出題大問数
2.0 問

長文1題あたり平均語数
627 語

- ☑ 内容一致（選択式）
- ☐ 内容一致（T or F）
- ☑ 空所補充
- ☑ 下線部言い換え
- ☑ 表題選択
- ☑ 下線部和訳
- ☐ 記述説明
- ☑ その他

表題選択や空所補充，下線部和訳問題など。解答時間には比較的余裕があるので，丁寧に取り組みたい。

大学名	明治学院大学	北里大学	南山大学
英文レベル※	 ★1.8 1……2……3……4	★2.6 1……2……3……4	★2.0 1……2……3……4
出題ジャンル	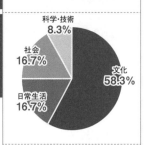 科学・技術 8.3% 社会 16.7% 日常生活 16.7% 文化 58.3%	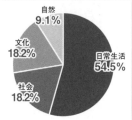 自然 9.1% 文化 18.2% 社会 18.2% 日常生活 54.5%	 産業 2.8% 科学・技術 8.3% 自然 13.9% 日常生活 27.8% 文化 47.2%
	長文問題の平均出題大問数 **3.0 問**	長文問題の平均出題大問数 **2.75 問**	長文問題の平均出題大問数 **3.0 問**
	長文1題あたり平均語数 **321 語**	長文1題あたり平均語数 **523 語**	長文1題あたり平均語数 **472 語**
設問形式	☑ 内容一致（選択式） ☐ 内容一致（T or F） ☐ 空所補充 ☐ 下線部言い換え ☐ 表題選択 ☐ 下線部和訳 ☐ 記述説明 ☑ その他	☑ 内容一致（選択式） ☐ 内容一致（T or F） ☑ 空所補充 ☑ 下線部言い換え ☐ 表題選択 ☐ 下線部和訳 ☐ 記述説明 ☑ その他	☑ 内容一致（選択式） ☐ 内容一致（T or F） ☑ 空所補充 ☑ 下線部言い換え ☐ 表題選択 ☐ 下線部和訳 ☐ 記述説明 ☑ その他
三浦先生Check!	論説文（英問英答）→会話文→要約のパターンが定着。150～180字の要約問題が特徴的。要約以外の問題は取り組みやすい。	空所補充，内容一致が中心で，文整序・文補充も。英文のテーマには専門性の高いものもある。医学部は特に難易度が高い。	英文の主題は文化や日常生活に関するものが多い。空所補充問題が多く，文法・語法の知識も問われる。文補充問題が特徴的。

※T or F：内容真偽判定問題

関西外国語大学

★ 2.4

1 ⋯⋯⋯ 2 ⋯⋯⋯ 3 ⋯⋯⋯ 4

自然 12.5%
社会 12.5%
文化 12.5%
日常生活 62.5%

長文問題の平均出題大問数
1.0 問

長文1題あたり平均語数
829 語

☑ 内容一致（選択式）
☐ 内容一致（T or F）
☑ 空所補充
☑ 下線部言い換え
☐ 表題選択
☐ 下線部和訳
☐ 記述説明
☐ その他

空所補充, 内容一致を中心に, 下線部の理由や具体例を選ぶ問題も。解答時間には余裕がある。高度な語彙力が求められる。

西南学院大学

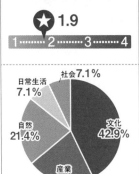

★ 1.9

1 ⋯⋯⋯ 2 ⋯⋯⋯ 3 ⋯⋯⋯ 4

社会7.1%
日常生活 7.1%
自然 21.4%
文化 42.9%
産業 21.4%

長文問題の平均出題大問数
1.75 問

長文1題あたり平均語数
538 語

☑ 内容一致（選択式）
☐ 内容一致（T or F）
☑ 空所補充
☑ 下線部言い換え
☐ 表題選択
☐ 下線部和訳
☐ 記述説明
☐ その他

選択肢が多いが, 内容一致は段落ごとに選択肢を検討するとよい。空所補充は文法・語法・語彙の知識を問うものが多い。

本データに記載の内容は,『2021 年受験用 全国大学入試問題正解 英語』〜『2024 年受験用 全国大学入試問題正解 英語』を旺文社編集部が独自に分析したものです。

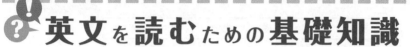
英文を読むための基礎知識

英文を読む上で，単語や熟語の知識が必要なのは当然である。しかし，語句の意味がわかれば英文を正しく理解できるというわけではない。英文は日本語とは異なる「構造」を持っているので，「構造」を把握することが英文を読むときには不可欠だ。

文型と文の要素

(1) 文型とは，英語の文のパターンを分類したものだ。英語の文には5つの文型がある。

第1文型：S + V
第2文型：S + V + C
第3文型：S + V + O
第4文型：S + V + O + O
第5文型：S + V + O + C

(2) そして，文型を構成する1つ1つのパーツのことを，文の要素と呼んでいる。これも5つある。

S（主語）：「〜は」「〜が」と訳す。**名詞**。
V（述語）：「〜する」「〜である」と訳す。**動詞**。
O（目的語）：「〜を」「〜に」と訳す。**名詞**。
C（補語）：決まった訳し方はない。**名詞**または**形容詞**。
M（修飾語）：決まった訳し方はない。**形容詞**または**副詞**。

句と節

「句」も「節」も，2語以上のカタマリを意味するが，以下のような違いがある。

「句」→〈S+V〉を含まないカタマリ 「節」→〈S+V〉を含むカタマリ

1. 句

（1）名詞句

S, O, C になる句。不定詞や動名詞のカタマリである。どちらも，「〜すること」と訳す場合が多い。

例 My desire is 〈to study abroad〉. 「私の希望は留学することだ」
　　S　　V　C

（2）形容詞句

名詞を修飾する句。不定詞，分詞，前置詞のカタマリがこれにあたる。

例 I have a lot of *homework* [to do]. 「私にはやるべき宿題がたくさんある」
　　S　V　　　　　　　O

（3）副詞句

名詞以外（主に動詞）を修飾する句。不定詞，分詞，前置詞のカタマリがこれにあたる。なお，分詞が副詞句を作ると，「分詞構文」と呼ばれ，【時】【理由】【付帯状況】などの意味を表す。

例 He *went* to America (to study jazz). 「彼はジャズの研究をするためにアメリカへ行った」
　　S　　V

to study jazz という不定詞のカタマリが went という動詞を修飾している。【目的】「〜するために」

例 He *entered* the room, (taking off his hat). 「彼は帽子を脱ぎながら部屋に入った」
　　S　　V　　　O

taking off his hat という分詞のカタマリ（分詞構文）が entered という動詞を修飾している。【付帯状況】「〜しながら」

例 I *got* (to the station) (at ten). 「私は10時に駅に到着した」
　　S　V

to the station と at ten という2つの前置詞のカタマリが，いずれも got という動詞を修飾している。

12

2. 節

（1）名詞節

S, O, C になる節。①従属接続詞（that / if / whether），②疑問詞，③関係詞が名詞節を作る。

① 従属接続詞とは，節を作るタイプの接続詞のこと。従属接続詞は数多くあるが，その中で**名詞節を作るの**は that「…こと」／ if「…かどうか」／ whether「…かどうか」の3つだけで，それ以外のすべての従属接続詞は副詞節しか作れない。

例 〈**That** you study Spanish now〉 is a good idea.
　　　S　　S　　V　　　O　　　　　V　　C

「あなたが今スペイン語を勉強する**こと**はいい考えだ」

例 I don't know 〈**if**〔**whether**〕 he will come here tomorrow〉.
　　S　　V　　　O　　　　　　　　　S　　　V

「明日彼がここに来るの**かどうか**わからない」

② **疑問詞**も名詞節を作る。

例 I don't know 〈**what** he wants〉. 「私は，彼が**何を**欲しがっているの**か**知らない」
　　S　　V　　　O　　　　S　　V

③ **一部の関係詞**も名詞節を作ることがある。これは，関係詞の中では少数派であり，関係詞の大半は，次に述べる形容詞節を作る。名詞節を作る関係詞は，what「…すること／…するもの」と how「…する方法」を押さえておこう。

例 〈**What** I want〉 is a new car. 「私が欲しい**もの**は新しい車だ」
　　S　　　S　　V　　　V　　C

例 This is 〈**how** I solved the problem〉.
　　S　　V　C　　　S　　V　　　O

「これが，私が問題を解決した**方法**だ（→このようにして私は問題を解決した）」

（2）形容詞節

名詞を修飾する働きをする節。これを作るのは**関係詞だけ**だ。

例 I have *a friend* 〔**who** lives in Osaka〕. 「私には大阪に住んでいる友人がいる」
　　S　V　　O　　　　　　　V

関係代名詞 who から始まるカタマリが a friend という名詞を修飾。

例 This is *the place* 〔**where** I met her first〕. 「ここは私が初めて彼女に会った場所だ」
　　S　V　　C　　　　　　　S　V　O

関係副詞 where から始まるカタマリが the place という名詞を修飾。

（3）副詞節

名詞以外（主に動詞）を修飾する節。従属接続詞はすべて，副詞節を作ることができる。

例 I like him （**because** he is generous）. 「彼は気前がいいので，私は彼が好きだ」
　　S　V　O　　　　　　　S　V　　C

従属接続詞 because から始まるカタマリが like という動詞を修飾している。

＊ 上の名詞節のところで出てきた that / if / whether は，名詞節だけではなく副詞節も作ることができる（ただし，that は so 〜 that … 構文など，特殊な構文に限られる）。if は「もし…すれば」，**whether** は「…であろうとなかろうと」の意味では**副詞節**である。

例 I will stay home （**if** it rains tomorrow）. 「もし明日雨が降ったら，私は家にいるつもりだ」
　　S　V　　　　　　　　　S　　V

従属接続詞 if から始まるカタマリが stay という動詞を修飾している。

このほか，「複合関係詞」と呼ばれる特殊な関係詞が副詞節を作ることができる。

例 I will reject your offer （**whatever** you say）. 「たとえ君が何を言っても，私は君の申し出を断ります」
　　S　V　　　O　　　　　　　　　　S　V

※ さらに詳しい解説は，本シリーズのレベル①（p.6〜15），レベル②（p.6〜19）を参照して下さい。

1 解答・解説

解 答

問1 (1) ④	(2) ④	(3) ①
問2 (ア) ③	(イ) ③	(ウ) ①
問3 オリンピックを開催することが観光客を引きつけ，収入を生み出すのに役立つかもしれないという認識がある		
問4 ①, ⑤		

解 説

問1

(1)「boycott とは，抗議や罰として，何かを買ったり使ったり参加したりするのを（　）することである」

① 「契約」　② 「使命」　③ 「許可」　④**「拒否」**

▶「ボイコット」は日本語になっている。また本文では difficulties の具体例として挙げられていることもヒントになる。

(2)「infrastructure とは，輸送や電力供給のような，国家や組織が適切に機能するために必要な（　）である」

① 「商品に対する需要」　　② 「見積もられている費用」

③ 「インフレ率」　　　　　④**「根本的な基盤」**

▶「インフラ」も日本語になっているし，設問の英文中の具体例もヒントになる。

(3)「budget とは特定の目的のために利用できる（　）である」

①**「金額」**　② 「利益」　③ 「エネルギー」　④ 「貯蓄」

▶ budget とは「予算」のこと。本文で，投資(investments)が負担をかける対象としているのもヒントになる。

問2

(ア) 選択肢を見ると，③のみ前置詞で，他は副詞の働きをする語句。文の構造に着目すると，there are 以下には**完全な文**があるので，（　**ア**　）tourism development の部分は構造上は**修飾語句**と考えられる。（　**ア**　）

の直後には名詞があるので，〈前置詞＋名詞〉とすれば修飾語句となる。なお，各選択肢の意味は以下の通り。①「やがて，まもなく」，②「他方で」，③「〜に加えて，〜だけでなく」，④「結果的に」。

（イ） 直前部分に these economic benefits are pragmatic とあることに注目。選択肢③を入れれば，they が these economic benefits を指し，are の後には pragmatic が省略されていると考えられるので，まず第一に，経済的利益が実際的なものか否かが問題となり，次に，**仮にそうだとして**（＝**経済的利益が実際的だとして**），どの程度費用を埋め合わせられるかが問題となる，という文脈になり，自然である。

（ウ） 空所の前後に名詞が並んでおり，いずれも the long-term benefits の具体例と考えられる。そこで，前後を対等に結ぶ as well as を入れる。**A as well as B** で「**B だけでなく A も，B と同様に A も**」の意味。A・B には文法上対等のものが入る。

問3

... there is an understanding that doing so could help attract tourists and generate income.

以下のポイントをおさえよう！

☑ that は**同格の接続詞**（⇒文法事項の整理①（21 ページ）参照）。直前の名詞 understanding の具体的な内容を説明する働き。「…という〜」と訳す。

☑ doing so の指す内容は，二重下線部直前の holding the Games「オリンピックを開催すること」。

☑ could は can の過去形だが，**過去を表すのではなく**，「（もしかすると）〜するかもしれない，〜する可能性がある」という【未来に関する見込み】を表す用法。

☑ help の用法は，help to do で「〜するのに役立つ」だが，to が省略されることがある。ここでも省略され，attract と generate という**2つの動詞の原形が and により並列されている**。

① 「多くの国家はオリンピックによる利益が費用を上回る可能性が高いと感じており，そのためオリンピックを開催することを望んでいる」

▶ 第1段落最終文と一致。

② 「オリンピック開催候補地の多くの都市は，インフラ構築を創り出すためには他の都市の注目を引きつける必要がある」

▶ そのような記述はない。また，第2段落第2文にはインフラが構築された結果，他の都市からの注目を引きつけてきた，との記述があるが，これとも一致しない。

③ 「オリンピック開催候補都市がオリンピックに期待している経済的恩恵は，常に幻想であることがわかってきた」

▶ 第2段落第1文と不一致。

④ 「多くの経済学的研究により，オリンピックを開催することによる利益は，おそらくマイナスの影響を増大させるであろうということがわかってきた」

▶ 第3段落第1文と不一致。マイナスの影響については第3段落第2文に記述があるが，これは研究によってわかったことではなく，考慮する必要性を筆者が指摘していることである。

⑤ 「政府はさまざまな施設，道路，建物を建設するために多額の金を使う必要があり，それが都市にとって多くの財政的困難をもたらす可能性がある」

▶ 第3段落第2文と一致。

⑥ 「高められた国際的評価，改善された公共福祉は，オリンピックから利点を奪ってしまうであろう」

▶ そのような記述はない。むしろこれらは第3段落第1文でオリンピック開催の利点として挙げられている。

▼

それでは次に，段落ごとに詳しくみていこう。
01

第1段落　文の構造と語句のチェック

¹The Modern Olympic Games were first held (in Athens) (in 1896).
　　　　　　S　　　　　　　　　V

²(Although the games have had to overcome many difficulties, 〔 including wars
　従接　　　S　　　　　V　　　　　　　O

and boycotts 〕), (for the most part), they have been held (every four years).
　　　　　　　　　　　　　　　　　　　S　　　V

³(In recent years), more countries have shown an interest 〔 in holding the
　　　　　　　　　　　S　　　　　　V　　　O

Games 〕(as there is an understanding 〈 that doing so could help 〈 attract
　　　　従接　　V　　　S　　　従接(同格)　S　　V　　O　V′

tourists and generate income 〉〉).
　O′　等接　V′　　O′

> 訳 ¹近代オリンピックが最初に行われたのは1896年のアテネであった。²オリンピックは，戦争やボイコットを含め，多くの困難を克服しなければならなかったのだが，概ね4年ごとに開催されてきた。³近年は，オリンピックを開催することが観光客を引きつけ，収入を生み出すのに役立つかもしれないという認識があるため，より多くの国々がオリンピック開催に関心を示すようになってきた。

語句
modern 形 現代の，近代の
hold 動 行う，開催する
　＊活用：hold-held-held
overcome 動 克服する，乗り越える
difficulty 名 困難
including ~ 前 ~を含めて
war 名 戦争
boycott 名 ボイコット

for the most part 熟 たいていは
recent 形 最近の
country 名 国，国家
understanding 名 理解，認識
attract 動 引きつける
tourist 名 観光客
generate 動 生み出す，創出する
income 名 収入，所得

¹Prospective host cities look to the many expected economic benefits and
　　　　S　　　　　　　　　V　　　　　　　　O　　　　　　　　　　　等接

indeed many studies have shown some distinct economic advantages 〔 in
　　　　　S　　　　　　V　　　　　　　　　　O

staging the games 〕. ²(In addition to tourism development) there are many
　　　　　　　　　　　　　　　　　　　　　　　　　　　　　　　　　　　　　V

other economic spin-offs 〔 such as infrastructure development 〕 〔 that have
　　　　　S　　　　　　　　　　　　　　　　　　　　　　　　　　　　　　　　関代

attracted the attention of many cities 〕. ³However, potential host communities
　V　　　　　　O　　　　　　　　　　　　　　　　　　　　　　　S

need to pose the question 〔 of 〈 whether, (in fact), these economic benefits are
　V　　　　　O　　　　　　①　　従接　　　　　　　　　　　S　　　　　　V

pragmatic 〉 and, (if they are), the extent 〔 to which such benefits actually
　C　　　　　等接　従接　S　V　　　②　　　　関代　　　S

offset the costs 〕〕.
　V　　　O

訳 ¹開催候補地の都市は，多くの期待される経済的恩恵を当てにしており，実際，多くの調査によれば，オリンピックを開催することには明確な経済的利点があることがわかってきた。²観光産業の発達に加え，インフラの構築といったような他の多くの経済的な副次効果があり，それらは多くの都市の注目を集めてきた。³しかし，開催候補地の地域社会は，これらの経済的利益が本当に実際的なものなのかどうか，また，仮にそうであるとして，それらの利益が実際にどの程度まで開催費用を埋め合わせるのか，といった問題を提起する必要がある。

Check! 第 2 文 … there are many other economic spin-offs such as infrastructure development that have attracted the attention of many cities.

▶ that は主格の関係代名詞。先行詞は直前の development ではなく，spin-offs。that の後が has ではなく have になっていることから，先行詞は複数形の名詞だとわかる。

Check! 第 3 文 … pose the question of whether, in fact, these economic benefits are pragmatic …

▶ 接続詞 whether は，名詞節を導けば「…かどうか」，副詞節を導けば「…であろうとなかろうと」の意味。ここでは前置詞 of の後にあるので名詞節。

語 句

prospective	形	期待される，今後そうなりそうな
host	名	主催者，開催地
look to ~	熟	~を当てにする，~に期待を寄せる
economic	形	経済的な
benefit	名	利益，恩恵
indeed	副	実際に，本当に
distinct	形	明らかな，目立った
advantage	名	利点，優位
stage	動	開催する，主催する
in addition to ~	熟	~に加えて，~だけでなく
tourism	名	観光事業，観光産業

development	名	発達，開発
spin-off	名	副産物，副次効果
such as ~	熟	（例えば）~のような
infrastructure	名	インフラ，社会基盤
attention	名	注意，注目
however	副	しかし
potential	形	可能性のある，潜在的な
community	名	地域（社会）
pose	動	提起する，提示する
pragmatic	形	実際的な
extent	名	程度，度合い
	▶ the extent to which S+V S が V する程度	
offset	動	相殺する，埋め合わせる
cost	名	費用

第 3 段落　文の構造と語句のチェック

[1]Many of the economic studies 〔 on the Olympics 〕 have emphasized the
S ／ V

long-term benefits 〔 such as newly constructed event facilities and infrastructure,
O ／ ① 等接

urban revival, enhanced international reputation and increased tourism, (as
② ／ ③ 等接 ④

---

well as improved public welfare, additional employment, local business
___①___ ___②___ ___③___

opportunities and corporate relocation)]. ²(In contrast), there are some
___ 等接 ___④___ V

potential negative impacts [that need to be considered], (for example)
S 関代 V

the high construction costs [of public sports infrastructure] and all the needed
___①___ 等接 ②

supporting investments [which can place a heavy burden (on the government
関代 V O

budget)]. ³Other problems include temporary crowding problems and property
S V O① 等接 O②

┌─ 従接 that 省略
rental increases. ⁴Nonetheless most host cities think ⟨the Games are a good bet⟩.
S V O S V C

訳 ¹オリンピックに関する経済学的研究の多くは，改善された公共福祉，さらに増えた雇用，地域のビジネスのチャンス，企業の移転のみならず，新たに建設されたオリンピック種目用施設やインフラ，都市の再生，高められた国際的評価，拡大した観光事業といったような，長期的な利益を強調してきた。²対照的に，考慮される必要のある潜在的なマイナスの影響もある。例えば，公共のスポーツ施設の高額な建設費，政府予算に重い負担をかける可能性のある，すべての必要とされる支援投資などである。³その他の問題としては，一時的な混雑の問題や不動産賃貸料の上昇といったものも含まれる。⁴それでも，大半の開催都市はオリンピックが間違いない選択であると考えているのだ。

語句

emphasize	動 強調する	**reputation**	名 評判，評価
long-term	形 長期的な	**increase**	動 向上させる，高める
newly	副 新たに	*A* **as well as** *B*	熟 B だけでなく A も
construct	動 建設する	**improve**	動 改善する，改良する
event	名 (オリンピックなどの)種目，試合	**public**	形 公共の
facility	名 施設，設備	**welfare**	名 福祉
urban	形 都市の，都会の	**additional**	形 さらなる，付加的な
revival	名 再生，復活	**employment**	名 雇用
enhance	動 高める，よくする	**local**	形 地域の
international	形 国際的な	**opportunity**	名 機会，チャンス
		corporate	形 企業の
		relocation	名 移転

in contrast	熟 対照的に	**budget**	名 予算
negative	形 マイナスの，よくない	**include**	動 含む
impact	名 影響	**temporary**	形 一時的な
consider	動 考慮する	**crowd**	動 混み合う，群がる
construction	名 建設	**property**	名 不動産
supporting	形 支援の，補助の	rental	名 賃貸料
investment	名 投資	**nonetheless**	副 それにもかかわらず，それで
burden	名 重荷，負担		もなお

▶place a burden on ～　～に重荷を負わせ
　　　　　　　　　　る，～に負担をかける
government 名 政府

bet　　　　　　名 賭け
　▶a good bet　安全な選択，まず間違いないこ
　　　　　　　　と

文法事項の整理 ①　【名詞＋ that 節】の識別

第 1 段落最終文の〈名詞＋that 節〉について見てみよう。

... there is an understanding **that** doing so could help attract tourists
and generate income.

■ **that 以下が不完全な文**（S や O，前置詞の後の名詞などが欠けた文）

➡ **that は関係代名詞**

※ S が欠けていれば**主格**，O や前置詞の後の名詞が欠けていれば**目的格**

例　This is the house that was designed by my father.

「これは私の父によって設計された家だ」

▶ that 以下に S が欠けているので，that は**主格の関係代名詞**。

例　This is the house that my father designed.

「これは私の父が設計した家だ」

▶ that 以下に O が欠けているので，that は**目的格の関係代名詞**。

例　This is the house that my father used to live in.

「これは私の父がかつて住んでいた家だ」

▶ that 以下に前置詞 in の後の名詞が欠けているので，that は**目的格
の関係代名詞**。

■ that 以下が完全な文

1) 前の名詞が「時」「場所」「理由(reason)」「方法(way)」

　➡ that は**関係副詞**

　　例　I don't like the way that my father talks to me.

　　「父の私に対する話し方が気に入らない」

　　　▶ that 以下は完全な文，前に「方法(way)」があるので，that は関係副詞。

2) その他

　➡ that は**同格の接続詞**

　　例　I couldn't accept the fact that we were wrong.

　　「私は，私たちが間違っているという事実を受け入れられなかった」

※同格の接続詞 that は，直前の抽象名詞(idea, fact, conclusion, belief など)の具体的内容を説明する働きをする。「…という〜」と訳すことが多い。

(第1段落最終文)

... there is an understanding that doing so could help attract tourists and generate income.

　▶ that 以下が完全な文なので，that は同格の接続詞。

(第2段落第2文)

... there are many other economic spin-offs such as infrastructure development that have attracted the attention of many cities.

　▶ that 以下が S の欠けた不完全な文なので，that は主格の関係代名詞(先行詞は spin-offs)。

(第3段落第2文)

... there are some potential negative impacts that need to be considered, ...

　▶ that 以下が S の欠けた不完全な文なので，that は主格の関係代名詞。

確認問題

1. 次の和訳と対応する英語の語句を，頭文字を参考にして書き，空欄を完成させよう。

（各1点×20）

①	o	動	克服する
②	f	t	m	p	熟	たいていは
③	p		形	期待される
④	d		形	明らかな
⑤	a		名	利点
⑥	i		名	社会基盤
⑦	c		名	地域(社会)
⑧	e		名	程度
⑨	e		動	強調する
⑩	c		動	建設する
⑪	f		名	施設
⑫	u		形	都市の
⑬	r		名	評判
⑭	i		動	改善する
⑮	e		名	雇用
⑯	i	c	熟	対照的に
⑰	i		名	投資
⑱	b		名	重荷
⑲	b		名	予算
⑳	t		形	一時的な

2. 次の[　]内の語句を並べ替えて，意味の通る英文を完成させよう。（各5点×2）

① Potential host communities need to pose [of / economic benefits / these / the / question / whether] are pragmatic.

② There are some potential [that / be / impacts / to / considered / negative / need].

3. 次の英文を和訳してみよう。(10 点)

In recent years, more countries have shown an interest in holding the Games as there is an understanding that doing so could help attract tourists and generate income.

ディクテーションしてみよう！

今回学習した英文に出てきた語句を，音声を聞いて＿＿＿に書き取ろう。

02   The Modern Olympic Games were first held in Athens in 1896. Although the games ❶＿＿＿＿＿＿＿＿＿＿ overcome many difficulties, including wars and boycotts, for the most part, they have been held every four years.   In recent years, more countries have ❷＿＿＿＿＿＿＿＿＿ ＿＿＿＿＿＿＿＿ holding the Games as there is an understanding that doing so could help attract tourists and generate income.

03   Prospective host cities look to the many expected economic benefits and indeed many studies have shown some distinct economic advantages in staging the games. ❸＿＿＿＿＿＿＿＿＿ tourism development there are many other economic spin-offs such as infrastructure development that have attracted the attention of many cities.   However, potential host communities need to ❹＿＿＿＿＿＿＿＿＿＿＿ of whether, in fact, these economic benefits are pragmatic and, if they are, the extent to which such benefits actually offset the costs.

04   Many of the economic studies on the Olympics have emphasized the long-term benefits such as newly constructed event facilities and infrastructure, urban revival, enhanced international reputation and ❺＿＿＿＿＿＿＿＿＿＿＿＿, as well as improved public welfare, additional employment, local business opportunities and corporate relocation.   In

24

contrast, there are some potential negative impacts that need to be considered, for example the high construction costs of public sports infrastructure and all the needed supporting investments which can place ❻_____ the government budget. Other problems include temporary crowding problems and property rental increases. Nonetheless most host cities think the Games are ❼_____.

確認問題の答

1. ① overcome　② for the most part　③ prospective　④ distinct　⑤ advantage
　⑥ infrastructure　⑦ community　⑧ extent　⑨ emphasize　⑩ construct　⑪ facility
　⑫ urban　⑬ reputation　⑭ improve　⑮ employment　⑯ in contrast　⑰ investment
　⑱ burden　⑲ budget　⑳ temporary

2. ① the question of whether these economic benefits （第2段落　第3文）
　② negative impacts that need to be considered （第3段落　第2文）

3. 近年は，オリンピックを開催することが観光客を引きつけ，収入を生み出すのに役立つかもしれないという認識があるため，より多くの国々がオリンピック開催に関心を示すようになってきた。（第1段落　最終文）

ディクテーションしてみよう！の答

❶ have had to　❷ shown an interest in　❸ In addition to　❹ pose the question
❺ increased tourism　❻ a heavy burden on　❼ a good bet

アドバイス ❺各単語の語尾と次の単語の語頭の音がつながる（連結）。
　　❺ increased の語尾の /t/ と，tourism の語頭の /t/ は同じ音なので1回しか発音されない（脱落）。
　　❼ good の語尾の /d/ と，bet の語頭の /b/ のように，発音の仕方が近い子音が重なる場合も脱落が起こり，前の子音 d がほとんど発音されなくなる。

問 （ア）この理論の信奉者がテレビで暗いニュースを見たとき，彼らは利潤追求が万能薬なのかどうか疑問に思うべきなのだが，そうではなく，彼らは悪いことをすべて市場の失敗のせいにしてしまう。

（イ）私たちはこの理論により，金を稼ぐことこそが人類に幸福をもたらす最善の方法だと思い込まされているので，自分自身を一次元的な人間に変質させようと努力しながら，熱狂的にその理論を模倣しているのだ

解 説

問

（ア）When believers in this theory see gloomy news on television, they should wonder whether the pursuit of profit is a cure-all, but, instead, they blame all the bad things on market failures.

以下のポイントをおさえよう！

☑ When は**副詞節を導く接続詞**で，この節は television まで。

☑ 主節は，they (= S) should wonder (= V) whether 〜 cure-all (= O) と，they (= S) blame (= V) all the bad things (= O) の 2 組あり，**等位接続詞 but が これらを並列**。

☑ whether は**名詞節を導き**，「…かどうか」の意味。

☑ instead は，instead of 〜「〜の代わりに，〜ではなくて」の of 以下が省略されたもの。ここでは，instead of wondering whether ... と考える（明らかなので訳す必要はない）。

☑ blame *A* on *B*「A を B のせいにする」

（イ）(And) since we are persuaded by this theory that making money is the best way to bring happiness to humankind, we enthusiastically imitate the theory, striving to transform ourselves into one-dimensional human

26

beings.

　以下のポイントをおさえよう！

☑ 接続詞 since は①「…以来」，②「…なので」の２つの意味があり，ここでは②の【理由】の意味。

☑ persuade は〈persuade＋（人）＋that ...〉「（人）に…ということを納得させる，思い込ませる」のパターン。ここでは受動態で使われている。

☑ that を同格の接続詞と考え，theory の内容を説明しているとすると，「…という理論によって何を納得させられているのか」が不明であり，不自然な解釈になる。したがって，that は **persuade の O となる名詞節を導く接続詞**と解するべき。

☑ bring *A* to *B* で「A を B に持ってくる，もたらす」。

☑ striving 以下は【付帯状況】を表す分詞構文（⇒文法事項の整理⑨（126 ページ）参照）。

☑ strive to *do*「～しようと努力する」

☑ transform *A* into *B* で「A を B に変化[変質，変形]させる」の意味。

▼

それでは次に，段落ごとに詳しくみていこう。
05

第1段落　文の構造と語句のチェック

¹Mainstream free-market theory assumes 〈 that you are contributing (to the
　　　　　S　　　　　　　　　　　V　　　 O従接　 S　　　V

society and the world) (in the best possible manner) (if you just concentrate
　　　等接　　　　　　　　　　　　　　　　　　　　　　　　　従接 S　　　 V

(on getting the most for yourself))〉. ²(When believers [in this theory] see
　　　　　　　　　　　　　　　　　　　　　　　 従接　　 S　　　　　　　　　 V

gloomy news (on television)), they should wonder 〈 whether the pursuit of
　　 O　　　　　　　　　　　　　 S　　 V　　　　 O　 従接　　　 S

profit is a cure-all 〉, but, instead, they blame all the bad things (on market
　 V　　 C　　　　　 等接　　　　　 S　 V　　　 O

failures). ³They have trained their minds (to believe 〈 that
　　　　　　　S　　　V　　　　　their minds　　　　V′　O′ 従接

well-functioning markets simply cannot produce unpleasant results 〉).
　　　　　　S　　　　　　　　　　V　　　　　O

> **訳** ¹主流派の自由市場理論は，自分のために最大限の物を得ることにのみ集中すれば，ありうる最善の方法で社会や世の中に貢献していることになる，ということを前提としている。²この理論の信奉者がテレビで暗いニュースを見たとき，彼らは利潤追求が万能薬なのかどうか疑問に思うべきなのだが，そうではなく，彼らは悪いことをすべて市場の失敗のせいにしてしまう。³彼らは自らの思考を，正しく機能している市場は絶対に不愉快な結果を生み出すことはあり得ないと思い込むよう訓練してしまっているのだ。

語句

mainstream	形	主流(派)の	pursuit	名 追求
free-market	形	自由市場の	profit	名 利益，利潤
theory	名	理論	cure-all	名 万能薬
assume	動	想定する，前提とする	**instead**	副 その代わりに，そうではなく
contribute to ～	熟	～に貢献する	**blame A on B**	熟 A を B のせいにする
society	名	社会	**failure**	名 失敗
manner	名	方法，やり方	**train**	動 訓練する，鍛錬する
concentrate on ～	熟	～に集中する	well-functioning	形 正しく機能している
believer	名	信者，信奉者	**simply**	副 〈否定語の前で〉全く～(ない)，どうしても～(ない)
gloomy	形	暗い，悲観的な		
wonder	動	…だろうかと思う	**produce**	動 生み出す
whether	接	…かどうか	**unpleasant**	形 不快な，いやな
			result	名 結果

第2段落　文の構造と語句のチェック

── 従接 that 省略

¹I think 〈 things are going wrong (not because of market failures)〉.　²The
　S　V　　O　　S　　V　　　C

problem is much deeper (than that).　³Mainstream free-market theory fails to
　S　　V　　C　　　　　　　　　　　　S　　　　　　　　V

capture the essence 〔 of 〈 what it is 〈 to be human 〉〉〕.
　　　　O　　　　　　　疑　仮S V　真S

28

訳 ¹私が思うに，事態が悪化しているのは市場の失敗のせいではない。²問題はそんなものよりはるかに深いのだ。³主流派の自由市場理論は，人間であるというのがいかなることなのか，その本質をとらえられていない。

語句

go wrong	熟 悪い方向に進む，うまくいかない	fail to *do*	熟 ～しない，～できない
		capture	動 とらえる，つかむ
		essence	名 本質，根本
because of ～	熟 ～のせいで	human	形 人間の，人間的な

第3段落　文の構造と語句のチェック

¹(In the conventional theory of business), we've created a one-dimensional
　　　　　　　　　　　　　　　　　　　　　　　　S　　　V　　　　　　　　　　　　

human being [to play the role of business leader]. ²We've insulated him (from
O　　　　　　　　　　　　　　　　　　　　　　　　　　　S　　　V　　　　O

the rest of life, the religious, emotional, political, and social). ³He is dedicated (to
　　　　　　　　└──同格──┘　①　　　　②　　　　③　　　④　　　　　S　V　　　C
　　　　　　　　　　　　　　　　　　　　　　　　　　　　等接

one mission only — maximize profit). ⁴He is supported (by other one-
　　　　　　　　　　　　　　　　　　　　　S　　V
　　　　　　　　　　　　　　　　　　　　　　　　　

dimensional human beings [who give him their investment money [to achieve
　　　　　　　　　　　　　　関代　V　　O₁　　　　　　O₂
　　　　　　　　　　　　　　　　　

that mission]]). ⁵(To quote Oscar Wilde), they know the price of everything
　　　　　　　　　　　　　　　　　　　　　　　S　　　V　　　　　　　　O①

and the value of nothing.
②
等接

訳 ¹従来のビジネス理論において，私たちはビジネス界のリーダーの役割を果たすべき一次元的な人間を創り出してきた。²私たちは，宗教的・感情的・政治的・社会的な事柄といったその他の生活局面からその人物を切り離してきたのだ。³その人物は，利益を最大化するという1つの使命のみに専念している。⁴その人物は，その使命を成し遂げるための投資金を与えてくれる他の一次元的な人間たちに支えられている。⁵オスカー・ワイルドの言葉を引用すると，彼らはあらゆる物の価格を知っているが，いかなる物の価値も知らないのだ。

conventional	形	伝統的な，従来の
create	動	創造する，創り出す
one-dimensional	形	一次元の
human being	名	人間
role	名	役割
▶ play a [the] role		役割を果たす，役を演じる
insulate	動	隔離する，分離する
rest	名	残り，その他
religious	形	宗教的な
emotional	形	感情的な
political	形	政治的な
social	形	社会的な
be dedicated to ～	熟	～に専念している，～に献身している
mission	名	使命
maximize	動	最大化する
support	動	支える，支援する
investment	名	投資，出資
achieve	動	達成する，成し遂げる
quote	動	引用する

第4段落　文の構造と語句のチェック

¹Our economic theory has created a one-dimensional world 〔 inhabited by those 〔 who devote themselves (to the game of free-market competition)〕〕, in which victory is measured (purely by profit). ²And (since we are persuaded (by this theory)〈 that 〈 making money 〉 is the best way 〔 to bring happiness to humankind 〕〉), we enthusiastically imitate the theory, (striving to transform ourselves into one-dimensional human beings). ³(Instead of theory imitating reality), we force reality to imitate theory.

> **訳** ¹私たちの経済理論は，自由市場競争というゲームに専念する人々が住む一次元的な世界を創り出してきた。そのゲームでは，勝利はあくまでも利益によって判断される。²そして私たちはこの理論により，金を稼ぐことこそが人類に幸福をもたらす最善の方法だと思い込まされているので，自分自身を一次元的な人間に変質させようと努力しながら，熱狂的にその理論を模倣しているのだ。³理論が現実を模倣するのではなく，私たちが現実に対して理論を模倣するように強いているのである。

語句

economic	形	経済の，経済学の
inhabit	動	住む，居住する
devote *oneself* to ~	熟	~に専念する， ~に献身する
competition	名	競争
victory	名	勝利
measure	動	評価する，判断する
purely	副	あくまでも，単に
persuade	動	思い込ませる，納得させる
humankind	名	人類，人間

enthusiastically	副	熱心に，熱狂的に
imitate	動	まねる，模倣する
strive	動	努力する，励む
transform *A* into *B*	熟	A を B に変化[変 質，変形]させる
instead of ~	熟	~の代わりに，~ではなくて
reality	名	現実
force	動	強制する，強いる

▶ force + O + to *do*　O に~するよう強制する，強いる

文法事項の整理 ②　動詞＋*A*＋前置詞＋*B*

第 1 段落第 2 文の〈動詞＋*A*＋前置詞＋*B*〉について見てみよう。

... but, instead, they **blame** all the bad things **on** market failures.

　〈動詞＋*A*＋前置詞＋*B*〉のパターンは，空所補充などの形式で出題される他，下線部和訳のポイントになることもある。以下に前置詞別に整理するので，覚えよう。

① **as**

1	regard [look on / think of / see / view / take] *A* as *B*	「A を B とみなす」
2	accept [acknowledge / recognize / identify] *A* as *B*	「A を B と認める」
3	describe [refer to] *A* as *B*	「A のことを B だと言う」
4	treat *A* as *B*	「A を B として扱う」
5	define *A* as *B*	「A を B と定義する」
6	strike [impress] *A* as *B*	「A に B だという印象を 与える」

※基本的に，**A ＝ B の関係が成立**する。ただし，6 だけは，文の S と B にイコール関係が成立する。

② **before**

put *A* before *B*	「A を B より優先する」＝ put *A* above *B*

③ **by**

1	mean *A* by *B*	「B という言葉で A を表す」
2	replace *A* by *B*	「A を B と交換する」= replace *A* with *B*

④ **for**

1	ask [call on] *A* for *B*	「A に B を求める」
2	depend on [rely on / count on / turn to / look to] *A* for *B*	「A に B を頼る，あてにする」
3	blame [criticize / condemn / denounce] *A* for *B*	「B のことで A を非難する」
4	scold *A* for *B*	「B のことで A を叱る」
5	punish *A* for *B*	「B のことで A を罰する」
6	thank *A* for *B*	「B のことで A に感謝する」
7	admire [praise] *A* for *B*	「B のことで A を称賛する」
8	excuse [forgive] *A* for *B*	「A の B を許す」
9	exchange *A* for *B*	「A を B と交換する」
10	substitute *A* for *B*	「B の代わりに A を用いる」
11	buy *A* for *B*	「B(金)を出して A(物)を買う」
12	pay *A* for *B*	「A(金)を B(物)の代金として払う」
13	take *A* for *B*	「A を B だと思う」
14	mistake *A* for *B*	「A を B と間違える」

※ 1・2 は【要求】，3 ～ 8 は【理由・関連】，9 ～ 14 は【交換】を表す for。

⑤ **from**

1	derive *A* from *B*	「A を B から引き出す」
2	demand *A* from *B*	「A を B に要求する」= demand *A* of *B*
3	expect *A* from *B*	「A を B に期待する」= expect *A* of *B*
4	order *A* from *B*	「A を B に注文する」
5	make *A* from *B*	「A を B から作る」cf. make *A* of *B*
6	protect *A* from *B*	「A を B から守る」= protect *A* against *B*
7	separate [isolate] *A* from *B*	「A を B から隔離する」
8	tell [know / distinguish] *A* from *B*	「A を B と区別する」
9	prevent [stop / keep / hinder] *A* from *B*	「A に B をさせない」
10	discourage [dissuade] *A* from *B*	「A に B をする気をなくさせる」
11	prohibit [ban] *A* from *B*	「A が B をするのを禁ずる」
12	disable *A* from *B*	「A が B をできなくする」

※ 1 ～ 5 は【出所】，6 ～ 8 は【分離・区別】，9 ～ 12 は【妨害】を表す from。

⑥ into

1	change [transform / turn] *A* into *B*	「A を B に変える」
2	make *A* into *B*	「A を B に加工する」
3	divide *A* into *B*	「A を B に分ける」
4	translate [put] *A* into *B*	「A を B に訳す」
5	persuade [talk] *A* into *B*	「A を説得して B させる」
6	cheat *A* into *B*	「A をだまして B させる」

※いずれも into が【変化】を表す。

⑦ of

1	remind *A* of *B*	「A に B を思い出させる」
2	inform *A* of *B*	「A に B を知らせる」
3	assure [convince / persuade] *A* of *B*	「A に B を納得させる」
4	warn *A* of *B*	「A に B を警告する」
5	accuse *A* of *B*	「A を B のことで告発する」
6	suspect *A* of *B*	「A に B の疑いをかける」
7	rob [deprive] *A* of *B*	「A から B を奪う」
8	relieve [ease] *A* of *B*	「A から B を取り除いて楽にさせる」
9	clear [rid] *A* of *B*	「A から B を取り除く」
10	cure *A* of *B*	「A の B を治療する」

※1～6は【関連・伝達】，7～10は【分離・剥奪】を表す of。

⑧ on

1	base *A* on *B*	「A を B に基づかせる」
2	blame *A* on *B*	「A を B のせいにする」
3	congratulate *A* on *B*	「A の B を祝う」
4	concentrate *A* on *B*	「A を B に集中させる」
5	impose [force] *A* on *B*	「A を B に課す，押し付ける」
6	spend *A* on *B*	「A(金)を B(物)に使う」

⑨ to

1	add *A* to *B*	「A を B に加える」
2	adapt [adjust] *A* to *B*	「A を B に適合させる」
3	apply *A* to *B*	「A を B に当てはめる，応用する」
4	ascribe [attribute] *A* to *B*	「A を B のせいにする」
5	compare *A* to *B*	「A を B にたとえる，A を B と比べる」
6	attach *A* to *B*	「A を B にくっつける」
7	convey [transmit] *A* to *B*	「A を B に伝える」
8	dedicate [devote] *A* to *B*	「A を B にささげる」
9	expose *A* to *B*	「A を B にさらす」

10	leave *A* to *B*	「A を B にまかせる」
11	limit [restrict / confine] *A* to *B*	「A を B に限る」

※いずれも to が【到達・付着】を表す。

⑩ **with**

1	connect [associate] *A* with *B*	「A を B と関連付ける」
2	link [combine] *A* with *B*	「A を B と結び付ける」
3	charge *A* with *B*	「A を B のことで責める」
4	help *A* with *B*	「A の B を助ける，手伝う」
5	provide [supply / furnish / serve / feed] *A* with *B*	「A に B を供給する」
6	present *A* with *B*	「A に B を贈る」
7	endow *A* with *B*	「A に B を授ける」
8	equip *A* with *B*	「A に B を備え付ける」
9	leave *A* with *B*	「A を B に預ける」
10	trust [charge] *A* with *B*	「A に B を委託する」
11	compare *A* with *B*	「A を B と比べる」
12	identify [equate] *A* with *B*	「A を B と同一視する」
13	mix [confuse] *A* with *B*	「A を B と混同する」
14	share *A* with *B*	「A を B と共有する」

※1〜4は【関連】，5〜10は【供給】，11〜14は【混合】を表す with。

　第1段落第2文の blame *A* on *B*，第4段落第1文の devote *A* to *B*，第2文の transform *A* into *B* などが，この〈動詞＋*A*＋前置詞＋*B*〉の形。

確認問題

1. 次の和訳と対応する英語の語句を，頭文字を参考にして書き，空欄を完成させよう。

/40点

（各1点 × 20）

① t ___ 　名 理論

② a ___ 　動 想定する

③ c ___ t ~ 　熟 ~に貢献する

④ c ___ o ~ 　熟 ~に集中する

⑤ p ___ 　名 追求

⑥ p ___ 　名 利益

⑦ b ___ *A* o *B* 　熟 A を B のせいにする

⑧ f ___ 　名 失敗

⑨ p ___ 　動 生み出す

⑩ u ___ 　形 不快な

⑪ e ___ 　名 本質

⑫ c ___ 　形 伝統的な

⑬ r ___ 　形 宗教的な

⑭ e ___ 　形 感情的な

⑮ m ___ 　動 最大化する

⑯ i ___ 　名 投資

⑰ a ___ 　動 達成する

⑱ q ___ 　動 引用する

⑲ i ___ 　動 住む

⑳ t ___ *A* i ___ *B* 　熟 A を B に変化させる

2. 次の[ ]内の語を並べ替えて，意味の通る英文を完成させよう。（各5点 × 2）

① I think things are going [failures / because / market / not / wrong / of].

② We've created a one-dimensional human [leader / the / play / to / business / of / being / role].

3. 次の英文を和訳してみよう。(10点)

Since we are persuaded by this theory that making money is the best way to bring happiness to humankind, we enthusiastically imitate the theory,

ディクテーションしてみよう！

今回学習した英文に出てきた語句を，音声を聞いて＿＿＿に書き取ろう。

06　　Mainstream free-market theory assumes that you are ❶＿＿＿＿＿＿ ＿＿＿＿＿＿ the society and the world in the best possible manner if you just concentrate on ❷＿＿＿＿＿＿＿＿＿＿ for yourself.　When believers in this theory see gloomy news on television, they should wonder whether the pursuit of profit is a cure-all, but, instead, they blame all the bad things on ❸＿＿＿＿＿＿＿＿＿.　They have trained their minds to believe that well-functioning markets simply cannot produce unpleasant results.

07　　I think things are going wrong not because of market failures.　The problem is much deeper than that.　Mainstream free-market theory fails to capture the essence of ❹＿＿＿＿＿＿＿ be human.

08　　In the conventional theory of business, ❺＿＿＿＿＿＿＿＿＿ a one-dimensional human being to play the role of business leader.　We've insulated him from ❻＿＿＿＿＿＿＿＿＿, the religious, emotional, political, and social.　He is ❼＿＿＿＿＿＿＿ one mission only — maximize profit.　He is supported by other one-dimensional human beings who give him their investment money to achieve that mission.　To quote Oscar Wilde, they know the price of everything and the value of nothing.

09　　Our economic theory has created a one-dimensional world ❽＿＿＿＿＿＿＿ those who devote themselves to the game of free-market competition, in which victory is measured purely by profit.   And since we are persuaded by this theory that making money is the best way to ⑨_____ to humankind, we enthusiastically imitate the theory, striving to transform ourselves into one-dimensional human beings. ⑩_____ theory imitating reality, we force reality to imitate theory.

確認問題の答

1. ① theory　　② assume　　③ contribute to　　④ concentrate on　　⑤ pursuit　　⑥ profit
   ⑦ blame, on　　⑧ failure　　⑨ produce　　⑩ unpleasant　　⑪ essence　　⑫ conventional
   ⑬ religious　　⑭ emotional　　⑮ maximize　　⑯ investment　　⑰ achieve　　⑱ quote
   ⑲ inhabit　　⑳ transform, into

2. ① wrong not because of market failures　（第2段落　第1文）
   ② being to play the role of business leader　（第3段落　第1文）

3. 私たちはこの理論により，金を稼ぐことこそが人類に幸福をもたらす最善の方法だと思い込まされているので，熱狂的にその理論を模倣している　（第4段落　第2文　抜粋）

ディクテーションしてみよう！の答

❶ contributing to　　❷ getting the most　　❸ market failures　　❹ what it is to　　❺ we've created
❻ the rest of life　　❼ dedicated to　　❽ inhabited by　　❾ bring happiness　　❿ Instead of

アドバイス〉 ❷ /t/ や /d/ の音が母音に挟まれるとら行のような音になる（フラッピング）。getting は「ゲッティング」というより「ゲリン」のように聞こえる。※ら行化するのはアメリカ英語。
❽ inhabited の語尾の /d/ と，by の語頭の /b/ のように，発音の仕方が近い子音が重なる場合，前の子音であるdがほとんど発音されなくなる（脱落）。

解答

問	(ア) ①	(イ) ③	(ウ) ③	(エ) ①	(オ) ④
	(カ) ②	(キ) ①	(ク) ②	(ケ) ①	(コ) ①
	(サ) ②	(シ) ①	(ス) ②	(セ) ④	

解説

問

(ア) discriminate against ～「～を差別する」が受動態になっている。

(イ) deny は第3文型(S＋V＋O)の場合は「O を否定する」の意味だが，第4文型(S＋V＋O₁＋O₂)の場合，**「O₁ に O₂ を与えない」**の意味。この第4文型を O₁ を主語にした受動態にすると，〈be denied＋O₂〉「O₂ を与えられない」となって，過去分詞 denied の後に名詞が続く形になる。

(ウ) 空所の前の do は**強調の助動詞**。空所の後にある bias「偏見，先入観」が O(目的語)になるような動詞を選ぶ。①「試す」，②「結び付けて考える」(associate *A* with *B*「A を B と結び付けて考える，A から B を連想する」)，③**「経験する」**，④「連絡を取る」。

(エ) シャツのボタン，ズボンのジッパーといった具体例から考えると，**「(右利きの人向けに)設計されて，デザインされて」**とするのが自然。②「発明されて」，④「注文されて」は文意に合わない。③については，be aimed at ～ で「～を対象にして，～に向けられて」の意味があるので，空所の後が for ではなく at であれば正解となり得る。

(オ) 「左手で使う」という内容にすべきなので，**【道具・手段】の前置詞 with** を入れる(**例** write **with** a pencil「鉛筆で書く」，cut meat **with** a knife「ナイフで肉を切る」)。by にも【手段】の意味はあるが，**【交通手段・通信手段】**を表し，**無冠詞**である点に注意(**例 by** train「電車で」，**by** telephone「電話で」)。

(カ) favor は動詞で用いると他動詞で，「～に有利になる，～にとって好都合である」の意味なので文意に合う。他の選択肢は，①「選択する」，

③「好む」，　④「支持する」。

(キ) 空所の直前には，… to get things specially made for us「私たち（＝左利き）のために特別に作られた物を入手するために…」とあるが，そういった物がなければ無理なのだから，「もし入手可能なら」とすれば自然な文脈になる。文意に合うのは if「もし…ならば」。

(ク) 操作する部分が右側に付いている自動販売機は左利きの人々にとって inconvenience「不便」であると考える。他の選択肢は，①「騒動，不安，妨害」，③「過ち」，　④「欠陥」。

(ケ) be accustomed to *doing*「～するのに慣れている」（＝be used to *doing*）

(コ) tend to *do*「～する傾向がある」。これ以外に to 不定詞と結び付くのは④だが，try to *do*「～しようとする」では主語との関係が合わない。

(サ) the difference between *A* and *B*「A と B の違い」

(シ) 空所直後の「,」（コンマ）は**同格**を表し，myself が続いているので，「私のアイデンティティ＝私自身」と考える。他の選択肢は，②「想像」，③「重要性」，④「自立，独立」。

(ス) 受動態になっており，もともとは〈動詞＋*A*＋to＋*B*〉のパターンであったと考えられる。convert *A* to *B* で「A を B に変える，転換する」の意味。「右利きに変えられるくらいなら～」とすれば文意に合う。他の選択肢を当てはめて検討すると以下のようになる。

① adapt *A* to *B*「A を B に順応させる」

③ exchange *A* to *B* という形はない。exchange *A* with *B*「B と A を交わす，やりとりする」，exchange *A* for *B*「A を B に取り替える」のパターンで使う。

④ transfer *A* to *B*「A を B に移転［移動］する」

(セ) otherwise は副詞で，1)「もしそうでなければ，さもないと」（＝if not），2)「その他の点では」（＝in every other respect），3)**「違ったふうに，違うやり方で」**（＝in a different way）の意味がある。ここでは 3) の意味で，文脈上「左利きではなく（生きること）」となる。他の選択肢は，①「全く，少しも」（※否定を強調），②「～なしで」（※前置詞なので，ここでは不適），③「どういうわけか，どうにかして」。

第1段落　文の構造と語句のチェック

¹〈 Being left-handed 〉 gives me some insights 〔 into 〈 what it is like 〈 to be a
S　　　　　　　　　 V　 O₁　　O₂　　　　　　　疑　仮S V　　　　　真S

minority 〉〉〕. ²That is（ because we lefties are discriminated against（ every day ）〉.
　　　　　　　　S　V　 従接　　 S　　　　　V

³Oh, it is not（ for serious things ）: we are not denied housing, jobs, medical
　　S　V　　　　　　　　　　　　　 S　 V　　　　　①　　　②　　 ③
　　　　　　　　　　　　　　　　　　　　　　　　　　　　　　　　O

care, or seats on a bus. ⁴However, we do experience anti-lefty bias（ in ways
　　 ④
　 等接　　　　　　　　　　　　　 S　 V　　　　　　O

　　関代 which 省略
〔 right-handed people probably never realize 〕). ⁵Did you know,（ for example ），
　　　　　S　　　　　　　　 V　　　　　　　　　　(V) S　V

　　　　　　　　①　　　　　　　　　②
〈 that shirt buttons and trouser zippers are designed（ for right-handed people ）〉?
O 従接　　　　　　　 等接 S　　　　　　 V

⁶Most kitchen tools,（ as well ）— can openers, ladles and sauce pans, and
　　S　　　　　　　　　　　　　　①　　　②　 等接　 ③　 等接

various knives and peelers — are ineffective, awkward, or impossible（ to use
　 ④　 等接　 ⑤　　　 V　 C①　　　 C②　 等接　 C③

（ with the left hand ）). ⁷（ Every day ）（ in school ）we must put up with such
　　　　　　　　　　　　　　　　　　　　　　　　　 S　　 V

things〔 as desks, pencil sharpeners, scissors, cutters, and three-ring binders 〕,
O　　①　　　　 ②　　　　 ③　　　 ④　 等接　 ⑤

　　　　　　　　　　　　　　　　　　　　①
all〔 which favor the right-handed person 〕. ⁸Musical instruments and sports
　 関代　 V　　　　 O　　　　　　　　　　　　　　　　　 等接 S

②
equipment, too, are made（ for right-handed people ）. ⁹We must either
　　　　　　　 V　　　　　　　　　　　　　　　　　　　 S

learn to play right-handed or spend extra money（ to get things〔 specially made
　 V　　　　　　 等接 V　　 O

for us]) ─ (<u>if</u> <u>they</u> <u>are</u> even <u>available</u>). ¹⁰<u>Then</u> there <u>is</u> <u>the mechanical world</u>.
　　　　　　　従接　S 　 V 　　　　　　　　C　　　　　　　　　　　 V 　　　　　　S

¹¹<u>Vending machines</u>, (with the controls to the right), <u>are</u> <u>a minor</u>
　　　　　　S　　　　　　　　　　　　　　　　　　　　　　　　　　　　V

<u>inconvenience</u>, <u>but</u> <u>power tools</u> <u>can be</u> <u>dangerous</u> (for us).
　　　C　　　　　　 等接　　 S　　　　 V　　　 C

> **訳** ¹左利きであることは，少数派であるのがどのようなことなのかについて，私に深い理解を与えてくれる。²それは，我々左利きは日々差別を受けているからだ。³いや，これは重大な事柄に対してではない。つまり，我々は住居や仕事や医療やバスの座席を認められていないのではない。⁴しかし，我々は，右利きの人々がおそらく絶対に気づかないであろう形で，左利きに不利に働く偏見を身をもって体験しているのだ。⁵例えば，シャツのボタンやズボンのジッパーが右利きの人向けにデザインされていることをご存じだっただろうか。⁶缶切り，おたま，シチュー鍋，さまざまなナイフや皮むき器といった，ほとんどの台所用具も，左手で使うには役に立たなかったり，扱いにくかったり，あるいは使えなかったりするのだ。⁷毎日，学校では，机，鉛筆削り，はさみ，カッター，3穴バインダーといったものに我慢をしなければならない。これらは皆，右利きの人に好都合なのだ。⁸楽器やスポーツ用品もまた，右利きの人に合わせて作られている。⁹我々は，右利きで使えるようになるか，あるいは，我々のために特別に作られた物を手に入れるために余分なお金を使うか，いずれかをしなければならない。そもそも，そういった物が入手可能であればの話だが。¹⁰そして今度は機械の世界が待ち構えている。¹¹自動販売機は，操作する部分が右側にあり，ちょっとした不便にすぎないが，電動工具は我々にとって危険な場合がある。

Check! 第1文：What is S like? で「Sはどのような人[物]か」の意味を表す(**例** What is the weather like?「天気はどうですか」)。この場合の like は前置詞。この間接疑問文が what S is like で，さらにこれが形式主語の it is ~ to do のパターンと結びつくと，what it is like to do「~することはどのようなことか」となる(**例** He doesn't know what it is like to be poor.「彼は貧乏であることがどのようなことか知らない」)。

語句

left-handed	形 左利きの
insight	名 (深い)理解，見識
minority	名 少数派
That is because ...	熟 それは…だからだ
lefty	名 左利きの人

discriminate against ~
熟 ~を差別する
deny A B 動 AにBを与えない，認めない
housing 名 住宅
medical 形 医療の
▶ medical care 医療ケア，医療
experience 動 経験する

anti-lefty	形	反左利きの，左利きに不利な	cutter	名	カッターナイフ
※ anti- は「反…，対…」を表す接頭辞			binder	名	バインダー，とじ込み表紙
bias	名	偏見，先入観	**favor**	動	有利である，好都合である
right-handed	形	右利きの	**musical**	形	音楽の
probably	副	たぶん，おそらく	**instrument**	名	器具
realize	動	わかる，気づく	▶ musical instrument 楽器		
trouser	形	ズボンの	**equipment**	名	装備，備品
zipper	名	ジッパー，チャック	**either *A* or *B***	熟	*A* か *B* のどちらか
tool	名	道具，用具	**extra**	形	余分の，追加の
as well	熟	～も（また）	**specially**	副	特別に，わざわざ
can opener	名	缶切り	**available**	形	入手可能な
ladle	名	おたま，ひしゃく	**mechanical**	形	機械の
sauce pan	名	シチュー鍋，外輪鍋	**vending machine**	名	自動販売機
peeler	名	皮むき器	control	名	制御装置，調整つまみ
ineffective	形	無益な，役に立たない	to the right	熟	右側に
awkward	形	扱いにくい，不便な	**minor**	形	さほど重要でない，ちょっと
put up with ～	熟	～を我慢する			した
such *A* as *B*	熟	*B* のような *A*	**inconvenience**	名	不便，不都合
sharpener	名	（鉛筆などを）削る道具	power tool	名	電動工具
scissors	名	はさみ	**dangerous**	形	危険な

第2段落 文の構造と語句のチェック

[1]Occasionally, however, there are a few advantages 〔 to being left-handed 〕.
（are = V, a few advantages = S）

[2]（ In sports ），（ particularly one-on-one situations 〔 such as tennis or boxing 〕），
（① 等接 ②）

we often have the advantage. [3]That is（ because we are accustomed（ to facing
（S V O）（S V 従接 S V C）

right-handed opponents ），and so are our opponents ）. [4]So, our left-handedness
（等接 V S）（S）

tends to confuse them. [5]（ In baseball ），（ as well ）, a left-handed batter is
（V O）（S V）

already（ one step ）closer（ to first base than a righty ）, which can make the
（C）（関代 V）

difference 〔 between being safe or out（ on a close play ）〕.
（O）

42

訳 ¹しかし，時々，左利きであることが有利になる点もいくつか存在する。²スポーツ，特にテニスやボクシングのような１対１の状況では，我々が有利になることが多い。³それは，我々は右利きの相手と対戦するのに慣れており，相手もそうだからだ。⁴だから，我々が左利きであることが相手を混乱させがちなのだ。⁵野球においても，左打者は右打者に比べてすでに１塁ベースに１歩近くなっており，きわどいプレーにおいてはそれがセーフかアウトかの違いを生み出す可能性もある。

Check! 第３文：... we are accustomed to facing right-handed opponents, and so are our opponents の so are our opponents は〈so＋V＋S〉「SもVする」の形。ここでは，are が V，our opponents が S で，「相手もそうである（＝右利きの相手と対戦するのに慣れている）」の意味。V の部分は前の文に合わせて，be 動詞，助動詞，do / does / did（一般動詞の文の場合）となる。

例 "I like baseball." "*So do I*."「私は野球が好きだ」「私もです」

語句

advantage	名	利点，有利	left-handedness	名 左利きであること
particularly	副	特に，とりわけ	tend to *do*	熟 ～する傾向がある，～しがちだ
one-on-one	形	１対１の，マンツーマンの	confuse	動 混乱させる
situation	名	状況	close	形 近い
such as ～	熟	（例えば）～のような	righty	名 右利きの人
be accustomed to ～	熟	～に慣れている（＊「～」は名詞または動名詞）	difference	名 違い
face	動	対戦する，対面する	close play	名 （アウト・セーフの判定が）きわどいプレー，クロスプレー
opponent	名	相手，敵		

第3段落 文の構造と語句のチェック

¹So, would(V) I(S) want to be(V) right-handed(C)? ²The answer(S) is(V) simple(C): No!

³Left-handedness(S) is(V) part(C) 〔 of my identity, myself 〕同格. ⁴I(S) **would sooner** cut off(V) my right arm(O) (**than** be converted to right-handedness). ⁵Left-handedness(S) is(V) **such** an integral part of me(C) (**that** 従接 I(S) could not imagine(V) 〈 living otherwise 〉(O)).

訳 ¹それでは，私は右利きになりたいのだろうか。²答えは簡単だ。ノーである。³左利きであることは，私のアイデンティティ，私自身の一部なのだ。⁴右利きに変えられるぐらいなら，私は右手を切断したほうがましだ。⁵左利きであることはまさに私の欠かせない一部なので，違う生き方をするのは想像できないほどである。

Check! 第4文の would sooner [rather] ... than ～（「...」，「～」はいずれも動詞の原形）は「～するぐらいなら…したい」の意味。

語句

simple	形 単純な，簡単な	convert *A* to *B*	熟 A を B に変える，転換する
identity	名 独自性，個性	right-handedness	名 右利きであること
would sooner ... than ～		**such ～ that ...**	熟 とても～なので…
	熟 ～するぐらいなら…したい	**integral**	形 不可欠の
cut off ～	熟 ～を切断する	**imagine**	動 想像する
		otherwise	副 別のやり方で，違ったふうに

文法事項の整理 ③　強調の助動詞 do

第1段落第4文の強調の助動詞 do について見てみよう。

However, we **do** experience anti-lefty bias in ways right-handed people probably never realize.

〈do / does / did＋原形〉は**動詞の強調**を表す。「確かに／実際に／本当に～する」などと訳す。**命令文の場合は「ぜひ～しなさい」**と訳す。

例 He does understand what you said.
「彼はあなたが言ったことをちゃんと理解していますよ」

例 "You didn't say that." "I did say that!"
「君はそんなことは言わなかったよ」「いや，確かに言った！」

例 Do come to see us.
「ぜひ会いにいらっしゃい」

（第 1 段落第 4 文）

However, we do experience anti-lefty bias in ways right-handed people probably never realize.

▶ do が動詞 experience を強調して，「実際に［まさに］体験する」の意。

確認問題

/40点

1. 次の和訳と対応する英語の語句を，頭文字を参考にして書き，空欄を完成させよう。

（各 1 点 × 20）

①	i	名	（深い）理解
②	m	名	少数派
③	d ～ a	熟	～を差別する
④	b	名	偏見
⑤	a	形	扱いにくい
⑥	p u w ～	熟	～を我慢する
⑦	f	動	有利である
⑧	i	名	器具
⑨	e	名	装備，備品
⑩	s	副	特別に，わざわざ
⑪	a	形	入手可能な
⑫	v m	名	自動販売機
⑬	m	形	さほど重要でない
⑭	i	名	不便
⑮	a	名	利点
⑯	p	副	特に，とりわけ
⑰	c	動	混乱させる
⑱	i	名	独自性

⑲	i	形	不可欠の
⑳	o	副	別のやり方で

2. 次の[ ]内の語句を並べ替えて，意味の通る英文を完成させよう。（各5点×2）

① We [in / anti-lefty bias / ways / experience / do] right-handed people probably never realize.

② Left-handedness is [of / that / integral / me / an / such / part] I could not imagine living otherwise.

3. 次の英文を和訳してみよう。（10点）

That is because we are accustomed to facing right-handed opponents, and so are our opponents.

*opponent （スポーツの試合での）相手，敵

ディクテーションしてみよう！

今回学習した英文に出てきた語句を，音声を聞いて＿＿＿に書き取ろう。

11   Being left-handed gives me some insights into ❶＿＿＿＿＿＿＿＿＿＿ to be a minority. That is because we lefties are discriminated against every day. Oh, it is not for serious things: we ❷＿＿＿＿＿＿＿＿＿＿ housing, jobs, medical care, or seats on a bus. However, we do experience anti-lefty bias in ways right-handed people probably never realize. Did you know, for example, that shirt buttons and trouser zippers are designed for right-handed people? Most kitchen tools, as well — can openers, ladles and sauce pans, and various knives and peelers — are ineffective, awkward, ❸＿＿＿＿＿ ＿＿＿＿＿＿＿＿＿＿＿＿＿ with the left hand. Every day in school we must ❹＿＿＿＿＿＿＿＿ such things as desks, pencil sharpeners, scissors, cutters, and three-ring binders, all which favor the right-handed person. Musical instruments and sports equipment, too, are made for right-handed people. We must either learn to play right-handed or spend extra money to

get things specially made for us — if they are ❺_____. Then there is the mechanical world. Vending machines, with the controls to the right, are a minor inconvenience, but power tools can be dangerous for us.

12　Occasionally, however, there are a few advantages to being left-handed. In sports, particularly one-on-one situations such as tennis or boxing, we often have the advantage. That is because we ❻_____ _____ facing right-handed opponents, and so are our opponents. So, our left-handedness tends to confuse them. In baseball, as well, a left-handed batter is already one step closer to first base than a righty, which can make the difference between being safe or out ❼_____.

13　So, would I want to be right-handed? The answer is simple: No! Left-handedness is part of my identity, myself. I ❽_____ cut off my right arm than be converted to right-handedness. Left-handedness is ❾_____ part of me that I could not imagine living otherwise.

確認問題の答

1. ① insight　② minority　③ discriminate against　④ bias　⑤ awkward　⑥ put up with
　⑦ favor　⑧ instrument　⑨ equipment　⑩ specially　⑪ available　⑫ vending machine
　⑬ minor　⑭ inconvenience　⑮ advantage　⑯ particularly　⑰ confuse　⑱ identity
　⑲ integral　⑳ otherwise

2. ① do experience anti-lefty bias in ways　（第1段落　第4文）
　② such an integral part of me that　（第3段落　最終文）

3. それは、我々は右利きの相手と対戦するのに慣れており、相手もそうだからだ。（第2段落　第3文）

ディクテーションしてみよう！の答

　❶ what it is like　❷ are not denied　❸ or impossible to use　❹ put up with
　❺ even available　❻ are accustomed to　❼ on a close play　❽ would sooner
　❾ such an integral

アドバイス　❻ accustomed の語尾の /d/ と to の /t/ で子音が2つ連続するため、前の /d/ の音はほとんど発音されなくなる（脱落）。

　❼ on の /n/ が後ろとつながり、「オンア」ではなく「オナ」のように聞こえる（連結）。

4 解答・解説

解答

問1 私たちの毎日の活動や行動により大気中の温室効果ガスが増えているが、その活動の多くは影響がわからないうちに設計され作られたものなので、完全に私たちの責任というわけではない。

問2 この科学者たちは、地球温暖化による強烈な影響をいくらかでも防ぐために全世界の温室効果ガス排出量を削減するための時間は、私たちにはわずかしか残されていないことを宣言した。

問3 これを達成できないと、何百万人もの人々が、熱波、干ばつ、洪水や暴風雨といった極限的な出来事の危険にさらされ、沿岸地域や都市は海面上昇に脅かされ、多くの生態系、動植物の種が深刻な絶滅の危機に瀕することになるから。

問4 生活の仕方を変えることは、私たちの健康や幸福にとってのみならず、私たちの生存にとっても重要となる。

問5 二酸化炭素排出量を算出することにより、自分が個人的に地球温暖化にどれほど関与しているのかを計算すること。

解説

問1

下線部の和訳は、「それは完全に私たちが悪いというわけではない」となる。**not entirely は「完全に[全く]〜というわけではない」の意味で、【部分否定】を表す**。it は同じ文の前半の many 〜 atmosphere を指す。具体的な説明としては、直後の文に書かれている理由を含めるべきだろう。

問2

These scientists declared that we have only a small window of time in which to reduce worldwide greenhouse gas emissions in order to prevent some of the drastic impacts of global warming.

以下のポイントをおさえよう！

☑ These scientists が S，declared が V，that ～ warming が O。

☑ declare は「宣言する」の意味。「明言する」「断言する」などの意味もある。

☑ window は［注］にある通り，「期間」の意味。

☑ in which 以下は time を修飾。〈前置詞＋whom[which]＋to *do*〉は不定詞の
　形容詞用法と同様の働きをし，「～するための」「～すべき」の意味。

例　I need a pen to write with.「書くためのペンが必要だ」
　　　＝ I need a pen with which to write.

☑ in order to *do* は「～するために」の意味で，【目的】を表す。

問3

　下線部**(ウ)**を受けて，直後の文で If we don't accomplish this「これを達成
しなければ」と，**実現しなかった場合の弊害**が the scientists, wrote のあとに
挙げられている。「すべて述べなさい」という設問なので，この段落に挙げら
れている内容を漏らさず書かなくてはならない。

　これらの弊害は，① many millions of people … floods and storms，② our
coasts and cities … rising sea levels，③ many ecosystems … danger of
extinction と**3つの〈S＋V〉を並列**して述べられているので，以下のようにまと
められる。

　　① 何百万人もの人々が，熱波，干ばつ，洪水や暴風雨といった極限的な出
　　　来事の危険にさらされる
　　② 沿岸地域や都市は海面上昇に脅かされる
　　③ 多くの生態系，動植物の種が深刻な絶滅の危機に瀕することになる

問4

Making changes in the way in which we live is key not only to our health
and happiness — but to our survival as well.

以下のポイントをおさえよう！

☑ 文頭の Making は動名詞。Making ～ we live が S，is が V，key 以下が C。

☑ 〈the way in which S＋V〉で「S が V するやり方，方法」。

☑ be key to ～ で「～への（解決，成功などへつながる）カギ[手がかり]であ

る」の意味。この key は「（〜にとって）重要な，必須の」という意味の形容詞。

☑ not only *A* but *B* as well は not only *A* but also *B* と同様の意味。

問5

　下線部の exercise は，ここでは「練習問題」の意味。this one simple exercise で「この1つの簡単な練習問題」。第5段落第1文では，筆者が自らの二酸化炭素排出量を算出しようとしたこと，第6段落第1，2文ではその結果の考察について述べられているので，下線部が指すのは，第5段落第1文 to figure out 〜 carbon footprint と考えてよい。

▼

それでは次に，段落ごとに詳しくみていこう。

第1段落　文の構造と語句のチェック

┌── 従接 that 省略

¹The truth is, 〈many 〔 of our daily actions and behaviors 〕 add
　S　　　　　V　C　S　　　　　　　　　　　　①　　　等接　　②　　　V

greenhouse gases (to the atmosphere)〉, and it's not entirely our fault. ²Many 〔
　　　　O　　　　　　　　　　　　　　　等接　S　V　　　　　　　C　　　　S

of the technologies, institutions, and ways of living 〔 that we embrace today 〕〕
　　　①　　　　　　②　　　等接　　③　　　関代　S　　V

were designed and created (before we understood 〈 what the consequences
　①　　　　　②　　　　　　　　　　　　　　　
　V　等接　V　　　従接　S　　V　　　O 疑　　　S

would be 〉).
　V

訳 ¹実は，私たちの毎日の活動や行動の多くは大気に温室効果ガスを加えていくが，そのことは完全に私たちの責任というわけではない。²今日私たちが受け入れている技術，制度，生活様式の多くは，それらの影響がどうなるかを理解する前に設計され作り出されたのだ。

語句

The truth is (that) ...	熟	実は…，本当は…
daily	形	毎日の
action	名	活動，行動
behavior	名	ふるまい，行動
add	動	加える
▶ add *A* to *B*		A を B に加える
greenhouse gas	名	温室効果ガス
atmosphere	名	大気

entirely	副	完全に，全く
▶ not entirely ~		完全に~というわけではない【部分否定】
fault	名	責任，落ち度
institution	名	(社会)制度，慣習
embrace	動	受け入れる，採り入れる
design	動	設計する，立案する
create	動	作り出す，創造する
consequence	名	影響，結果

第2段落 文の構造と語句のチェック

¹But （ in December 2007 ） （ at the annual United Nations Framework
_{等接}

Convention on Climate Change in Bali ）, 200 of the world's leading climate
_S

scientists issued a major call to arms. ²These scientists declared 〈 that we have
_V _O _S _V _{O 従接} _S _V

only a small window of time 〔 in which to reduce worldwide greenhouse gas
_O _{関代} _{V′}

emissions （ in order to prevent some of the drastic impacts of global warming ）〕〉.
_{O′} _{V′} _{O′}

> 訳 ¹しかし，2007年12月に，バリ島で行われた国連気候変動枠組条約年次大会において，世界の主要な気候科学者の200人が重要な呼びかけを行った。²この科学者たちは，地球温暖化による強烈な影響をいくらかでも防ぐために全世界の温室効果ガス排出量を削減するための時間は，私たちにはわずかしか残されていないことを宣言した。

語句

annual	形	毎年の，年次の
climate	名	気候
leading	形	主要な，一流の
issue	動	発する，出す
major	形	主要な，重大な
declare	動	宣言する，明言する
reduce	動	削減する

worldwide	形	世界中の
emission	名	排出(量)
in order to *do*	熟	~するために
prevent	動	防ぐ，予防する
drastic	形	強烈な
impact	名	影響，衝撃
global warming	名	地球温暖化

¹(In the next 10 to 15 years), (they said), emissions must begin to decline
　　　　　　　　　　　　　　主節の挿入
　　　　　　　　　　　　　　S　V　　　　S　　　　　　　　V

(each year) (rather than grow) — and (by 2050), emissions must be *half*
　　　　　　　　　　　　　　　　等接　　　　　　　　　　S　　　　　V　　　　C

⟨ what they were (in 1990)⟩. ²(If we don't accomplish this), (the scientists
　　(of)
　関代　S　V　　　　　　　　　　　　　　　　　　　　　　　　　　主節の挿入
　　　　　　　　　　　　　　　　　　　　　　　　　　　　　　　　S

wrote), *many millions of people will be at risk* (*from extreme events* [*such as*
　V　　　　　S　　　　　　　　　V　　　C

heat waves, drought, floods and storms]), *our coasts and cities will be*
　　①　　　　②　　　③　等接　④　　　　　　　　　　　等接
　　　　　　　　　　　　　　　　　　　　　　S

threatened (*by rising sea levels*), *and many ecosystems, plants and*
　V　　　　　　　　　　　　　　　　　等接　　　　　　　　　　　等接

animal species will be in serious danger of extinction.
　　　　S　　　　V　　　C

> 訳 ¹彼らが言うには，今後 10 〜 15 年で，排出量は増加するどころか毎年減少し始めなくてはならず，2050 年までには，排出量は1990 年の排出量の半分になっていなければならない。²これを達成できない場合，科学者たちによると，何百万人もの人々が，熱波，干ばつ，洪水や暴風雨といった極端的な出来事の危険にさらされ，沿岸地域や都市は海面上昇に脅かされ，そして多くの生態系，動植物の種が深刻な絶滅の危機に瀕することになるであろう。

Check! 第 1 文の they said，第 2 文の the scientists wrote はいずれも主節が挿入されている。

語句

decline	動	減少する，低下する	drought	名 干ばつ
rather than ~	熟 ~というよりむしろ		flood	名 洪水
accomplish	動 達成する	storm	名 嵐，暴風(雨)
at risk (from ~)	熟 (~の)危険にさらされて	coast	名 沿岸(地帯)
		threaten	動 脅かす
extreme	形 極端な，極限的な	level	名 高さ，水位
event	名 出来事	ecosystem	名 生態系
heat wave	名 酷暑，熱波	in danger of ~	熟 ~の危機に瀕して
		extinction	名 絶滅

第4段落　文の構造と語句のチェック

^{1}That's a lot 〔 to digest 〕. ^{2}But（ rather than being overwhelmed ）, let's start
　　　S　V　C　　　　　　　　　　　　　　等接　　　　　　　　　　　　　　　　　　　　V

（ with 〈 what you can do today 〉）. ^{3}One person can make a huge difference.
　　　　　関代　S　V　　　　　　　　　S　　　　　V　　　O

^{4}〈 Making changes in the way 〔 in which we live 〕〉 is key （ not only to our
　S　　　　　　　　　　　　　　　　関代　S　V　　　　V　C　　　　　　　　　

health and happiness — but to our survival as well ）.
　　　　①　　　　　　　　　　　　　　②

> **訳** ^{1}これらをすべて受け入れるのは大変なことだ。^{2}しかし、呆然（ぼうぜん）としていないで、今日でき
> ることから始めよう。^{3}1 人の人間でも大きな違いを生み出すことは可能だ。^{4}生活の仕
> 方を変えることは、私たちの健康や幸福にとってのみならず、私たちの生存にとっても重
> 要となる。

Check! 第 4 文 not only *A* but also *B*「A だけでなく B も」は、only の代わりに
just / simply / merely が使われることもあり、but also *B* の部分も、but *B* /
but *B* as well / but *B* too などの形もある。第 4 文は not only *A* but *B* as well
のパターン。

語句

digest	動	（知識などを）消化する、会得する
overwhelm	動	呆然とさせる、困惑させる
huge	形	巨大な、莫大（ばくだい）な
key	形	重要な

not only *A* but *B* as well		
	熟	A だけでなく B も
health	名	健康
happiness	名	幸福
survival	名	生き残ること、生存

第5段落　文の構造と語句のチェック

^{1}（ Not too long ago ）, I decided to figure out 〈 just how much I personally was
　　　　　　　　　　　　　　S　　V　　　　　O　　　　　疑　　　　S

contributing to global warming 〉（ by calculating my carbon footprint ）. ^{2}The
　　V　　　　　　O　　　　　　　　　　　　V'　　　　　　O'

measure of our impact is often called a carbon footprint （ because carbon dioxide
　　　　S　　　　　　　V　　　　　C　　　　　　　　　従接　　　　S

$\underset{\text{V}}{\text{is}}$ $\underset{\text{C}}{\underline{\text{the most common greenhouse gas}}}$).

> **訳** ¹それほど前のことではないが，私は自分の二酸化炭素排出量を算出することにより，個人的に地球温暖化にどれほど関与しているのかを計算してみることにした。²二酸化炭素が最も一般的な温室効果ガスであるため，私たちが与える影響の程度は，よく carbon footprint（二酸化炭素排出量）と呼ばれる。

語句

figure out ~	熟	~を計算する，（計算して）~を出す	
personally	副	個人的に，自分自身で	
contribute to ~	熟	~の一因となる，~に関与する	

calculate	動	計算する，算出する
carbon footprint	名	二酸化炭素排出量
measure	名	程度
carbon dioxide	名	二酸化炭素
common	形	普通の，ありふれた

第6段落 文の構造と語句のチェック

¹(Considering ⟨ that $\underset{\text{S}}{\text{I}}$ $\underset{\text{V①}}{\underline{\text{live}}}$ (in an eco-friendly apartment building), $\underset{\text{V②}}{\underline{\text{recycle}}}$,
　　　　　　従接

$\underset{\text{V③}}{\underline{\text{walk}}}$ (to work), $\underset{\text{等接}}{\underline{\text{and}}}$ (no longer) $\underset{\text{V④}}{\underline{\text{own}}}$ $\underset{\text{O}}{\text{a car}}$ ⟩), $\underset{\text{S}}{\text{I}}$ $\underset{\text{V}}{\underline{\text{assumed}}}$ ⟨ $\underset{\text{O}}{\underline{\text{my impact}}}$ [on the （従接 that 省略）

planet] $\underset{\text{V}}{\underline{\text{would be}}}$ $\underset{\text{C}}{\underline{\text{relatively low}}}$). ²$\underset{\text{仮S}}{\text{It}}$ $\underset{\text{V}}{\underline{\text{turns out}}}$ ⟨ $\underset{\text{真S 従接}}{\text{that}}$ (because $\underset{\text{S}}{\text{I}}$ $\underset{\text{V}}{\underline{\text{fly}}}$ so often), 従接

$\underset{\text{S}}{\underline{\text{my carbon footprint}}}$ $\underset{\text{V}}{\text{is}}$ $\underset{\text{C}}{\underline{\text{much higher}}}$ (than $\underset{\text{S}}{\text{I}}$ $\underset{\text{V}}{\underline{\text{thought}}}$)⟩. ³⟨ $\underset{\text{V'}}{\underline{\text{Doing}}}$ （関代 which 省略）

$\underset{\text{O'}}{\underline{\text{this one simple exercise}}}$ ⟩ quickly $\underset{\text{V①}}{\underline{\text{showed}}}$ $\underset{\text{O}_1}{\underline{\text{me}}}$ $\underset{\text{O}_2}{\underline{\text{changes}}}$ [$\underset{\text{S}}{\text{I}}$ $\underset{\text{V}}{\underline{\text{could make}}}$ (to $\underset{\text{V'}}{\underline{\text{lower}}}$

$\underset{\text{O'}}{\underline{\text{my carbon footprint}}}$)] $\underset{\text{等接}}{\underline{\text{and}}}$ $\underset{\text{V②}}{\underline{\text{inspired}}}$ $\underset{\text{O}}{\underline{\text{me}}}$ $\underset{\text{C}}{\underline{\text{to do more}}}$.

> **訳** ¹私はエコ集合住宅に住んでおり，リサイクルもし，徒歩で通勤し，もう車も所有していないということを考慮すると，私が地球に与える影響は比較的小さいであろうと思い込んでいた。²ところが，私は非常に頻繁に飛行機で移動するため，私の二酸化炭素排出量は思っていたよりもはるかに多いということが判明したのだ。³このような単純な練習問題を1つ解くことで，自分の二酸化炭素排出量を減らすためにできる変化があっという間にわかったし，もっと多くのことをやろうという刺激になった。

語 句

considering that ... 熟 …ということを考
慮すれば
eco-friendly 形 環境に優しい
apartment 名 アパート
recycle 動 リサイクルする，再利用する
no longer ~ 熟 もはや~ない
own 動 所有する
assume 動 (当然)…と思う

the planet 名 地球
relatively 副 比較的
it turns out that ... 熟 …ということがわ
かる
fly 動 飛行機で移動[旅行]する
exercise 名 練習(問題)，課題
quickly 副 すぐに，即座に
lower 動 減らす
inspire 動 奮起させる，刺激する

文法事項の整理 ④　部分否定

第1段落第1文の【部分否定】について見てみよう。

The truth is, many of our daily actions and ... to the atmosphere, and it's **not entirely** our fault.

部分否定とは，「全部が~というわけではない」「いつも~というわけではない」といった，"**例外を認める否定**"。

■副詞による部分否定

not + always	「いつも[必ずしも]~というわけではない」
not + necessarily	「必ずしも~というわけではない」
not + everywhere	「どこでも~というわけではない」
not + quite altogether completely entirely wholly	「全く[完全に]~というわけではない」
not + very much so too	「あまり[それほど／たいして]~というわけではない」

■代名詞・形容詞による部分否定／全体否定

	2者	3者以上
部分否定	**not＋both**：形代 「両方〜というわけではない」	**not＋all**：形代 **not＋every**：形 「すべて〜というわけではない」
全体否定	**not＋either**：形代 　　（*either＋not は×） **neither**：形代 「どちらも〜ない」	**not＋any**：形代 　　（*any＋not は×） **no**：形 / **none**：代 「全く［1つも］〜ない」

※形：形容詞の働き，つまり，直後に名詞がつく。
　代：代名詞の働き，つまり，単独でSやOになれる。
　形代：上記の両方の働きを持つ。

（第1段落第1文）

... it's not entirely our fault.

▶ not entirely が部分否定で「完全に〜というわけではない」の意味。

（第5段落第1文）

Not too long ago, ...

▶ not too が部分否定で「それほど〜というわけではない」の意味。

確認問題

/40点

1. 次の和訳と対応する英語の語句を，頭文字を参考にして書き，空欄を完成させよう。

(各1点×20)

No.	頭文字	品詞	和訳
①	a	名	大気
②	i	名	(社会)制度
③	e	動	受け入れる
④	c	名	結果
⑤	a	形	毎年の
⑥	l	形	主要な
⑦	i	動	発する
⑧	d	動	宣言する
⑨	e	名	排出(量)
⑩	d	形	強烈な
⑪	d	動	減少する
⑫	a	動	達成する
⑬	e	形	極端な
⑭	f	名	洪水
⑮	t	動	脅かす
⑯	d	動	消化する
⑰	s	名	生き残ること
⑱	c	動	計算する
⑲	c　　d	名	二酸化炭素
⑳	r	副	比較的

2. 次の[ ]内の語を並べ替えて，意味の通る英文を完成させよう。(各5点×2)

① Many [be / people / risk / will / from / of / at / millions] extreme events such as heat waves, drought, floods and storms.

② It [so / because / fly / that / out / turns / I] often, my carbon footprint is much higher than I thought.

3. 次の英文を和訳してみよう。(10 点)

The truth is, many of our daily actions and behaviors add greenhouse gases to the atmosphere, and it's not entirely our fault.

ディクテーションしてみよう！

今回学習した英文に出てきた語句を，音声を聞いて＿＿＿に書き取ろう。

15   The truth is, ❶＿＿＿＿＿＿＿＿ daily actions and behaviors add greenhouse gases to the atmosphere, and it's not entirely our fault. Many of the technologies, institutions, and ❷＿＿＿＿＿＿＿＿ that we embrace today were designed and created before we understood what the consequences would be.

16   But ❸＿＿＿＿＿＿＿＿ at the annual United Nations Framework Convention on Climate Change in Bali, 200 of the world's leading climate scientists issued a major call to arms. These scientists declared that we have only a small window of time ❹＿＿＿＿＿＿＿ ＿＿＿＿＿ worldwide greenhouse gas emissions in order to prevent some of the drastic impacts of global warming.

17   In the ❺＿＿＿＿＿＿＿＿＿, they said, emissions must begin to decline each year rather than grow — and by 2050, emissions must be *half* what they were in 1990. If we don't accomplish this, the scientists wrote, *many millions of people will be at risk from extreme events such as heat waves, drought, floods and storms, our coasts and cities will be threatened by rising sea levels, and many ecosystems, plants and animal species will be* ❻＿＿＿＿＿＿＿＿＿＿＿.

18   That's a lot to digest. But rather than being overwhelmed, let's start with what you can do today. One person can make a huge difference.

Making changes in the way in which we live is key not only to our health and happiness — ❼_____ as well.

19　Not too long ago, I decided to figure out just how much I personally was contributing to global warming by calculating my carbon footprint. ❽_____ is often called a carbon footprint because carbon dioxide is the most common greenhouse gas.

20　Considering that I live in an eco-friendly apartment building, recycle, walk to work, and no longer own a car, I assumed my impact on the planet would be ❾_____. It turns out that because I fly so often, my carbon footprint is much higher than I thought. Doing this one simple exercise quickly showed me ❿_____ to lower my carbon footprint and inspired me to do more.

5　解答・解説

解答

問1	社主[経営者]は強い政治的見解を持っており，大統領を公然と批判した音楽家の音楽を流すことを折にふれて拒絶してきた。
問2	アメリカ人は絶え間ないジレンマに直面している。つまり，言論の自由の権利と，子供たちを保護し，品位の水準を維持する必要性との釣り合いをいかにして取るかという問題である。
問3	アメリカの子供たちは，テレビを見たり，コンピュータを使用したり，テレビゲームをしたりして過ごす時間が多すぎる結果，運動不足になっているから。
問4	コンピュータを所有し，テレビよりコンピュータに時間を費やす人々は教育レベルや社会経済上のレベルが高く，他方，コンピュータを所有しない人々は貧しい生活を送っているという，コンピュータ所有の有無による格差。

解説

問1

The owner has strong political views, and he has on occasion refused to play music of musicians who publicly criticized the president.

以下のポイントをおさえよう！

☑ owner は，この文脈では，クリアチャンネルという会社のオーナー(社主)。

☑ on occasion「時々，時折」

☑ refuse to *do*「～することを拒否する」

☑ 関係代名詞 who の導く節が musicians を修飾。

問2

Americans face a constant dilemma — how to balance the right to free speech with the need to protect children and maintain standards of decency.

以下のポイントをおさえよう！

☑ face は動詞で「〜に直面する」の意味。

☑ dilemma は日本語でも「ジレンマ」というので,そのように訳してもよい。「板挟み」「二者択一の難問」などの訳も可。

☑ **―(ダッシュ)は言い換えを表す記号。**「つまり」「すなわち」などと訳すとよい。

☑ how to *do*「〜する方法,どのように〜すべきか」

☑ balance *A* with *B*「A と B の両立を図る,A と B の釣り合いを取る」

☑ the need to *do*「〜する必要性」。to 以下は **protect ... と maintain ... が and で並列されている。**

☑ maintain は多義語で,①「維持する」,②「主張する」,③「扶養する」,④「支持する」などの意味を持つ。ここでは①の意味。

問3

2型糖尿病については第2段落最終文後半で言及されており,この前に原因が書かれているので,第2段落第2文,および最終文前半をまとめる。

問4

第4段落全体をまとめる。

「デジタル・ディバイド」の定義は第4段落第1文にある。

コンピュータを所有する人々と,所有しない人々の,それぞれの特徴をまとめればよい。

▼

それでは次に,段落ごとに詳しくみていこう。
21

第1段落 文の構造と語句のチェック

¹There <u>are</u> <u>several issues</u> 〔 raised by the technological revolution 〕. ²The <u>first</u>
 V   S   S

<u>is</u> <u>the merging</u> 〔 of technology providers 〕. ³<u>A single company</u> <u>can</u> now <u>provide</u>
V   C   S   V

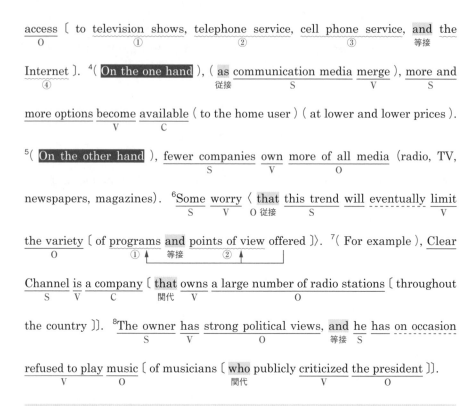

access 〔 to television shows, telephone service, cell phone service, and the
　O　　　　　①　　　　　　　　②　　　　　　　　　③　　　　　　　　等接

Internet 〕. ⁴(On the one hand), (as communication media merge), more and
　　④　　　　　　　　　　　　　　　　従接　　　　S　　　　　　V　　　　S

more options become available (to the home user) (at lower and lower prices).
　　　　　　　V　　　　C

⁵(On the other hand), fewer companies own more of all media (radio, TV,
　　　　　　　　　　　　　　　S　　　　　V　　　O

newspapers, magazines). ⁶Some worry 〈 that this trend will eventually limit
　　　　　　　　　　　　　　S　　V　　O 従接　　S　　　will　　　　　　V

the variety 〔 of programs and points of view offered 〕〉. ⁷(For example), Clear
　　O　　　　①　　　等接　　②

Channel is a company 〔 that owns a large number of radio stations 〔 throughout
　　S　　V　　C　　　関代　V　　　　　　　O

the country 〕〕. ⁸The owner has strong political views, and he has on occasion
　　　　　　　　　　　　S　　V　　　　O　　　等接　S

refused to play music 〔 of musicians 〔 who publicly criticized the president 〕〕.
　V　　　　O　　　　　　　　　　関代　　　　V　　　　O

訳 ¹技術革命によって提起される問題点がいくつか存在する。²第一の問題は，技術提供事業者の合併である。³現在では１つの会社が単独で，テレビ番組，電話サービス，携帯電話サービス，インターネットへの利用権を提供することができる。⁴一方では，通信メディアが合併するにつれ，ますます多くの選択肢がますます低価格で家庭のユーザーに利用可能となる。⁵他方では，すべてのメディア(ラジオ，テレビ，新聞，雑誌)の中の多くを所有する会社は少なくなる。⁶この傾向は結局，提供される番組や視点の多様性を限定してしまうであろうと心配する人もいる。⁷例えば，クリアチャンネルは全国的に多数のラジオ局を有する会社である。⁸社主は強い政治的見解を持っており，大統領を公然と批判した音楽家の音楽を流すことを折にふれて拒絶してきた。

語句

issue	名	問題，論点
raise	動	提起する
technological	形	科学技術の
revolution	名	革命，変革
merge	動	合併する，結合する

technology	名	科学技術
provider	名	提供(事業)者
single	形	たった１つの，単一の
company	名	会社
provide	動	提供する
access	名	権利，利用権

show	名	(テレビやラジオの)番組	offer	動	提供する，提示する
cell phone	名	携帯電話	a large number of ~	熟	多数の~
on the one hand ~, on the other hand ...			radio station	名	ラジオ局
	熟	一方で~，他方で…	throughout ~	前	~の至る所に，~のあちらこちらに
communication	名	通信			
option	名	選択肢	owner	名	所有者
available	形	利用可能な	political	形	政治的な
own	動	所有する	view	名	見解
trend	名	傾向，動向	on occasion	熟	時々
eventually	副	結局，最終的に	refuse	動	拒否する
limit	動	制限する，限定する	publicly	副	公式に，公然と
variety	名	多様性	criticize	動	批判する
point of view	名	見解，観点，見方	president	名	大統領

第2段落 文の構造と語句のチェック

¹Another challenge is the effect [of all this technology] [on children]. ²Some
　　　S　　　　　　V　　C

worry 〈 that American children and young people are spending too much time
V　　O 従接　　　　　　S　　　　　　　　　V　　　　　O
　┌─ (in)　　　　　　┌─ (in)　　　　　　┌─ (in)
(watching television), (using their computers), and (playing video games)〉.
①　　　　　　　　　②　　　　　　　　　等接 ③

³Clearly, they are not getting enough exercise, and the lack of physical activity
　　　　S　　V　　　　　O　　等接　　　　　S

has led to serious problems [of childhood obesity and a sharp rise [in the
V　　　　O　　　　　　　①　　　等接　②

number of children [with type 2 diabetes]]].

訳 ¹もう１つの難題は，こういった科学技術のすべてが子供たちに与える影響である。²アメリカの子供たちや若者たちは，テレビを見たり，コンピュータを使ったり，テレビゲームをしたりするのに，あまりに多くの時間を費やしていると心配する人もいる。³明らかに，

63

子供たちは十分な運動をしておらず，身体を使う活動が不足していることにより，幼少期の肥満と，2型糖尿病を患う子供たちの数の急増という深刻な問題が生じてきた。

Check! spend の用法は，①〈spend＋O＋(in) *doing*〉「～するのに O を費やす」，② spend *A* on *B*「B のために A を費やす」の2つを知っておこう。第2文は①のパターン。

語句

challenge	名	課題，難題
effect	名	影響
▶ the effect of *A* on *B*		A が B に与える影響
clearly	副	明らかに
exercise	名	運動
lack	名	不足
physical	形	身体的な，肉体の
activity	名	活動
lead to ～	熟	～を引き起こす，～の原因となる
childhood	名	子供時代
obesity	名	肥満
sharp	形	急激な
rise	名	増加，上昇
diabetes	名	糖尿病

第3段落 文の構造と語句のチェック

¹Others worry more (about the quality of 〈 what children are watching (on TV)〉 and 〈 what they are seeing (on the Internet)〉〉. ²Americans face a constant dilemma — 〈 how to balance the right to free speech (with the need〔 to protect children and maintain standards of decency 〕)〉. ³(Because Americans place such a high value (on individual freedom, particularly freedom of speech)), they have traditionally been very hesitant (to censor, or even restrict, the flow of information 〔 by any means of communication 〕). ⁴True

64

censorship occurs (when the government sets the standard); Most Americans
<u>censorship</u> <u>occurs</u> (when <u>the government</u> <u>sets</u> <u>the standard</u>); <u>Most Americans</u>
S   V   従接   S   V   O   S

would prefer ⟨ that the entertainment industry regulate itself ⟩, and the movie
<u>would prefer</u> ⟨ that <u>the entertainment industry</u> <u>regulate</u> <u>itself</u> ⟩, and <u>the movie</u>
V   O 従接   S   V   O   等接

industry does have a rating system for films. 5(Now that many American
<u>industry</u> <u>does have</u> <u>a rating system for films</u>. 5(Now that <u>many American</u>
S   V   O   従接

children have access [to the Internet]), there is a debate [over ⟨ whether and
<u>children</u> <u>have</u> <u>access</u> [to the Internet]), there <u>is</u> <u>a debate</u> [over ⟨ whether and
S   V   O   V   S   等接

how to regulate it ⟩]. 6(For example), there have been arguments [over
how to regulate it ⟩]. 6(For example), there <u>have been</u> <u>arguments</u> [over
V   S

⟨ whether public libraries should deny Internet users access [to certain
⟨ whether <u>public libraries</u> <u>should deny</u> <u>Internet users</u> <u>access</u> [to certain
従接   S   V O_1 O_2

websites]⟩].

訳 1子供がテレビで見ているものや，インターネット上で閲覧しているものの品質につい
てより不安に思う人もいる。2アメリカ人は絶え間ないジレンマに直面している。つまり，
言論の自由の権利と，子供たちを保護し，品位の水準を維持する必要性との釣り合いをい
かにして取るかという問題である。3アメリカ人は個人の権利，とりわけ言論の自由に高い
価値を置いているので，いかなる通信手段によるものであれ，情報の流れを検閲すること
に，あるいは制限することにさえ，伝統的に非常に抵抗を覚えてきた。4本当の検閲が起こ
るのは，政府が基準を設定したときである。ほとんどのアメリカ人は，娯楽産業が自主規
制してくれる方がよいと思うであろうし，また，映画産業は映画に対する等級付けシステ
ムを実際に持っている。5今や多くのアメリカの子供たちがインターネットにアクセスでき
るので，それを規制すべきかどうか，また，どのように規制するのかについて論争が起こ
っている。6例えば，公共図書館がインターネット利用者に一定のウェブサイトへのアクセ
スを認めないようにすべきかどうかをめぐって議論がなされてきた。

Check! 第6文の deny には第3文型(S+V+O)で「Oを否定する」，第4文型(S
+V+O_1+O_2)で「O_1にO_2を与えない，認めない」の意味がある。ここでは第
4文型(deny が V，Internet users が O_1，access to certain websites が O_2)。

語句

quality	名	質, 性質
face	動	直面する
constant	形	絶え間ない
dilemma	名	ジレンマ, 板挟み
balance *A* **with** *B*	熟	A と B の両立を図る, A と B の釣り合いを取る
right	名	権利
speech	名	言論
protect	動	保護する
maintain	動	維持する
standard	名	基準, 水準
value	名	価値
▶ place a high value on ~		~に高い価値を置く, ~を重視する
individual	形	個人の
particularly	副	特に
traditionally	副	伝統的に
be hesitant to *do*	熟	~するのをためらっている, ~することに消極的である

restrict	動	制限する
flow	名	流れ
information	名	情報
means	名	手段
communication	名	通信
occur	動	起こる
government	名	政府
set	動	定める, 決める
prefer	動	より好む, より良いと思う
entertainment	名	娯楽
industry	名	産業, 業界
regulate	動	規制する
rating	名	評価, 等級付け
now that ...	接	今や…なので
debate	名	論争, 議論
argument	名	論争, 議論
public	形	公の, 公共の
deny *A B*	動	A に B を与えない
certain	形	一定の

第4段落　文の構造と語句のチェック

¹Finally, there **is** a concern 〔 about the growing "digital divide," the gap
〈V〉〈S〉　　　　　　　　　　　　　　　　　　　　　　　└──同格──┘

(own computers)

〔 between Americans 〔 who own computers 〕 and those 〔 who do not 〕〕〕. ²People
　①　　　　　　　関代　V　　　O　　　②　　　　　関代　　　　　　　　　　S

〔 who have more education and are higher (on the socioeconomic scale)〕 are
関代　V　　　O　　　等接　V　　C

— (in)

likely to spend less time (watching television) and more time (on their
V　　　　　O　　　　　　　　　　　　　　　　　等接　　　O

66

computers). ³Many〔 of those〔 on the other side of the digital divide 〕, those
 　　　　　　　　　 S
 　　　　　　　　　　　　　　　　　　　　　　　　　　　└──同格──┘

〔 who do not own computers 〕〕, live (in poverty), and some belong (to minority
 関代　V　　　　O　　　　　　 V　　　　　　　　　　　等接　 S　　 V

populations).

訳 ¹最後に，ますます高まる「デジタル・ディバイド」，つまり，コンピュータを所有する
アメリカ人と所有しないアメリカ人との格差に対する懸念がある。²教育レベルがより高
く，社会経済上の尺度でより高い方にいる人々は，テレビを見て過ごす時間がより少なく，
コンピュータに費やす時間がより多くなる可能性が高い。³デジタル・ディバイドの対極に
ある人々，つまりコンピュータを所有しない人々の多くは，貧しい生活をし，中には少数
派集団に属する者もいる。

語句

concern	名	不安，懸念
growing	形	増大する，高まっている
divide	名	隔たり，格差
▶ digital divide		情報格差
gap	名	格差，隔たり
education	名	教育，教養
socioeconomic	形	社会経済的な

scale	名	基準，尺度
be likely to *do*	熟	～しそうだ，～する可能性が高い
poverty	名	貧しさ，貧困
▶ live in poverty		貧しい生活をする
belong to ～	熟	～に属する
minority	形	少数(派)の
population	名	集団，人々

文法事項の整理 ⑤　接続詞 whether

第3段落第5文の接続詞 whether について見てみよう。

Now that many American children have access to the Internet, there
is a debate over **whether** and how to regulate it.

接続詞 whether は，**名詞節を導く用法**と，**副詞節を導く用法**がある。
　名詞節の場合は「…かどうか」，副詞節の場合は「…であろうとなかろ
うと」の意味を表す。

例 Whether it is true or not doesn't matter.

　　　　　　　S　　　　　　　V

「それが本当かどうかは問題ではない」

▶ whether の導く節が S になっているので，**名詞節**。

※形式主語のパターンもあり。

　上記例文は It doesn't matter whether it is true or not. と書き換え可。

例 Whether it is true or not, I will do my best.

　　　　　　　　　　　　　S　　V　　O

「それが本当であろうとなかろうと，私は最善を尽くす」

▶ whether の導く節が動詞 do を修飾しているので，**副詞節**。

※名詞節を導く whether が O になる場合，**if に置き換え可能**。

例 I don't know whether [if] it is true or not.

　 S　　V　　　　　　　　　O

「私はそれが本当かどうか知らない」

（第3段落第5文）

Now that many American children have access to the Internet, there is a debate over whether and how to regulate it.

▶ whether to *do* (or not) で「～すべきかどうか」の意味。名詞句を導く。

（第3段落第6文）

For example, there have been arguments over whether public libraries should deny Internet users access to certain websites.

▶ whether は名詞節を導き，「…かどうか」の意味。if にも同じ意味があるが，この文のように前置詞 (over) の後に置けるのは whether のみ。

確認問題

1. 次の和訳と対応する英語の語句を，頭文字を参考にして書き，空欄を完成させよう。

(各1点×20)

①	i	名	問題
②	r	名	革命
③	t	名	科学技術
④	o	名	選択肢
⑤	t	名	傾向
⑥	v	名	多様性
⑦	r	動	拒否する
⑧	c	名	課題
⑨	p	形	身体的な
⑩	o	名	肥満
⑪	f	動	直面する
⑫	p	動	保護する
⑬	m	動	維持する
⑭ be	h	t *do*	熟 ～するのをためらっている
⑮	m	名	手段
⑯	g	名	政府
⑰	r	動	規制する
⑱	c	名	不安
⑲ be	l	t *do*	熟 ～しそうだ
⑳	p	名	貧しさ

2. 次の[ ]内の語を並べ替えて，意味の通る英文を完成させよう。(各5点×2)

＊文頭に来るべき語も小文字で示してある。

① As communication media merge, more [to / options / available / more /

and / become] the home user at lower and lower prices.

② [many / to / have / that / children / now / access / American] the Internet, there is a debate over whether and how to regulate it.

3. 次の英文を和訳してみよう。(10 点)

... there have been arguments over whether public libraries should deny Internet users access to certain websites.

ディクテーションしてみよう！

今回学習した英文に出てきた語句を，音声を聞いて＿＿＿＿に書き取ろう。

22　　There are several issues ❶＿＿＿＿＿＿ the technological revolution. The first is the merging of technology providers. A single company can now provide access to television shows, telephone service, cell phone service, and the Internet. On the one hand, as communication media merge, more and more options ❷＿＿＿＿＿＿＿＿＿ to the home user at lower and lower prices. On the other hand, fewer companies own ❸＿＿＿＿＿ ＿＿＿＿＿ (radio, TV, newspapers, magazines). Some worry that this trend will eventually limit the variety of programs and points of view offered. For example, Clear Channel is a company that owns a large number of radio stations throughout the country. The owner has strong political views, ❹＿＿＿＿＿＿＿＿＿＿＿＿ refused to play music of musicians who publicly criticized the president.

23　　Another challenge is ❺＿＿＿＿＿＿ all this technology on children. Some worry that American children and young people are spending too much time watching television, using their computers, and playing video games. Clearly, they are not getting enough exercise, and the lack of physical activity ❻＿＿＿＿＿ serious problems of childhood obesity and a sharp rise in the number of children with type 2 diabetes.

24　　Others worry more about the quality of what children are watching on TV and what they are seeing on the Internet. Americans face a constant dilemma — how to balance ❼_____ with the need to protect children and maintain standards of decency. Because Americans place such a high value on individual freedom, particularly freedom of speech, they have traditionally been very hesitant to censor, or even restrict, the flow of information by any ❽_____

_____. True censorship occurs when the government sets the standard; Most Americans would prefer that the entertainment industry regulate itself, and the movie industry does have a rating system for films. Now that many American children have access to the Internet, there is a debate over whether and how to regulate it. For example, ❾_____

_____ over whether public libraries should deny Internet users access to certain websites.

25 Finally, there is a concern about the growing "digital divide," the gap between Americans who own computers and those who do not. People who have more education and ❿_____ the socioeconomic scale are likely to spend less time watching television and more time on their computers. Many of those on the other side of the digital divide, those who do not own computers, ⓫_____, and some belong to minority populations.

確認問題の答 1. ① issue ② revolution ③ technology ④ option ⑤ trend ⑥ variety
⑦ refuse ⑧ challenge ⑨ physical ⑩ obesity ⑪ face ⑫ protect ⑬ maintain
⑭ hesitant to ⑮ means ⑯ government ⑰ regulate ⑱ concern ⑲ likely to ⑳ poverty
2. ① and more options become available to （第１段落　第４文）
② Now that many American children have access to （第３段落　第５文）
3. 公共図書館がインターネット利用者に一定のウェブサイトへのアクセスを認めないようにすべきかどうかをめぐって議論がなされてきた。（第３段落　最終文　抜粋）

ディクテーションしてみよう！の答 ❶ raised by ❷ become available ❸ more of all media
❹ and he has on occasion ❺ the effect of ❻ has led to ❼ the right to free speech
❽ means of communication ❾ there have been arguments ❿ are higher on ⓫ live in poverty

アドバイス ❸ more の /r/ の音と後ろの of の /ə/ の音がつながり「ロ」のように聞こえる（連結）。
❹代名詞，前置詞，接続詞，冠詞などの機能語は，強形・弱形という２種類の発音を持ち，原則として弱形で，例外的に文中で重要な意味を持つ場合は強形で発音される。he の弱形は /(h)i/，強形は /hi:/ であり，ここでは弱形。つまり，/h/ の音がほぼ発音されず，「ヒー」というより「イ」に近い音になる。この /i/ の音が前の and の /d/ とつながり，「ディ」のように聞こえる（連結）。

問	(1) ①	(2) ③	(3) ①	(4) ④	(5) ②

解 説

問

(1)「記事によれば，『平均的なイギリス人』にとっての時間配分の正しい順位（最も量の少ないものから多いものへ）はどれか」

①**「電話；新聞；Ｅメール；ラジオ；テレビ」**

②「テレビ；Ｅメール；新聞；ラジオ；電話」

③「テレビ；新聞；Ｅメール；電話；ラジオ」

④「電話；Ｅメール；テレビ；ラジオ；新聞」

▶ 第2段落によれば，電話(28分)＜新聞(31分)＜Ｅメール(34分)＜ラジオ(62分)＜テレビ(173分)の順。

(2)「記事によれば，デジタルビデオレコーダーにより何の増加となったか」

①「マルチタスク処理」

②「Ｅメールのトラフィック(ネット上のデータ流通量)」

③**「テレビ視聴」**

④「携帯電話のメール入力」

▶ 第5段落参照。

(3)「記事の中で用いられている統計によれば，6年前にイギリス人は1年におよそ何回，携帯電話のメールを打ったか」

①**「560回」**　②「760回」　③「960回」　④「1,260回」

▶ 第8段落第2文参照。1人あたり1,700通が，6年前の3倍以上である，との記述がある。そこで，1,700÷3を計算する。

(4)「記事によれば，若者たちはどんな種類のメディア関連の行為に携わっているか」

①「インターネットから違法にメディアのコンテンツをダウンロードしている」

②「運転中に携帯電話のメールを打ち，それにより事故を起こしている」

③「コンピュータよりもテレビや携帯電話をはるかに多く利用している」

④「テレビを見ながら携帯電話を使用している」

▶ 第9段落最終文に using more than one device とある。

(5)「記事によれば，メディア消費の将来的な傾向はどのような型に向かって
いると思われるか」

①「テレビが注目を集めるような型」

②「さまざまな機器が同時に使用されるような型」

③「携帯電話のメールがメッセージ1通ごとに料金を請求されるような型」

④「新聞とラジオの果たす役割が増加の一途をたどるような型」

▶ 第10段落最終文 They'll use a computer and a mobile phone, or tweet
when they're watching television. は具体例であり，要するに複数の機器
を同時使用するという内容。

それでは次に，段落ごとに詳しくみていこう。

第1段落　文の構造と語句のチェック

^{1}A study has revealed the surprising extent 〔 to which we rely on modern
　　S　　　V　　　　　O　　　　　　　　　関代　S　　V

media 〕. ^{2}(According to Ofcom, the media regulator), the average Briton
　O　　　　　　　　　　　　└──同格──┘　　　　　　　　S

spends more than seven hours (a day) — or almost half their waking hours —
　V　　　　　O　　　　　　　　　　等接　　　　　O

　　　(in)
(watching television, texting, sending e-mails and reading newspapers). ^{3}We
　　①　　　　②　　　　③　　　　　等接　　　④　　　　　　　　S

are sending four times as many texts (a day) (as in 2004) and spending
　V　　　　O　　　　　　　　　　　　　　　　　　　等接　　V
　　　　　　　　　　　　　　　　　　　　　　　　　(are)

almost a quarter of our time (on the Internet) (on social-networking sites),
　　　　O

主節の挿入

(the study found).
　　 S 　　　 V

訳 ¹ある調査により，私たちが現代のメディアに頼っている驚くべき程度が明らかになった。²メディア規制機関であるオフコムによると，平均的なイギリス人は１日に７時間以上，つまり起きている時間のほぼ半分を，テレビを見たり，携帯電話のメールを打ったり，Ｅメールを送ったり，新聞を読んだりして過ごしている。³調査の結果，私たちは 2004 年に比べ４倍もの携帯メールを１日に送信しており，インターネットに接続している時間のほぼ４分の１をソーシャルネットワークのウェブサイトで過ごしているとわかった。

Check! 第１文の extent の基本パターンは，to ～ extent「～の程度にまで」。extent が先行詞となり，関係代名詞が続くと，〈the extent to which S＋V〉となり，「S が V する程度」「どの程度 S が V するか」の意味になる。.

Check! 第 2，3 文の spend の用法は，それぞれ〈spend＋O＋(in) *doing*〉「～してO を費やす［過ごす］」，spend *A* on *B*「B に A を費やす」のパターン。

語 句

study	名	研究，調査	**average** 形	平均的な
reveal	動	明らかにする	Briton 名	イギリス人
surprising	形	驚くべき	**waking** 形	起きている
extent	名	程度	**text** 動	（携帯電話で）メールを打つ／
rely on ～	熟	～に頼る	名	（携帯電話の）メール
modern	形	現代の	**quarter** 名	4 分の 1
media	名	マスメディア，マスコミ	**spend *A* on *B*** 熟	A を B に費やす
according to ～	熟	～によれば	social-networking 名	ソーシャルネットワーク（特にインターネットを利用した交流）
regulator	名	規制機関	site 名	ウェブサイト，ホームページ

第 2 段落　文の構造と語句のチェック

¹(In total), <u>an average person's digital day</u> <u>includes</u> <u>173 minutes</u> 〔 spent
　　　　　　　　　 S 　　　　　　　　　　　　　　 V 　　　 O①

┌ (spent)

watching television 〕, <u>62 minutes</u> 〔listening to the radio 〕, <u>34 minutes</u> 〔reading
　　　　　　　　　　　 O② 　　　　　　　　　　　　　　　　　　　　 O③

┌ (spent)　　　　　　　　　　　　　　　　　　　┌ (spent)

e-mails 〕, <u>31 minutes</u> 〔reading newspapers 〕 and <u>28 minutes</u> 〔making calls 〕.
　　　　　　 O④ 　　　　　　　　　　　　　　 等接 　　 O⑤

74

訳 ¹合計すると，平均的な人のデジタルな 1 日には，テレビを見て過ごす 173 分，ラジオを聞く 62 分，E メールを読む 34 分，新聞を読む 31 分，そして電話をかける 28 分が含まれている。

語 句

in total	熟 合計して	include	動 含む
digital	形 デジタル(式)の	make a call	熟 電話をかける

第 3 段落 文の構造と語句のチェック

¹(Buoyed by the success of shows 〔 such as *The X Factor* and *Britain's Got*
　　　　　　　　　　　　　　　　　　　　　　①　　　　 等接　　　　②

Talent 〕), we are watching more TV (than at any time since 1992). ²Another
　　　　　 S　　 V　　　 O

study found 〈 that the average viewer tuned in (for three hours and 45 minutes
 S　　 V　 O従接　　　　　 S　　　　　 V

a day)(last year)〉.

訳 ¹X ファクターやブリテンズ・ゴット・タレントといったショー番組が成功したことで勢いづいて，私たちは 1992 年以降のどの時期と比べてもテレビを多く見ている。²別の調査では，平均的な視聴者は昨年，1 日につき 3 時間 45 分，チャンネルを合わせていることがわかった。

語 句

buoy	動 元気づける，鼓舞する	another	形 別の，もう 1 つの
success	名 成功	viewer	名 視聴者
at any time	熟 どんなときも，いつでも	tune in	熟 テレビのチャンネル[ラジオの周波数]を合わせる

第 4 段落 文の構造と語句のチェック

¹"Live evening TV still remains the main entertainment event 〔 of the day 〕,"
　 S　　　　　　 V　　　 C

said James Thickett, Ofcom's director of research. ²"(Although mobile and
 V　　　 S　　　└─同格─┘　　　　　　　　　　　　　従接

computer use is up), families still like 〈 coming together (into the living room)
　　　　　S　V　　　S　　　 V　 O

(to watch Simon Cowell (on big high-definition screens))〉."

訳 ¹「生放送の夜のテレビは今なお1日の主たる娯楽イベントであり続けている」と，オフコムの調査責任者であるジェームズ・シケットは述べた。²「携帯電話とコンピュータの利用が上昇しているが，各家庭は依然として，大型の高解像度画面でサイモン・コーウェルを見るために居間に集まってくるのが好きなのだ」

語句

live	形	生放送の	research	名	研究，調査
remain	動	〜のままである	mobile	名	携帯電話
main	形	主たる，主要な	use	名	使用，利用
entertainment	名	娯楽	come together	熟	集まる
director	名	責任者，管理者	high-definition	形	高解像度の
			screen	名	画面，スクリーン

第5段落　文の構造と語句のチェック

¹TV has also been boosted (by strong growth 〔 in the use of digital video
　S　　　　　　　V　　　　　　　　　①

recorders 〕 — (37 per cent of households now own one) — and the introduction
　　　　　　　　挿入
　　　　　　　　　　　S　　　　　　V　 O　　等接　　②

〔 of high definition 〕).

訳 ¹テレビはまた，デジタルビデオレコーダーの利用が著しく増加したこと（現在，37％の世帯が所有）や高画質の導入によって伸びてきた。

語句

boost	動	増大させる，伸ばす	household	名	家族，世帯
strong	形	著しい，目立つ	own	動	所有する
growth	名	増加，増大	introduction	名	導入，採用
			definition	名	鮮明度，画質

第6段落　文の構造と語句のチェック

¹"High definition has enhanced the viewing experience," Mr. Thickett said.
　　S　　　　　 V　　　　　　　 O　　　　　　　 S　　　 V

²"(Even though investment in TV has fallen), the effect has been outweighed
　　　従接　　　　　S　　　　　　V　　　　　　S　　　　　　V

(by high definition and digital video recorders)."
　　　①　　　　　　等接　　　　②

訳 ¹「高画質がテレビの視聴という体験をより豊かなものにした」とシケット氏は述べた。
²「テレビに対する投資は減ったが，高画質とデジタルビデオレコーダーがその影響を上回ったのだ」

語句

enhance	動	高める，より良くする
viewing	名	（テレビの）視聴
experience	名	経験，体験
even though ...	接	…だけれども

investment	名	投資，出資
effect	名	影響
outweigh	動	～に勝る，～より重要である

▶ be outweighed by ～　～が(主語を)上回る

第7段落　文の構造と語句のチェック

¹More than five million homes now have access 〔 to HD channels 〕.
　　S　　　　　　　　　　　　　　　　V　　O

訳 ¹500万世帯以上が現在，高解像度チャンネルを利用できる。

語句

million	形	百万の

have access to ～	熟	～を利用[入手]できる
channel	名	チャンネル，周波数帯

第8段落　文の構造と語句のチェック

¹(Helped by increasing numbers of mobile phone contracts 〔 that include
　　　　　　　　　　　　　　　　　　　　　　　　　　　　　　　　関代　V

"unlimited texting" 〕), consumers sent record numbers of texts (last year).
　　　　O　　　　　　　　　S　　　V　　　　　O

²More than 100 billion messages were sent, (equal to 1,700 for every person in
　　　　　　S　　　　　　　　　V

Britain — a figure 〔 that is more than triple the number 〔 sent six years ago 〕〕).
　　　└─同格─┘　関代　V　　　　　　　　　　C

77

Check! 第 1 文 Helped by ... は【理由】または【付帯状況】を表す分詞構文。Helped の前に Being が省略されている。

語句

increase	動	増加する
contract	名	契約
unlimited	形	無制限の
consumer	名	消費者
record	名	記録

▶ a record number of ~ /
record numbers of ~
記録的な数の~，史上最多の~

billion	形	10 億の
equal to ~	熟	~に等しい
figure	名	数値，数字
triple	形	3 倍の

第 9 段落　文の構造と語句のチェック

¹The study also offered a glimpse〔into a new Internet-enabled future〕,(as it
　S　　　　　V　　　　O　　　　　　　　　　　　　　　　　　　　　　　従接 S

surveyed people〔aged 16 to 24〕).　²(Unlike older generations), they spent
　V　　　O　　　　　　　　　　　　　　　　　　　　　　　　　　　　　S　　V

more than half of their "media time" (on computers and mobile phones),
　　　　　　　O　　　　　　　　　　　　　　　　①　　　等接　　②

(shunning television).　³They consumed less media output overall, (at six
　V′　　　O′　　　　　　　S　　V　　　　　O

hours and 35 minutes a day), but they multi-tasked more effectively — (with
　　　　　　　　　　　　　　　等接　S　　　V　　　　　　　　　　　　　付帯状況

　　　　　　　　　　┌─ (in)
two thirds of that time spent (using more than one device)).
　　　S′　　　　　　　V′

訳 ¹その調査は16歳から24歳の人々を対象に行われたため，インターネットによって可能となる新しい未来を垣間見ることもできた。²もっと上の世代とは異なり，彼らは「メディア時間」の半分以上をコンピュータや携帯電話に費やし，テレビは避けていた。³彼らは全体的に見てメディア制作物の消費が少なく，1日あたり6時間35分であったが，より効率的に複数のことを同時に行っていて，その時間の3分の2は2つ以上の電子機器を使用して過ごしていた。

 第2文の shunning television は【付帯状況】を表す分詞構文。

 最終文の with two thirds of that time spent using more than one device は〈with＋名詞＋過去分詞〉の形で，【付帯状況】を表している。

語句

offer	動	提供する		generation	名	世代
glimpse	名	ちらりと見えること		shun	動	避ける
enable	動	可能にする		consume	動	消費する
▶~ -enabled		~によって可能となる		output	名	生産(物)，制作(物)
future	名	未来，将来		overall	副	全般的に，全体的に
survey	動	調査する		multi-task	動	複数の処理を同時に行う
unlike	前	~と違って		effectively	副	効果的に，効率的に
				device	名	装置，器具

第10段落　文の構造と語句のチェック

¹(If spread out), the total time 〔 spent (by those aged 16 to 24) (consuming
　　　(it was)
　　従接　　　　　　　S

media)〕 was just under ten hours. ²"We were really surprised (at 〈 how many
　　　　　V　　　　　C　　　　　　S　　V　　　　　　　C　　　　疑

different types of media a teenager could use (at once)〉)," Mr. Thickett said.
　　　　　　O　　　　　　S　　　V　　　　　　　　　　　S　　　　V

³"They'll use a computer and a mobile phone, or tweet (when they're watching
　　①　　　　　　　　　　　　　　　　　　　②(they'll)
　S　　V　　　　　　O　　　　　　等接　V　　従接　S　　　V

television)."
　　O

¹延べにすると，16歳から24歳の人々がメディアを利用して過ごす合計時間は10時間弱であった。²「10代の若者が同時に利用できるメディアの種類がいかに多いかを知って，私たちは本当に驚いた」とシケット氏は述べた。³「彼らはコンピュータと携帯電話を使ったり，テレビを見ながらツイッターに投稿したりするようになるだろう」

語句

spread out ~	熟 ~を引き延ばす	teenager	名 10代の若者
total	形 合計の	at once	熟 同時に，一度に
		tweet	動 ツイッター（現 X）に投稿する

文法事項の整理 ⑥　副詞節中の〈S＋be〉の省略

第10段落第1文の副詞節中の〈S＋be〉の省略について見てみよう。

If spread out, the total time spent by those aged 16 to 24 consuming media was just under ten hours.

　時・条件・譲歩を表す副詞節中の〈S＋be〉は，**S が主節の S と同じなら省略することができる。**

> 例　She fell asleep (while *she was* watching television).　**←時の副詞節**
> 　　　　　　　　　　　　　　省略可
> 　　　「彼女はテレビを見ている間に眠ってしまった」

> 例　This machine will be of great use (if *it is* properly used).
> 　　　　　　　　　　　　　　　　　　　　　　省略可
> 　　　　　　　　　　　　　　　　　　　　　　　　　**←条件の副詞節**
> 　　　「この機械は適切に使えば非常に役立つだろう」

> 例　I didn't drink water (though *I was* thirsty).　**←譲歩の副詞節**
> 　　　　　　　　　　　　　　　　　省略可
> 　　　「のどが渇いていたが，私は水を飲まなかった」

※副詞節中の S が主節の S と同じでなくても，文脈上明らかな場合は省略されることがある。

例 I will finish this work by tomorrow (if *it is* possible).
省略可
「可能ならば明日までにこの仕事を終えるつもりだ」

（第10段落第1文）

If spread out, the total time spent by those aged 16 to 24 consuming media was just under ten hours.

▶ If の後に it was が省略されている。it は文全体の S である the total time。

確認問題

1. 次の和訳と対応する英語の語句を，頭文字を参考にして書き，空欄を完成させよう。 /40点

（各1点×20）

①	r	動	明らかにする
②	s	形	驚くべき
③	q	名	4分の1
④	i	動	含む
⑤	s	名	成功
⑥	e	名	娯楽
⑦	r	名	研究
⑧	h	名	家族
⑨	o	動	所有する
⑩	i	名	導入
⑪	e	動	高める
⑫	o	動	〜に勝る
⑬	m	名	百万／形 百万の
⑭	c	名	契約
⑮	c	名	消費者

⑯	f	名	数値
⑰	o	動	提供する
⑱	g	名	世代
⑲	e	副	効果的に
⑳	d	名	装置

2. 次の [ ] 内の語を並べ替えて，意味の通る英文を完成させよう。(各5点×2)

① A study has revealed the surprising [we / on / which / rely / to / modern / extent] media.

② We were really surprised [types / media / many / how / at / of / different] a teenager could use at once.

3. 次の英文を和訳してみよう。(10点)

If spread out, the total time spent by those aged 16 to 24 consuming media was just under ten hours.

ディクテーションしてみよう！

今回学習した英文に出てきた語句を，音声を聞いて_____に書き取ろう。

27・36

27　A study has revealed the surprising extent to which we rely on modern media.　According to Ofcom, the media regulator, the average Briton spends more than ❶_____ — or almost half their waking hours — watching television, texting, sending e-mails and reading newspapers.　We are sending four times as many texts a day as in 2004 and spending ❷_____ on the Internet on social-networking sites, the study found.

28　In total, an average person's digital day includes 173 minutes spent watching television, 62 minutes listening to the radio, 34 minutes reading e-mails, 31 minutes reading newspapers and 28 minutes making calls.

29　Buoyed by the success of shows such as *The X Factor* and *Britain's*

Got Talent, we are watching more TV ❸_____ since
1992. Another study found that the average viewer ❹_____ for three
hours and 45 minutes a day last year.

30   "Live evening TV still remains the main entertainment event of the
day," said James Thickett, Ofcom's director of research. "Although mobile
and computer use is up, families still like coming together into the living
room to watch Simon Cowell on big high-definition screens."

31   TV has also been boosted by strong growth in the use of digital video
recorders — 37 per cent of households ❺_____ — and the
introduction of high definition.

32   "High definition has enhanced the viewing experience," Mr. Thickett
said. "Even though investment in TV ❻_____, the effect has been
outweighed by high definition and digital video recorders."

33   More than five million homes now have access to HD channels.

34   Helped by increasing numbers of mobile phone contracts that include
"unlimited texting", consumers sent record numbers of texts last year. More
than 100 billion messages were sent, equal to 1,700 for every person in
Britain — ❼_____ more than triple the number sent six
years ago.

35   The study also offered a glimpse into a new Internet-enabled future,
as it surveyed people ❽_____. Unlike older generations, they
spent more than half of their "media time" on computers and mobile phones,
shunning television. They consumed ❾_____,
at six hours and 35 minutes a day, but they multi-tasked more effectively —
with two thirds of that time spent using more than one device.

36   ❿_____, the total time spent by those aged 16 to 24
consuming media was just under ten hours. "We were really surprised at
how many different types of media a teenager could use at once," Mr.
Thickett said. "⓫_____ a computer and a mobile phone, or tweet
when they're watching television."

1. ① reveal ② surprising ③ quarter ④ include ⑤ success ⑥ entertainment ⑦ research ⑧ household ⑨ own ⑩ introduction ⑪ enhance ⑫ outweigh ⑬ million ⑭ contract ⑮ consumer ⑯ figure ⑰ offer ⑱ generation ⑲ effectively ⑳ device

2. ① extent to which we rely on modern （第1段落 第1文）
   ② at how many different types of media （第10段落 第2文）

3. 延べにすると，16歳から24歳の人々がメディアを利用して過ごす合計時間は10時間弱であった。 （第10段落 第1文）

ディクテーションしてみよう！の答

❶ seven hours a day ❷ almost a quarter of our time ❸ than at any time ❹ tuned in
❺ now own one ❻ has fallen ❼ a figure that is ❽ aged 16 to 24
❾ less media output overall ❿ If spread out ⓫ They'll use

アドバイス ❼ /t/ の音が母音に挟まれるとら行のような音になる（フラッピング）。that is は「ザットイズ」というより「ザリズ」のように聞こえる。

❿ if の後に S＋be 動詞が省略されるという文法事項を理解していないと聞き取りにくい。

⓫ they will が短縮形の they'll となった場合，-'ll の部分は明確に発音されない。後ろが原形であることや文意もヒントにしないと聞き取りにくいだろう。

解答

問1	②, ⑥			
問2	(ア) ③	(イ) ①	(ウ) ③	(エ) ③

解説

問1

① 「環境保護論者は，ヒマラヤ山脈の氷河が溶けてバングラデシュの三角州に洪水を起こしているのではないかと懸念している」

▶ 第1段落最終文に if the Himalayan glaciers melt, the rivers' flow will decrease drastically 「ヒマラヤの氷河が溶けると河川の流水量が激減するであろう」とあり，これと不一致。

② **「以前は米を栽培していた農家が，現在は塩水でエビを育てている」**

▶ 第1段落第3文と一致。

③ 「洪水は干ばつ以上にバングラデシュの農家にとって大きな危険を意味する」

▶ 第1段落第2文と不一致。

④ 「昨年，異常な量の降雨により，バングラデシュ北西部では氷河が溶けてしまった」

▶ 第3段落第4文に the annual rains failed completely 「例年の雨が完全に降らなくなってしまった」とあり，これと不一致。

⑤ 「アイヌヌ・ニシャット氏は氷河が溶けたことによる河川の流水量の増加に勇気付けられている」

▶ 第3段落第1文には worries him most 「最も彼を心配させている」とあり，これと不一致。

⑥ **「インドで建設されたダムはバングラデシュで河川の流水量が減少した主たる原因である」**

▶ 第5段落第1文と一致。

⑦ 「気候の変化はバングラデシュの農業に多大な影響を与えているため，塩

分に耐性のある新種のマングローブが開発されてきた」

▶ 第6段落第1文に a strain of rice「米の品種」とあり，これと不一致。なお，〜 -resistant は「〜に耐性のある」の意味。

【問2】

下線部，および各選択肢の意味は以下の通り。

(ア) catastrophic「壊滅的な」（※catastrophe「大惨事」の形容詞形）

① continuous「連続的な」，② regular「定期的な」，**③ terrible「ひどい，非常に悪い」**，④ worldwide「全世界的な」

(イ) withstand「耐える，持ちこたえる」

① endure「耐える，持ちこたえる」，② overcome「克服する」，③ reach「到着する」，④ understand「理解する」

(ウ) resort to 〜「〜(手段)に頼る」

① dig away 〜「〜を掘り崩す，掘って取り除く」，② keep from 〜「〜を避ける」，**③ rely on 〜「〜に頼る」**，④ tend to 〜「〜に気を配る，〜の世話をする」（※後に名詞が来た場合。tend to *do* は「〜する傾向がある」の意味）

(エ) strain「品種，種族」

① difficulty「困難」，② sound「音」，**③ type「種類」**，④ worry「心配，悩み」

▼

それでは次に，段落ごとに詳しくみていこう。

🔊 37

第1段落 文の構造と語句のチェック

¹(Well known for its annual floods), Bangladesh may seem the last place 〔 in
   S   V   C

the world 〕〔 to worry about a drying up of the rivers 〔 that flow (from the
                                                         関代 V

Himalayas)〕〕. ²But the country is as much at risk from drought (as it is from
              等接 S   V   C

(at risk)

86

flooding). ³Already farmers 〔 who used to grow rice 〕 have turned (to farming
　　　　　　　　　　S　　関代　　　V　　　　O　　　　V

shrim) (because the water 〔 in their fields 〕 has turned so salty (nothing
　　　　　　従接　　　S　　　　　　　　　　　　　　V　　　C　　　　　S

　　　　　　　　　　　　　　　　　　　　　　　　　　　　　　　┌─ 従接 that 省略

will grow there)). ⁴Bangladesh is the front line of global warming, (with rivers
　V　　　　　　　　　　S　　　V　　　　　　　C　　　　　　　　　　　　　①

〔 drying up 〕, and increasingly unusual weather conditions 〔 that include
　　　　　　　等接　　　　　　　　　②　　　　　　　　　　　　　関代　　　V

out-of-season tornadoes 〕 and tides 〔 that have stopped changing 〕). ⁵The
　　　　O　　　　　　等接　③　関代　　　V　　　　O

entire country is one huge delta, 〔 formed by the Ganges, Brahmaputra and
　　S　　　　V　　　C　　　　　　　　　　　　　①　　　　　②　　　等接

Meghna rivers 〕. ⁶Flooding may seem to be Bangladesh's greatest enemy, but
　③　　　　　　　　S　　　V　　　　　　　　　C　　　　　　　等接

(in fact) the rivers are its lifeline. ⁷They are the main source of fresh water
　　　　　　S　　　V　　C　　　　　　S　　V　　　　C

〔 for a country 〔 where agriculture represents 21 per cent of the economy 〕〕.
　　　　　　　　関副　　S　　　　V　　　　　O

⁸And environmentalists fear 〈 that (if the Himalayan glaciers melt),
等接　　　S　　　　　　V　O 従接　従接　　　　S　　　　V

the rivers' flow will decrease drastically 〉.
　　S　　　　V

訳 ¹バングラデシュは毎年の洪水でよく知られており，ヒマラヤ山脈から流れてくる河川
が干上がることなど全く心配の要らない場所のように思えるかもしれない。²しかし，その
国は洪水による危険と同程度に，干ばつの危険にもさらされている。³既に，かつては米を
栽培していた農家が，エビの養殖に転向している。彼らの水田の水は，何も育たないほど
に塩分を含むようになってしまったからである。⁴バングラデシュは地球温暖化の最前線で
あり，干上がる河川，季節外れのトルネードを含むますます異常な天候状態，満ち引きが
なくなった海水などをかかえている。⁵国全体が，ガンジス川，ブラマプトラ川，メグナ川
によって形成される１つの巨大な三角州になっている。⁶洪水はバングラデシュの最大の
敵のように思えるかもしれないが，実際には河川はバングラデシュの生命線である。⁷それ
らの河川は，農業が経済の21％に相当する国家にとって，真水の主たる供給源なのであ

る。⁸ そして，環境保護論者たちは，ヒマラヤの氷河が溶けると河川の流水量が激減するのではないかと心配している。

🌀 Check! 第1文 Well known for its annual floods, ... は分詞構文。文頭に Being を補って考える。ここでは【理由】を表す（▶ As it is well known for its annual floods, ...）

🌀 Check! 第1文 the last ~ to *do* は「最後に…する~」の他，「決して…しない~」の意味もある。

語句

annual	形 毎年の	**condition**	名 状況，状態
flood	名 洪水／動 水浸しにする		▶ weather condition 気象状況，天候状態
the last ~ to *do*	熟 決して…しない~	**include**	動 含む
in the world	熟 全く，断じて（＊否定の強調）	out-of-season	形 季節外れの
dry up	熟 枯渇する，干上がる	**tornado**	名 トルネード（大雷雨をともなう竜巻）
flow	動 流れる／名 流れ，流水量	**tide**	名 潮流，潮の干満
country	名 国	**entire**	形 全体の，全部の
at risk from ~	熟 ~の危険にさらされて	**huge**	形 巨大な
drought	名 干ばつ	**form**	動 形成する
flooding	名 洪水，（河川の）氾濫	**enemy**	名 敵
already	副 既に	**in fact**	熟 実は，実際には
farmer	名 農民，農家の人	lifeline	名 生命線，頼みの綱
used to *do*	熟 かつては~した	**main**	形 主要な
grow	動 栽培する，（農作物を）育てる	**source**	名 源，供給源
turn to ~	熟 ~に転向する，~に取りかかる	**fresh**	形 淡水の，真水の
farm	動 養殖する，飼育する	**agriculture**	名 農業
shrimp	名 エビ	**represent**	動 ~に当たる，相当する
field	名 水田，畑	**economy**	名 経済
salty	形 塩を含んだ，塩気の多い	**environmentalist**	名 環境保護論者
front line	名 最前線，最先端	**fear**	動 恐れる，心配する
global warming	名 地球温暖化	**glacier**	名 氷河
increasingly	副 ますます	**melt**	動 溶ける
unusual	形 異常な	**decrease**	動 減少する
		drastically	副 大幅に，急激に

第2段落　文の構造と語句のチェック

┌── 従接 that 省略
¹Most people tend to think 〈 the main risk 〔 in Bangladesh 〕 is a catastrophic
　　　S　　　　V　　　　　　O　　　　S　　　　　　　　　　　　　　　　　V

flood 〔 from rising sea levels 〕〉. ²But the country has a defense 〔 against that 〕: a
　C　　　　　　　　　　　　　　　　　等接　　 S　　　　 V　　 O

series of seawalls 〔 along the coast 〕 〔 which should be able to withstand
　　　　　　　　　　　　　　　　　　　　　　関代　　　　　　　　V

predicted rises 〔 in the sea level 〕〕. ³There is no defense 〔 against drought 〕.
　　O　　　　　　　　　　　　　　　　　　　　　　V　　S

> **訳**　¹ほとんどの人々は，バングラデシュの主たる危険は海面上昇による壊滅的な洪水だと
> 考えがちだ。²しかし，その国はそれに対する防御方法を持っている。予測される海面上昇
> に持ちこたえられるはずの，海岸沿いに連なる防潮堤である。³干ばつに対しては防御方法
> がない。

語句

tend to *do*	熟	～する傾向がある	**a series of ~**	熟	一連の～
catastrophic	形	壊滅的な	seawall	名	防波[潮]堤
sea level	名	平均海面	**coast**	名	海岸，沿岸
defense	名	防御(物)	**withstand**	動	耐える，持ちこたえる
			predict	動	予測する

第3段落　文の構造と語句のチェック

　　　　　　　　　　　　　　　　　　　　　　　　　　　　従接 that 省略 ──┐
¹Professor Ainun Nishat, one of the country's leading climate experts, says 〈 it
　　　　S　　　　　　　　　└─同格─┘　　　　　　　　　　　　　　　　V　　O

　　　　　　　　　　　　　　　　──強調構文──
is the melting of the Himalayan glaciers that worries him most — (more than
　　　　　　　　　　S　　　　　　　　　　　　　V　　　O

rising sea levels or changing local weather patterns)〉. ²"(At the moment),
　　　　　①　　　　等接　　　　　　②

we're probably seeing a slight increase 〔 in the river flow 〕 (because of the
　S　　　　　　　V　　　O

glaciers melting)," he says. ³"But what happens (in two to five years) (when
　　　　　　　　　　S　V　　等接　　S　　　V　　　　　　　　　　　　従接

the glaciers are gone)?" ⁴The northwest faced an unprecedented drought (last
　　　　　S　　　V　　　　　　　　　　　　S　　　　V　　　　　　　　O

year), (after the annual rains failed completely). ⁵Farmers had to resort to
　　　　　　従接　　　S　　　　V　　　　　　　　　　　　S　　　　V

　　　　　　　　　　　　　　　　　　　　　　┌── 従接 that 省略
〈 pumping ground water 〉 (to survive), but they fear 〈 the ground water
O　　　　　　　　　　　　　　　　　　　　等接　S　　V　O　　S

will dry up (if the rains fail again)〉.
　　V　　　　従接　S　　V

訳 ¹アイヌン・ニシャット教授は，その国の主要な気象専門家の１人であるが，海面上昇
や地域の天候パターンの変化以上に，最も心配なのはヒマラヤ山脈の氷河が溶けることだ
と述べている。²「現在のところ，氷河が溶けることによる川の流水量の増加はおそらくわ
ずかなものしか見られていない」と彼は言う。³「しかし，２〜５年後氷河がなくなったとき，
何が起こるだろうか。」⁴北西地方は昨年，毎年の雨が完全に降らなくなってしまった後，
いまだかつてない干ばつに直面した。⁵農家は生き延びるために地下水のくみ上げに頼らざ
るを得なかったが，もしまた雨が降らなくなったら，その地下水も干上がってしまうので
はないかと恐れている。

語句

professor	名	教授
leading	形	一流の，主要な
expert	名	専門家
worry	動	心配させる
local	形	地域の
at the moment	熟	現在，今のところ
probably	副	おそらく
slight	形	わずかな
increase	名	増加
be gone	熟	なくなる，消える

northwest	名	北西部，北西地方
face	動	直面する
unprecedented	形	前例のない，空前の
fail	動	(供給などが)止まる，足りなくなる
completely	副	完全に
resort to〜	熟	〜(手段)に頼る
pump	動	くみ上げる
ground water	名	地下水
survive	動	生き残る，生き延びる

第４段落　文の構造と語句のチェック

¹(In the southwest), trees 〔 in the famous Sundarbans National Park,
　　　　　　　　　　　　　S
　　　　　　　　　　　　　　┌──同格──┐
home to the world's largest remaining population of wild tigers 〕, are dying out
　　　　　　　　　　　　　　　　　　　　　　　　　　　　　　　　　　　V

— and falling river levels may be one reason. ²Bangladeshi scientists believe
　等接　　　　　 S　　　　　　　 V　　 C　　　　　　　　 S　　　　　　　 V

┌── 従接 that 省略
⟨the trees are dying (because of rises [in salt levels] [in the mangrove
 O　 S　　 V

swamps])⟩. ³That could be (because rising sea levels are flooding the swamps),
　　　　　　　 S　　 V　　 従接　　 S　　　　　　 V　　　　 O

but it could also be ⟨that the river flow has decreased (in recent years)⟩.
等接 S　　　　　　 V　 C従接　 S　　　　　　 V

訳 ¹南西地方では，有名なスンダルバンス国立公園，現存する世界最大の野生のトラの個
体群の生息地であるが，そこの樹木が絶滅しつつある—それも，川の水位が下がっている
ことが１つの理由であるのかもしれない。²バングラデシュの科学者たちは，マングロー
ブの湿地帯において塩分濃度が上昇しているせいで樹木が枯れつつあると考えている。³そ
れは，海面上昇により湿地帯が冠水していることが理由でもあり得ようが，河川の流水量
が近年減少している可能性もあるのである。

語句
southwest　名 南西部，南西地方
home　名 生息地
　▶ be home to ～　～が住んでいる，～の生
　　　　　　　　　息地である

remaining　形 残っている
population　名 (生物の)個体群
die out　熟 絶滅する
it could be that ...
　　　　　熟 …ということがあり得る

第5段落 文の構造と語句のチェック

¹(So far), the reduction [in flow] is purely [due to dam projects [upstream
　　　　　　　　 S　　　　　　 V

in India]]. ²But experts fear ⟨the loss of fresh water would be far more drastic
　　　　　 等接　 S　　 V　 O　　　　 S　　　　　　 V　　 C
　　　　　　　　　　　┌── 従接 that 省略

(if the Himalayan glaciers melt and the rivers start to dry up)⟩. ³Already
 従接　　 S　　　　　 V　 等接　 S　　 V

Bangladesh is fighting a losing battle [against rising salt levels]. ⁴Its farmers
 S　　　 V　　　 O　　　　　　　　　　　　　　　　　　 S

can only produce 8 tons of rice per hectare, (compared with 17 tons in China).
　　 V　　　　 O

訳 ¹今までのところ，流水量の減少はあくまでも，川の上流のインドにおけるダム事業計画が原因である。²しかし，もしヒマラヤの氷河が溶け，河川が干上がり始めた場合には，真水の減少ははるかに強烈になるのではないかと専門家は懸念している。³既にバングラデシュは，上昇する塩分濃度との勝ち目のない戦いをしている。⁴バングラデシュの農家は，1ヘクタールあたり中国の17トンに対して，わずか8トンの米しか生産できないのだ。

語句

so far	熟	今までのところ
reduction	名	減少
purely	副	あくまでも，全く
be due to ~	熟	~のせいである
dam	名	ダム
project	名	(事業)計画
upstream	副	上流で

loss	名	減少，低下
drastic	形	劇的な，猛烈な
losing battle	名	勝ち目のない戦い，負け戦
produce	動	生産する
per	前	~ごとに，~につき
hectare	名	ヘクタール(10,000 m²)
compared with [to] ~		
	熟	~と比べると，~に対して

第6段落 文の構造と語句のチェック

¹(Faced with potentially disastrous effects on agriculture), the country
〈S〉

has come up with a strain of rice 〔 that grows (in salty water)〕. ²"We
〈V〉 〈O〉 関代 〈V〉 〈S〉

are fighting climate change (on the front line)," Professor Nishat told
〈V〉 〈O〉 〈S〉 〈V〉

The Independent (earlier this year). ³"But the battle has to be integrated
〈O〉 等接 〈S〉 〈V〉

(across all countries)." ⁴Bangladesh has good reason 〔 to feel angered (over
〈S〉 〈V〉 〈O〉 〈V'〉 〈C'〉

global warming)〕. ⁵Its annual carbon emissions total only 0.172 tons per person,
〈S〉 〈V〉 〈O〉

(compared to 21 tons in the US). ⁶(If the rivers dry up), it would leave
従接 〈S〉 〈V〉 〈S〉 〈V〉

Bangladesh completely at the mercy of the rains.
〈O〉 〈C〉

訳 ¹農業に対して壊滅的な影響となるかもしれない事態に直面して，その国は塩水でも育つ米の品種を考え出した。²ニシャット教授は「私たちは最前線で気候変化と戦っている」と，今年の早い時期に『インディペンデント』紙に話した。³「しかし，その戦いは国家の枠を超えて一本化されなくてはならないのだ。」⁴バングラデシュが地球温暖化に対して腹を立てるのももっともである。⁵その国の年間の二酸化炭素排出量の合計は，1人あたりアメリカの21トンに対して，わずか0.172トンにすぎない。⁶もし河川が干上がってしまったら，バングラデシュは完全に雨のなすがままになってしまうであろう。

Check! 第1文 Faced with potentially disastrous effects on agriculture, ... は分詞構文。文頭に Being を補って考える。ここでは【理由】を表す（▶ As it is faced with potentially disastrous effects on agriculture, ...）

語句

(be) faced with ~ 熟 ~に直面して
potentially 副 可能性として，潜在的に
disastrous 形 壊滅的な，破壊的な
effect 名 影響
come up with ~ 熟 ~を思いつく
strain 名 品種

integrate 動 統合する，一本化する
have good reason to do
　　　　　　熟 ~するのはもっともだ
be [feel] angered 熟 怒る
total 動 合計で~になる
at the mercy of ~ 熟 ~のなすがままに，
　　　　　　　　　　~に翻弄されて

文法事項の整理 ⑦　強調構文

第3段落第1文の強調構文を見てみよう。

... **it is** the melting of the Himalayan glaciers **that** worries him most

　強調構文とは，It is ~ that ... の形で，「~」の部分を強調する表現。基本的には「…するのは~だ」と訳すが，「~こそ…する」「まさに~が…する」などの訳し方も可。

例　My brother bought a new car last month.
　　　　①　　　　　　　②　　　　③

→強調構文にすると…

①**を強調**：It was <u>my brother</u> that [who] bought a new car last month.
　　　　　「先月新車を買ったのは私の兄だ」

②**を強調**：It was a new car that my brother bought last month.
　　　　　「私の兄が先月買ったのは新車だ」

③**を強調**：It was last month that my brother bought a new car.

「私の兄が新車を買ったのは先月だ」

※It is 〜 that ... の形は形式主語（仮主語）の場合もあるので，区別に注意しよう。

■ **It is 〜 that ... 識別方法**（※ It の指示対象が前にない場合）

「〜」が形容詞		形式主語
「〜」が名詞	「...」が完全な文	
	「...」が不完全な文	
「〜」が副詞		強調構文
「〜」が前置詞＋名詞		

（第 3 段落第 1 文）

... it is the melting of the Himalayan glaciers that worries him most ...

it is と that の間には**名詞**が挟まっている。that 以下は worries が V，him が O，つまり，S が欠けた**不完全な文**。よって，**強調構文**とわかる。

確認問題

1. 次の和訳と対応する英語の語句を，頭文字を参考にして書き，空欄を完成させよう。

（各 1 点 × 20）

/40点

①	d	名	干ばつ
②	f	名	水田
③	g ⎯ w	名	地球温暖化
④	u	形	異常な
⑤	a	名	農業
⑥	d	動	減少する
⑦	p	動	予測する
⑧	e	名	専門家
⑨	u	形	空前の

⑩　r 　　　 t ～　　　　　熟　～(手段)に頼る

⑪　be h 　 t ～　　　　　熟　～が住んでいる

⑫　d 　 o 　　　　　　　　熟　絶滅する

⑬　s f 　　　　　　　　　熟　今までのところ

⑭　be d 　 t ～　　　　　熟　～のせいである

⑮　l 　　　　　　　　　　名　減少

⑯　c 　　　 w ～　　　　　熟　～と比べると

⑰　d 　　　　　　　　　　形　壊滅的な

⑱　c 　 u w ～　　　　　熟　～を思いつく

⑲　i 　　　　　　　　　　動　統合する

⑳　a t m 　 o ～　　　　熟　～のなすがままに

2. 次の [ ] 内の語を並べ替えて，意味の通る英文を完成させよう。(各5点×2)

① Already farmers [rice / to / have / grow / used / who / turned] to farming shrimp.

② Faced with potentially disastrous effects on agriculture, the country [a / with / come / rice / strain / has / up / of] that grows in salty water.

3. 次の英文を和訳してみよう。(10点)

It is the melting of the Himalayan glaciers that worries him most — more than rising sea levels or changing local weather patterns.

ディクテーションしてみよう！

今回学習した英文に出てきた語句を，音声を聞いて＿＿＿＿に書き取ろう。

38　　Well known for its annual floods, Bangladesh may seem the last place in the world to worry about a drying up of the rivers that flow from the Himalayas.　But the country is ❶＿＿＿＿＿＿＿＿＿＿ from drought as it is from flooding. Already farmers who used to grow rice have turned to farming shrimp because the water in their fields ❷_____

_____ nothing will grow there. Bangladesh is the front line of global warming, with rivers drying up, and increasingly unusual weather conditions that include out-of-season tornadoes and tides that have stopped changing. The entire country is one huge delta, formed by the Ganges, Brahmaputra and Meghna rivers. Flooding may seem to be Bangladesh's greatest enemy, but in fact the rivers are its lifeline. They are the main ❸_____ for a country where agriculture represents 21 per cent of the economy. And environmentalists fear that if the Himalayan glaciers melt, the rivers' flow will decrease drastically.

39   Most people tend to think the main risk in Bangladesh is a catastrophic flood from rising sea levels. But the country has a defense against that: a series of seawalls along the coast which should be able to withstand ❹_____ the sea level. There is no defense against drought.

40   Professor Ainun Nishat, one of the country's leading climate experts, says it is the melting of the Himalayan glaciers that worries him most — more than rising sea levels or changing local weather patterns. "At the moment, we're probably seeing ❺_____ the river flow because of the glaciers melting," he says. "But what happens in two to five years when the glaciers are gone?" The northwest faced an unprecedented drought last year, after the annual rains failed completely. Farmers ❻_____ pumping ground water to survive, but they fear the ground water will dry up if the rains fail again.

41   In the southwest, trees in the famous Sundarbans National Park, home to the world's largest remaining population of wild tigers, are dying out — and falling river levels may be one reason. Bangladeshi scientists believe the trees are dying because of rises in salt levels in the mangrove swamps. That could be because rising sea levels are flooding the swamps, but ❼_____ that the river flow has decreased in recent years.

42　So far, the reduction in flow is ❽_____ dam projects upstream in India. But experts fear the loss of fresh water would be far more drastic if the Himalayan glaciers melt and the rivers start to dry up. Already Bangladesh is fighting a losing battle against rising salt levels. Its farmers ❾_____ 8 tons of rice per hectare, compared with 17 tons in China.

43　Faced with potentially disastrous effects on agriculture, the country has ❿_____ a strain of rice that grows in salty water. "We are fighting climate change on the front line," Professor Nishat told *The Independent* earlier this year. "But the battle has to be integrated across all countries." Bangladesh has good reason to feel angered over global warming. Its annual carbon emissions total ⓫_____ _____, compared to 21 tons in the US. If the rivers dry up, it would leave Bangladesh completely at the mercy of the rains.

確認問題の答

1.　① drought　② field　③ global warming　④ unusual　⑤ agriculture　⑥ decrease
　　⑦ predict　⑧ expert　⑨ unprecedented　⑩ resort to　⑪ home to　⑫ die out　⑬ so far
　　⑭ due to　⑮ loss　⑯ compared with　⑰ disastrous　⑱ come up with　⑲ integrate
　　⑳ at the mercy of

2.　① who used to grow rice have turned　（第 1 段落　第 3 文）
　　② has come up with a strain of rice　（第 6 段落　第 1 文）

3.　海面上昇や地域の気候パターンの変化以上に，彼にとって最も心配なのは，ヒマラヤ山脈の氷河が溶けることだ。　（第 3 段落　第 1 文）

ディクテーションしてみよう！の答

　　❶ as much at risk　❷ has turned so salty　❸ source of fresh water　❹ predicted rises in
　　❺ a slight increase in　❻ had to resort to　❼ it could also be　❽ purely due to
　　❾ can only produce　❿ come up with　⓫ only 0.172 tons per person

アドバイス　❻ had　to と resort　to は /d/ と /t/，/t/ と /t/ の連続であるが，どちらも個々に発音されることはなく，後ろの /t/ の発音 1 回で済ませる（脱落）。
　　　　　　❾ can の /n/ の音と後ろの only の /o/ の音がつながり「ノ」のように聞こえる（連結）。

解答

問1	②	問2	④	問3	③	問4	④	問5	③
問6	①	問7	①	問8	②	問9	④	問10	①

解説

問1

直後に many over-optimistic images … という名詞句が続いているので文法的には前置詞が入る。

前置詞の場合の各選択肢の意味は，

①「～として」　②**「～と同様に」**　③「～とは違って」　④「～なしで」

となる。

over-optimistic は「楽観的すぎる」の意味で，over- がついていることから批判的な意味合い（見通しが甘い，実際にはうまくいかない）が読み取れる。

文の後半は it is a bit of an illusion「それはちょっとした幻想である」となっており，これも同様の批判的な意味合いが読み取れる。

以上により，②が文意に合う。

問2

①は本文で言及されていない。

②第2段落第4文の the person in the driver's seat ～ may also fail to intervene「運転席に乗っている人も介入しないかもしれない」という部分に相当するが，助動詞 may を用いていることからもわかるように，可能性があるというだけであって，この事故のケースで「判明した」わけではない。

③の「コンピュータの誤作動」については，第2段落第4文の For example の後に具体例として挙げられているが，これは同段落第3文 could introduce new risks「新たなリスクをもたらすことになりうる」の具体例であって可能性にすぎず，これも「判明した」わけではない。

第2段落最終文の That is what appears to have happened in the crash. からも，判明していることは何もないと言えるので，④が正解となる。

問3

① 「自動運転車の背後にある技術によってもたらされる危険性について懸念を表明する人はほとんどいない」

② 「これらの近代的で強力な車両で使われている新しい技術を理解している人はほとんどいない」

　　＊ apprehend「理解する」

③ 「これらの新しい車で使われている技術は予測しがたい事故を引き起こすかもしれない」

　　＊ predict「予測する」

④ 「これらの近代的な車に適用されている技術はあまりに強力なために正しく評価されていない」

　　＊ unappreciated「正しく評価されていない，価値を認められていない」

　下線部の構造は the technology が S, could introduce が V, new risks が O で，「技術が新たなリスクをもたらす」が大まかな意味。

　また，risks の後には that few people appreciate「ほとんどの人々が正しく理解していない」という関係詞節が続く。

　この内容に最も近いものは③。

問4

　change は他動詞で用いると「変える，変化させる」。introduce は「（新しい物事を）取り入れる，もたらす」。

　空所(エ)は the nature「本質」が目的語として続いているので changes が適切。空所(オ)は new kinds of errors「新たな種類の過ち」が目的語として続いているので introduces が適切。

問5

① 「確立した理論」

　　＊ established「確立した」

② 「隠された前提[想定]」

　　＊ conceal「隠す」

③ 「証明されていない仮説」

＊unproven「証明されていない」／ hypothesis「仮説」

④「裏目に出た状況」

　＊misguided「見当違いの，裏目に出た」／ circumstance「状況」

　空所の後の that 以下には完全な文が続いているため，この that は空所に入る語を説明する同格の接続詞と考えられる。that 以下の意味は「技術が衝突や死亡事故を減らしてくれるだろう」。これは第1・2段落の内容からも，早まった判断であることがわかる。

　そこで，③が正解となる。

問6

①「**自信を持っている**」

②「疑っている」

③「よくわかっている」

④「理解していない」

　文頭の Even as ... は「…にもかかわらず，…なのに」という意味で，though と同様に【譲歩】を表す。そこで，主節 American roads are becoming less safe「アメリカの道路の安全性は低下しつつある」と逆の方向性になるように考える。

　また，bet はもともと「賭け」の意味なので，place a big bet で「大金を賭ける」が直訳。

　以上により①が文意に合う。

問7

①「**国会議員および州議会議員は将来の人々の命を救うための法案を準備することに時間を費やしてきたが**」

　＊lawmaker「立法者，議員」／ bill「法案」

②「専門家は将来のリスクに関してより深刻な懸念があると警告してきたので」

③「役人が将来の死亡率増加に対抗すべきときに」

④「しかしそれにもかかわらず死亡事故のない明るい未来を期待する」

　＊nevertheless「にもかかわらず」

as opposed to ～ は「～ではなく，～とは反対に」の意味。ここでは，下線部直前の now と下線部の some time in the distant future「遠い未来のいつか」が対比されている。議員は未来には関心があるが現在には関心がない，という指摘をしている文脈。

問8

第7段落前半で，交通事故を減らしている国々が紹介されており，これらの国々は自動運転車の最新技術に頼るのではなく，in the old-fashioned way「古風なやり方で」事故を減らしてきたとある。

そして，下線部以降で挙げられている具体的な方法は，以下の通り。

①車の減速(第7段落第5文)

②歩行者が車に注意しなくても済むように道路を変更(第7段落第6文)

③シートベルトの着用促進(第7段落第7文)

④厳格な運転者教育と試験(第7段落最終文)

この中で「交通事故の減少」に直接結びつきそうにないのは②である。

問9

① 「政府はこれらの問題を解決するために十分速やかに取り組んでいないし，産業界もしていない」

② 「自動車業界は将来ではなく今，金を儲ける必要がある」

③ 「そのために自動運転車は禁止も規制もされるべきではない」

④ 「私たちは最速の方法ではなく，責任ある方法でそれを行う必要がある」

第8段落第1文(Mr. Sullenberger is worried that the rush to develop automated cars will lead to many unforeseen problems.)で，自動運転車の開発を急ぐことへの懸念が表明されており，また空所前の Even though there is a sense of urgency to prevent human-caused accidents(人為的な事故を防ごうと焦る気持ちがあるとはいえ)という譲歩の関係から，自動運転車の拙速な導入をしないよう警告する内容が入ると考えられる。よって，④が適切。

問10

① 「自動運転車の時代だって？　まず考えよ」

② 「再びアメリカの道路を安全にすること」

③ 「自動運転車の可能性と将来性」

④「交通規制方法の新旧対決」

テーマは自動運転車。以下の部分から読み取れるように，筆者は自動運転車を拙速に導入することへの異議を唱えている。

▶ 第1段落最終文：But like many over-optimistic images of the future, it is a bit of an illusion.

▶ 第2段落第2文：But a recent fatal crash suggests that some of these cars are not ready for the busy American roads …

▶ 第4段落：What concerns him and other safety experts is that industry executives and government officials are rushing to put self-driving cars on the road without appropriate safeguards and under the unproven hypothesis that the technology will reduce crashes and fatalities.

▶ 第8段落第1文：Mr. Sullenberger is worried that the rush to develop automated cars will lead to many unforeseen problems.

以上により，正解は①。

▼

それでは次に，段落ごとに詳しくみていこう。

第1段落 文の構造と語句のチェック

¹The promise 〔 of self-driving cars 〕 can be attractive. ²Imagine
　　S　　　　　　　　　　　　　　　　　 V　　C　　　　　　 V

〈 taking a nap or watching a movie (in a comfortable armchair) (while being
　　O　　　①　等接　　②　　　　　　　　　　　　　　　　　　　　　　従接

shuttled safely home (after a long day 〔 at work 〕)))〉. ³But (like many over-
　　　　　　　　　　　　　　　　　　　　　　　　　　　　　　等接

optimistic images 〔 of the future 〕), it is a bit of an illusion.
　　　　　　　　　　　　　　　　　 S V 　a bit of an illusion
　　　　　　　　　　　　　　　　　　　　　　C

訳 ¹自動運転車の将来性は魅力的なものでありうる。²長い一日の仕事の後，安全に家まで送り届けられる間，快適な肘掛け椅子に腰かけてうたた寝したり映画を見たりすることを

想像してみてください。³しかし，未来についての多くの楽観的すぎるイメージと同様に，それはちょっとした幻想である。

語句

promise	名	将来性，前途の有望さ	
self-driving	形	自動運転の	
attractive	形	魅力的な	
imagine	動	想像する	
take a nap	熟	うたた寝する，昼寝をする	
comfortable	形	心地よい，快適な	

armchair	名	肘掛け椅子
shuttle	動	（人を）運ぶ，往復させる
at work	熟	働いて，勤務して
over-optimistic	形	楽観的すぎる
image	名	イメージ，印象
a bit of ~	熟	ちょっとした~
illusion	名	幻想，勘違い

第2段落　文の構造と語句のチェック

¹Automated cars may indeed make commuting more pleasurable (while
S　　　　　　　V　　　　　　　O　　　　　　C　　　　　　従接

preventing accidents and saving many lives) — someday. ²But a recent fatal
①　　　　　　等接　　　②　　　　　　　　　　等接　　　S

crash suggests ⟨ that some of these cars are not ready (for the busy American
V　　O 従接　　　　S　　　V　　C

roads)⟩ : a lot of sensors and software turned this car (into a high-tech vehicle
①　　　②
　　　　　　等接　　S　　　V　　O

┌ 関代 which 省略
[you might see (in a science fiction movie)]). ³(In fact), the technology
S　　V　　　　　　　　　　　　　　　　　　　　　　S

[that powers these vehicles] could introduce new risks [that few people
関代　V　　O　　　　V　　　　O　　　関代　　S

appreciate]. ⁴(For example), (when a computer [controlling the car] does
V　　　　　　　　　　従接　　S　　　　　　　　　V

not hit the brakes (to avoid a car crash)), the person [in the driver's seat] —
O　　　　　　　　　　　　　　S

many automated cars [on the road today] still require someone to be there (in
S　　　　　　　　　　　V　　O　　　C

case of an emergency) — may also fail to intervene (because the driver trusts
V　　　　　　　従接　　S　　V

the car <u>too</u> much（<u>to</u> pay close attention to the road））. ⁵<u>That</u> <u>is</u> ⟨<u>what</u> <u>appears</u>
　　　O　　　　　　　　　　　　　　　　　　　　　　　　　　S　V　C　関代

<u>to have happened</u>（in the crash ））.
　　　V

訳 ¹自動運転車は確かに，事故を防いで多くの人命を救いつつ，通勤をより楽しくしてくれるかもしれない—いつかは。²しかし，最近起こったある衝突死亡事故は，このような車の一部はアメリカの交通量の多い道路を走行するには準備が整っていないことを示している。多くのセンサーやソフトウェアがこの車をSF映画で見るようなハイテク車両に変えた。³実際，このような車両に動力を供給する技術はほとんどの人々が正しく理解していない新たなリスクをもたらすことになりうる。⁴例えば，車を操るコンピュータが車の衝突を避けるためにブレーキを踏まなかったら，運転席に座っている人(今日路上を走る自動運転車の多くは，緊急事態に備えて誰かがそこにいることをまだ必要としている)も介入しないかもしれないのだ。なぜなら，運転手は車を信頼しすぎて道路に細心の注意を払わないからだ。⁵この衝突事故において起こったのはそのようなことだったと思われる。

語句

automate	動 自動化[機械化]する	**science fiction**	名 SF(空想科学小説)
indeed	副 実際に，確かに	**power**	動 動力[電力]を供給する
commute	動 通勤する	**introduce**	動 取り入れる，もたらす
pleasurable	形 楽しい，愉快な	**appreciate**	動 正しく理解[認識]する
someday	副 いつか，そのうち	**require**	動 必要とする
fatal	形 死にいたる	**in case of ~**	熟 ~の場合に(備えて)
crash	名 衝突(事故)	**emergency**	名 緊急[非常]事態
busy	形 交通量が多い，賑やかな	**fail to** *do*	熟 ~しない，~できない
sensor	名 センサー(感知装置)	**intervene**	動 介在[介入]する
turn *A* **into** *B*	熟 A を B に変える	**trust**	動 信用[信頼]する
high-tech	形 ハイテクの，先端技術の	**pay attention to ~**	熟 ~に注意を払う
vehicle	名 乗り物，車両	**close**	形 綿密な，注意深い

第3段落　文の構造と語句のチェック

¹"<u>Technology</u> <u>does not eliminate</u> <u>error</u>, <u>but</u> <u>it</u> <u>changes</u> <u>the nature</u>〔of errors
　　　S　　　　　　V　　　　　　O　　等接　S　V　　　　O

〔<u>that</u> <u>are made</u> ）〕, <u>and</u> <u>it</u> <u>introduces</u> <u>new kinds of errors</u>," <u>said</u> <u>Chesley</u>
　関代　V　　　　　等接　S　　V　　　　　O　　　　　　　V

<u>Sullenberger</u>, the former US Airways pilot〔<u>who</u> <u>landed</u> <u>a plane</u>（in the Hudson
　S　　└─同格─┘　　　　　　　　　　　　　関代　V　　O

River）（in 2009）（after its engines were struck（by birds）））]．²He now sits

（従接　　　S　　　　V　　　　　　　　　　　　　　S　　　　V

（on a Department of Transportation advisory committee〔on automation〕）．

³"We have to realize〈that it's not a solution〔for everything〕〉．"

S　　　　V　　　　O従接　S　V　　　C

> **訳** ¹「技術は過ちをなくすものではなく，犯される過ちの本質を変えて，新たな種類の過ち
> をもたらすものである」と，2009年にエンジンに鳥がぶつかった後にハドソン川に飛行
> 機を着水させた，元USエアウェイズのパイロットであるチェズレイ・サレンバーガー氏
> は言った。²彼は現在，運輸省の自動化諮問委員会の一員となっている。³「私たちは，それ
> （自動運転）があらゆることに対する解決策ではないことを認識しなければならない。」

語句

eliminate	動 排除する，なくす		**department**	名 （米国政府の）省
nature	名 性質，本質		**transportation**	名 輸送，交通
former	形 元，かつての		advisory	形 助言を与える，諮問[顧問]の
land	動 着陸させる		**committee**	名 委員会
strike	動 打つ，当たる		**automation**	名 自動化
sit on ~	熟 ~の一員[委員]である，~を 務める		**realize**	動 認識する，気づく
			solution	名 解決策，解決法

第4段落 文の構造と語句のチェック

¹〈What concerns him and other safety experts〉is〈that industry executives

S 関代　V　　　　①等接　　　②O　　　　　　V　C 従接　　　　　①

and government officials are rushing to put self-driving cars（on the road）

等接②　　S　　　　　　V　　　　　O

（without appropriate safeguards）and（under the unproven hypothesis〈that

①　　　　　　　　　　　　　　等接　②　　　　　　　　　　　　　　従接（同格）

the technology will reduce crashes and fatalities〉〉〉．

S　　　　V　　①　　　　②

S　　　　V　　　等接　O

105

> **訳** ¹彼や他の安全の専門家が懸念するのは，業界幹部や政府当局者が，適切な安全対策もなく，技術が衝突や死亡事故を減らしてくれるだろうという未検証の仮説のもとで，急いで自動運転車を路上で走らせようとしていることである。

語句

concern	動	心配させる
expert	名	専門家
executive	名	経営陣，役員
government	名	政府
official	名	職員，公務員
rush to *do*	熟	慌てて[急いで] ～する

appropriate	形	適切な
safeguard	名	予防手段，保護対策
unproven	形	証明[立証]されていない
hypothesis	名	仮説
reduce	動	減らす，削減する
fatality	名	死亡者(数)，死亡事故

第5段落 文の構造と語句のチェック

¹(Even as officials place a big bet ⟨ that autonomous cars will solve many of
　　従接　　　S　　　V　　　O　　従接(同格)　　　S　　　　　V

our safety problems ⟩), American roads are becoming less safe. ²More than
　　　O　　　　　　　　　　S　　　　　V　　　　C

37,000 people were killed (in 2016), (up 5.6 percent from 2015).
　　S　　　　　V

³The death toll is estimated to be more than 40,000 (in 2017).
　　S　　　　　V　　　　C

> **訳** ¹自動運転車が安全問題の多くを解決するということに役人が大きな賭けをしているにもかかわらず，アメリカの道路の安全性は低下しつつある。²2016年には37,000人を超える人々が命を落としており，2015年から5.6%増加している。³2017年には死亡者数が40,000人を超えると推定されている。

語句

even as ...	熟	…にもかかわらず，…なのに
place a bet	熟	賭ける

autonomous	形	自立した，自主的な
toll	名	犠牲者[死傷者]数
estimate	動	推定する，見積もる

第6段落　文の構造と語句のチェック

[1]Experts〔who are skeptical（about the unstoppable march of technology）〕
　　S　　　関代　V　　C

say〈fatalities are rising（because public officials have become so fond（of the
V　O　　S　　　V　　　　従接　　　S　　　　　　V　　　　　C

shiny new thing）（that they have taken their eyes（off problems
　　　　　　　　　　　　S　　V　　　　　O

〔they could be solving today〕)))). [2]（In the federal government and most
　S　　　V　　　　　　　　　　　　　　　　　①　　　　　等接　　②

states）, there appears to be little interest〔in making policies（with proven
　　　　　　　　V　　　　S

track records of saving lives now）,（as opposed to some time in the distant

future）〕.

訳 [1]歯止めがきかない科学技術の進歩に懐疑的な専門家は，死亡者数が増加している理由は，役人がピカピカの新しいものを好むあまり，今日解決できているはずの問題から目をそらしてきたからなのだ，と言う。[2]連邦政府やほとんどの州においては，遠い未来のいつかではなく，今人命を救うことにおける確かな実績がある政策を立案することにほとんど関心がないようだ。

語句

skeptical 形 懐疑的な，疑い深い	**policy** 名 政策
unstoppable 形 止められない，抑制できない	**proven** 形 証明［立証］された
march 名 進展，進歩	track record 名 実績，業績
shiny 形 ピカピカの，光り輝く	**as opposed to ～** 熟 ～ではなく，～とは
take A off B 熟 A を B から離す，はずす	反対［対照的］に
federal 形 連邦（政府）の	distant 形 遠い，遠く離れた

107

¹<u>Other industrialized countries</u> <u>have made</u> <u>great progress</u> (in reducing traffic
　　　　S　　　　　　　　　　　　　V　　　　　　O

crashes) (over the last two decades). ²<u>Road fatality rates</u> 〔 in <u>Canada</u>,
　　　　　　　　　　　　　　　　　　　　　　　　　S　　　　　　　　　①

<u>France</u>, <u>Germany</u> and <u>Sweden</u> 〕, (for example), <u>are</u> now <u>less than half the rate</u>
　②　　　③　　　等接　④　　　　　　　　　　　　V　　　　　　　C

〔 in the United States 〕. ³<u>And</u> no, <u>these countries</u> <u>don't have</u> <u>loads of</u>
　　　　　　　　　　　　　　等接　　　　　S　　　　　　V

<u>self-driving cars</u>. ⁴<u>They</u> <u>have reduced</u> <u>accidents</u> (in the old-fashioned way).
　　　O　　　　　　S　　　　V　　　　　O

⁵<u>Some of them</u> <u>have worked</u> (to slow down traffic); <u>speed</u> <u>is</u> <u>a leading killer</u>.
　　S　　　　　　V　　　　　　　　　　　　　　　　　S　　V　　　C

　　　　　　　　　　　　　　　　　　　　┌─ 従接 that 省略
⁶<u>They</u> <u>have made</u> <u>changes</u> (to roads) (so <u>pedestrians</u> <u>will not have to pay</u>
　S　　　V　　　　O　　　　　　　　　　従接　　S　　　　　V

<u>much attention</u> (to cars)). ⁷<u>European regulators</u> <u>have encouraged</u> <u>the use of</u>
　　O　　　　　　　　　　　　　　　S　　　　　　　　V

<u>seatbelts</u> (by putting visual reminders (even in the back seat)). ⁸<u>Germany</u>
　O　　　　　　　　　　　　　　　　　　　　　　　　　　　　　　S

　　　　　　　　　　　　　　　　　　　①　　　　　　　②
<u>requires</u> much more rigorous <u>driver education</u> and <u>testing</u> (than most
　V　　　　　　　　　　　　　　O　　　　等接　　　　従接

<u>American states</u> <u>do</u>).
　　S　　　　　V

> 訳 ¹他の先進工業国は過去20年間で交通事故の減少において大きく進歩した。²例えば，カナダ，フランス，ドイツ，スウェーデンの交通事故による死亡率は，今やアメリカの半分以下である。³そして，これらの国々は自動運転車が多いわけではない。⁴これらの国々は古風なやり方で事故を減らしてきたのである。⁵車を減速させるよう取り組んできた国もある。スピードは主たる死亡原因なのだ。⁶歩行者が車にあまり注意しなくても済むように道路に変更を加えた。⁷ヨーロッパの規制当局は後部座席にも視覚的な注意書きを付けることによりシートベルトの着用を促進してきた。⁸ドイツではアメリカのほとんどの州よりもはるかに厳格な運転者教育と試験を義務づけている。

語句

industrialized	形	産業[工業]化した
make progress	熟	進歩[前進]する
decade	名	10年間
rate	名	割合, 比率
loads [a load] of ~	熟	多くの~
old-fashioned	形	古風な, 旧式の
slow down ~	熟	~の速度を落とす, ~を減速させる
leading	形	主要な, 先頭に立つ

killer	名	死をもたらすもの, 死亡原因
pedestrian	名	歩行者
regulator	名	監督[監査]機関, 規制当局
encourage	動	促進する, 助長する
visual	形	視覚的な
reminder	名	思い出させるもの, (思い出させるための)注意
rigorous	形	厳格な
education	名	教育

第8段落 文の構造と語句のチェック

¹Mr. Sullenberger is worried (that the rush 〔 to develop automated cars 〕
　　　　S　　　　　V　worried　従接　the rush
　　　　　　　　　　　C

will lead to many unforeseen problems). ²"(Even though there is a sense of
V　　　　　O　　　　　　　　　　従接　　　　V

urgency 〔 to prevent human-caused accidents 〕), we need to do it (in a
S　　　　　　　　　　　　　　　　　　　　　S　　V　　O

responsible way, not the fastest way)."

> **訳** ¹サレンバーガー氏は自動運転車の開発を急ぐことは多くの予想外の問題につながるのではないかと心配している。²「人為的な事故を防ごうと焦る気持ちがあるとはいえ,我々は最速の方法ではなく,責任ある方法でそれを行う必要がある。」

語句

rush	名	急ぎ, あわただしさ
unforeseen	形	予期しない, 予想外の
urgency	名	緊急(性), 切迫

human-caused	形	人間が引き起こした, 人為的な
responsible	形	責任のある

文法事項の整理 ⑧　so (that) S＋V の整理

第6段落第1文の so 〜 that S＋V について見てみよう。

Experts who are skeptical about the unstoppable march of technology say fatalities are rising because public officials have become **so** fond of the shiny new thing **that** they have taken their eyes off problems they could be solving today.

1）so 〜 that S＋V【結果】【程度】

　so 〜 that S＋V（「〜」は形容詞・副詞）は，「とても〜なので S は V する」【結果】，「S が V するほど〜」【程度】の意味を表す。

　　例　He is so poor that he cannot own a car.
　　　　「彼はとても貧しいので車を所有することができない」→【結果】
　　　　「彼は車を所有できないほど貧しい」→【程度】

　※**否定文**では【程度】の意味になる。

　　例　He isn't so poor that he cannot own a car.
　　　　「彼は車を所有できないほど貧しいわけではない」→【程度】

（第6段落第1文）
... because public officials have become so fond of the shiny new thing that they have taken their eyes off problems they could be solving today.

　▶ so 〜 that S＋V が【結果】を表す。

2）so that S＋V【目的】

　so that S＋V は「S が V するために，S が V できるように」【目的】の意味を表す。この場合，V は〈**can** / **may** / **will ＋原形**〉となるのが一般的。

　　例　He studied hard so that he could pass the examination.
　　　　「彼は試験に合格できるよう一生懸命に勉強した」

（第7段落第6文）

They have made changes to roads so pedestrians will not have to pay much attention to cars.

▶ so S＋V が【目的】を表す。so の後に that が省略されている。

3）so that S＋V【結果】

　so that S＋V が「だから S は V した，その結果 S は V した」【結果】の意味を表すこともある。この場合，**so の前に「，」（コンマ）がつく**ことが多い。

　例　He studied hard, so that he passed the examination.
　　　「彼は一生懸命に勉強したので，試験に合格した」

※上記1）～3）のいずれの場合にも，**that は省略可能**。

確認問題

1. 次の和訳と対応する英語の語句を，頭文字を参考にして書き，空欄を完成させよう。

/40点

（各1点×20）

①	a	形	魅力的な
②	i	名	幻想
③	c	動	通勤する
④	f	形	死にいたる
⑤	v	名	乗り物
⑥	e	名	緊急事態
⑦	e	動	排除する
⑧	a	名	自動化
⑨	o	名	公務員
⑩	a	形	適切な

⑪	h	名	仮説	
⑫	e	動	見積もる	
⑬	s	形	懐疑的な	
⑭	f	形	連邦の	
⑮	a　o　　t ~	熟	~ではなく	
⑯	m　p	熟	進歩する	
⑰	o	形	古風な	
⑱	r	名	思い出させるもの	
⑲	r	形	厳格な	
⑳	r	形	責任のある	

2. 次の[　]内の語を並べ替えて，意味の通る英文を完成させよう。(各5点×2)

① The technology [could / these / powers / introduce / that / vehicles] new risks.

② Germany requires [and / rigorous / education / more / much / driver] testing than most American states do.

3. 次の英文を和訳してみよう。(10点)

They have made changes to roads so pedestrians will not have to pay much attention to cars.

ディクテーションしてみよう！

今回学習した英文に出てきた語句を，音声を聞いて＿＿＿に書き取ろう。

45 / 52

45　The promise of self-driving cars can be attractive.　Imagine
❶＿＿＿＿＿＿＿＿ or watching a movie in a comfortable armchair while being shuttled safely home after a long day at work.　But like many over-optimistic images of the future, it is ❷＿＿＿＿＿＿＿＿＿＿.

46 Automated cars may indeed make commuting more pleasurable while preventing accidents and ❸_____ — someday. But a recent fatal crash suggests that some of these cars are not ready for the busy American roads: a lot of sensors and software turned this car into a high-tech vehicle you might see in a science fiction movie. In fact, the technology that powers these vehicles could introduce new risks that few people appreciate. For example, when a computer controlling the car does not hit the brakes ❹_____, the person in the driver's seat — many automated cars on the road today still require someone to be there in case of an emergency — may also fail to intervene because the driver trusts the car too much to pay close attention to the road. That is what appears to have happened in the crash.

47 "Technology does not eliminate error, but it changes the nature of ❺_____, and it introduces new kinds of errors," said Chesley Sullenberger, the former US Airways pilot who landed a plane in the Hudson River in 2009 after its engines were struck by birds. He now sits on a Department of Transportation advisory committee on automation. "We have to realize that it's not a solution for everything."

48 ❻_____ and other safety experts is that industry executives and government officials are rushing to put self-driving cars on the road without appropriate safeguards and under the unproven hypothesis that the technology will reduce crashes and fatalities.

49 Even as officials place a big bet that autonomous cars will solve many of our safety problems, American roads are becoming less safe. More than 37,000 people were killed in 2016, up 5.6 percent from 2015. The death toll ❼_____ more than 40,000 in 2017.

50 Experts who are skeptical about the unstoppable march of technology say fatalities are rising because public officials have become so fond of the shiny new thing that they have ❽_____ problems they could be solving today. In the federal government and most states, there appears to be little interest in making policies with proven track records of saving lives now, as opposed to some time in the distant future.

51   Other industrialized countries have made great progress in reducing traffic crashes over the last two decades. Road fatality rates in Canada, France, Germany and Sweden, for example, are now less than half the rate in the United States. And no, these countries don't have loads of self-driving cars. They have reduced accidents in the old-fashioned way. Some of them have worked to slow down traffic; speed is a leading killer. They have made changes to roads so pedestrians will not have to pay much attention to cars. European regulators have ❾_____

_____ seatbelts by putting visual reminders even in the back seat. Germany requires much more rigorous driver education and testing than most American states do.

52   Mr. Sullenberger is worried that the rush to develop automated cars will lead to many unforeseen problems. "Even though ❿_____

_____ urgency to prevent human-caused accidents, we need to do it in a responsible way, not the fastest way."

確認問題の答

1. ① attractive   ② illusion   ③ commute   ④ fatal   ⑤ vehicle   ⑥ emergency   ⑦ eliminate
   ⑧ automation   ⑨ official   ⑩ appropriate   ⑪ hypothesis   ⑫ estimate   ⑬ skeptical
   ⑭ federal   ⑮ as opposed to   ⑯ make progress   ⑰ old-fashioned   ⑱ reminder   ⑲ rigorous
   ⑳ responsible
2. ① that powers these vehicles could introduce （第2段落　第3文）
   ② much more rigorous driver education and （第7段落　最終文）
3. 歩行者が車にあまり注意しなくても済むように道路に変更を加えた。 （第7段落　第6文）

ディクテーションしてみよう！の答

❶ taking a nap   ❷ a bit of an illusion   ❸ saving many lives   ❹ to avoid a car crash
❺ errors that are made   ❻ What concerns him   ❼ is estimated to be   ❽ taken their eyes off
❾ encouraged the use of   ❿ there is a sense of

アドバイス ❷ bit of an illusion はそれぞれの単語の語尾と次の単語の語頭の音がつながる（連結）。
❽ their の語尾と eyes の語頭がつながり、「ラ」の音になる（連結）。

解答

問1 ⑤	問2 ⑤	問3 ③	問4 ⑤	問5 ①
問6 ③				

解説

問1

garment(s) は「衣服」，microfiber(s) は「マイクロファイバー［超極細合成繊維］」。本文の主題が「衣服から放出される繊維」である（特に明確なのは第6段落の中ほどにある microfiber released by garments という表現）点に注目する。

… one person could <u>release</u> almost 300 million polyester （　**ア**　） per year to the environment …

（**ア**）は動詞 release の O（目的語）の位置にあるので，「放出される側」，つまり，microfibers が入る。

… more than 900 million to the air by simply <u>wearing</u> the （　**イ**　）.

（**イ**）は動詞 wear の O（目的語）の位置にあるので，garments が入る。

… in preventing （　**ウ**　） from <u>being emitted</u> to the environment.

prevent O from *doing* で「O が〜するのを妨げる，O が〜しないようにする」の意味。つまり，（**ウ**）は being emitted「放出される」の主体なので，microfibers が入る。

問2

dedicated は，「（人が）献身的な，熱心な」，「（施設や機器などが）専用の，専門の」という2つの意味を持つ形容詞（同意語は devoted）。ここでは，laboratory「実験室，研究所」を修飾しているので後者の意味。

上記の知識がなかったとして，a dedicated clean laboratory の意味を推測すると，衣類から放出されるマイクロファイバーの量を計測するという目的の実験室なので，このような微細な物質を把握するには不純物をなくさなければならないであろうと考えられる。その意味で，clean は単に「清潔な」の意味で

115

はなく「無塵の，無菌の」といった意味であろう。したがって，dedicated も，その場に不純物が入り込まないよう，その実験に特化したものでなくてはならない。このように考えれば，「専用の，専門の」の意味が自然だと判断できる。

問3

各選択肢の意味は，①「貴重な」，②「革新的な」，③**「通常の」**，④「想像できない」，⑤「鮮明な」。

... then performing a sequence of movements simulating a mix of real life activities.

simulating(＜ simulate)に注目しよう。simulate は「模擬する，擬似的に作り出す」の意味。名詞形の simulation は「シミュレーション」として日本語になっているので推測できるだろう。ここでは，衣類から放出されるマイクロファイバーの量を計測するために，実験室内で服を着用して生活を模擬的に行うことを意味している。服を着用するのは「通常の」生活で行うことなので，正解は③となる。

問4

各選択肢の意味は，①「除外する」，②「それとなく示す」，③「計測する」，④「過大評価する」，⑤**「過小評価する」**。

第6段落第1文(Recently, more evidence has been accumulating on the presence of synthetic microfibers not only in the water, but also in the air.「最近，合成マイクロファイバーが水中だけでなく空気中にも存在することに関する証拠が蓄積してきた」)より，これまでの研究では水中のマイクロファイバーだけに目を向けていたことがわかる。さらに空所の直後では，... since they did not take into account the quantities released directly into the air「空気中に直接放出される量を考慮していなかったため」とあるので，合成繊維の環境への悪影響を「過小評価」していたと考えられる。

問5

この文章で紹介されている研究は，衣服が環境に放出するマイクロファイバーについて，①着用することによる空中への放出，②洗濯することによる水中への放出の両面を検証している。以下，①を点線，②を波線で示す。

（第 1 段落）

... how many fibers were released when they were being worn and washed.

（第 3 段落）

... could release almost 300 million polyester microfibers per year to the environment by washing their clothes, and more than 900 million to the air by simply wearing the garments.

（第 6 段落前半）

... on the presence of synthetic microfibers not only in the water, but also in the air.

（第 6 段落後半）

... can release fewer microfibers to both air and water.

（第 8 段落）

... the greatest release during both washing and wearing, ...

（第 11 段落前半）

... the emission of fibers while wearing clothes is likely of a similar amount as that from washing them.

（第 11 段落後半）

... both release to the （　**オ**　） and release due to laundering; ...

なお，laundering「洗浄，洗濯」は知らなくても，同語源の laundry「洗濯（物）」は「ランドリー」として日本語になっているので推測できるだろう。以上により，空所には air を入れるのが適切だとわかる。

問6

① 「昔の洗濯機に比べて，最新式の洗濯機の方が，繊維を放出する量が 10 分の 1 なので，環境への害がより少ない」

▶ 洗濯機についての記述はない。

② 「合成繊維による大気汚染についての従来の知見が，今回の実験でさらに確認された」

▶ 問 4 の解説参照。従来の研究では洗濯によって水中に放出される合成繊維が計測の対象になっていたが，新たな研究では衣服の着用により空中

に放出される合成繊維に着目し，これを測定している。したがって，適切でない。

③ **「今回の実験結果によれば，織り方が密なポリエステルよりも，織り方が粗い綿・ポリエステル混合の方が，着用時に多くの繊維を放出する」**

▶ 第8段落最終文と一致。本文では loosely woven「ゆるく織られた」，tightly woven「しっかりと織られた」という表現を用いているが，これらがそれぞれ「織り方が粗い」「織り方が密な」に対応する。

④ **「環境保持のためには，洗濯時の繊維の放出量よりも着用時の繊維の放出量に注意すべきである」**

▶ 第11段落の最初の部分で，… the emission of fibers while wearing clothes is likely of a similar amount as that from washing them.「衣服を着用する際の繊維の放出量が，おそらく洗濯時と同程度だ」とある。つまり，両者は同程度に注意すべきだということになるので，適切でない。

▼

それでは次に，段落ごとに詳しくみていこう。 🔊 53

第1段落 文の構造と語句のチェック

¹(In a first-of-its-kind study), <u>some scientists</u> <u>compared</u> <u>four different items</u>
　　　　　　　　　　　　　　　　　　　S　　　　　V

<u>of polyester clothing</u> (including one blended with cotton) <u>and</u> ⟨ how many fibers
　　O①　　　　　　　　　　　　　　　　　　　　　　　　　　　等接 O②疑　　　S

　　　　　　　　　　　　　　　　　　　　　　① 等接 ②
<u>were released</u> (<u>when</u> <u>they</u> <u>were being worn and washed</u>)⟩.
　　V　　　　　　　　従接　S　　　　V

> **訳** ¹その類いでは初めての研究で，科学者たちはポリエステルの衣類4点（綿との混紡1点を含む）において，それらが着用されたり洗濯されたりしたときにどれほど多くの繊維が放出されるかを比較した。

118

語句

first-of-its-kind	形 その種で初めての，前例のない	including	前 ～を含めて
compare	動 比較する	blend	動 混合する
item	名 品目，項目	cotton	名 綿
clothing	名 衣類	fiber	名 繊維
		release	動 放出する／名 放出

第2段落 文の構造と語句のチェック

[1]The results showed 〈 that up to 4,000 fibers per gram of fabric
　　S　　　　V　　　O 従接　　　　　　　　　　　S

could be released (during a conventional wash), (while up to 400 fibers per
　　V　　　　　　　　　　　　　　　　　　　　　　　　従接　　　　　　　S

gram of fabric could be released (by items of clothing) (during just 20 minutes
　　　　　　　　　　　V

of normal activity)))．

訳 [1]その結果，普通の洗濯時には生地1グラムあたり最大4,000本の繊維が放出される一方，通常の活動を20分間行うだけで生地1グラムあたり最大400本の繊維が衣類から放出される可能性があることが示された。

語句

up to ～	熟 最大で～	fabric	名 生地，布地
per	前 ～あたり，～につき	conventional	形 普通の，平凡な
		normal	形 通常の，正常な

第3段落 文の構造と語句のチェック

[1](Scaled up), the results indicate 〈 that one person could release almost 300
　　　　　　　　　　S　　　V　　　O 従接　　S　　　　　V

million polyester microfibers per year (to the environment) (by washing their
　　　　　　　　O①

　　　　　　　　　　　　　　　　　┌ polyester microfibers per year 省略
clothes), and more than 900 million ↓ (to the air) (by simply wearing the
　　　　　等接　　　　O②

garments)〉．

訳 ¹以上の結果は，規模を大きくしてみると，人間1人が衣類を洗濯することにより，年間3億本近くのポリエステルのマイクロファイバーを環境に放出し，また衣服を着るだけで9億本以上を空気中に放出する可能性があるということを示している。

語句

scale up	熟 規模を拡大する	microfiber	名 マイクロファイバー
			［超極細合成繊維］
indicate	動 示す	**garment**	名 衣服

第4段落 文の構造と語句のチェック

¹(In addition), there were significant differences (depending on ⟨ how
                     V   S   疑

the garments were made ⟩); the researchers conclude ⟨ that clothing design and
   S   V   S   V   O従接   ①   S 等接

②
manufacturers have a major role [to play] (in preventing microfibers from
             V   O   S′

being emitted (to the environment)))⟩.
  V′

訳 ¹さらに，衣類の作り方によっても重大な相違があった。研究者は，衣類のデザインとメーカーが環境へのマイクロファイバーの放出を防ぐ上で重要な役割を果たすと結論付けている。

語句

significant	形 重大な，重要な	**design**	名 デザイン
depending on ～	熟 ～次第で，～によって	**manufacturer**	名 製造業者，メーカー
conclude	動 結論付ける	**emit**	動 放出する

第5段落 文の構造と語句のチェック

¹The research, [published in the journal Environmental Science and Technology],
  S   └同格┘

was conducted (by scientists [at the Institute for Polymers, Composites and
  V   ①

Biomaterials of the National Research Council of Italy (IPCB-CNR) and the
　　　　　　　　　　　　　　　　　　　　　　　　　　　　　　等接　②

University of Plymouth 〕). ²It builds (on their previous studies 〔 which showed
　　　　　　　　　　　　　　　S　V　　　　　　　　　　　　　　関代　　　V

── 従接 that 省略

〈¹large quantities of fibers are released (during the laundry process)〉〕]).
　　O　　　　　　　　　　　　S　　　V

訳 ¹この研究は，「環境科学技術」誌において発表されたが，イタリア国立研究協議会のポリマー・コンポジット・バイオマテリアル研究所(IPCB-CNR)とプリマス大学の科学者によって行われた。²それは，洗濯の過程で繊維が大量に放出されることを示した，彼らの以前の研究をもとにしている。

語句

publish	動	発表する，公表する
journal	名	専門誌，定期刊行物
conduct	動	行う

build on ～	熟	～をもとにする，～を足がかりにする
previous	形	以前の，これより前の
quantity	名	量
laundry	名	洗濯

第6段落 文の構造と語句のチェック

¹Dr. Francesca De Falco, Research Fellow at IPCB-CNR said: "Recently, more
　S　　　　　　　　└─同格─┘　　　　　　　　　　　V

evidence has been accumulating 〔 on the presence of synthetic microfibers 〔 not
　S　　　　V

only in the water, but also in the air 〕〕. ²That is 〈 why we decided to design this
　　　　　　　　　　　　　　　　　　　S　V　C　　関副 S　　　　　V

set of experiments (to study microfiber 〔 released by garments to both
　　　O

environments 〕)〉. ³This is a type of pollution 〔 that should be mainly tackled
　　　　　　　　　　S　V　　　　C　　　　　　　関代　　　　　　　　　V

(at its source, the fabric itself)〕, but we investigated the influence 〔 of different
　　　└─同格─┘　　　　　　　　等接 S　　V　　　　　O

textiles 〕〔 on the release 〕. ⁴Results have shown 〈 that tightly woven textiles
　　　　　　　　　　　　　　　S　　　V　　　　O 従接　　　　　S

<u>can release</u> <u>fewer microfibers</u> (to both air and water)⟩."
    V   O

訳 [1]IPCB-CNR の研究フェローであるフランチェスカ・デ・ファルコ博士は以下のように述べた。「最近,合成マイクロファイバーが水中だけでなく空気中にも存在することに関する証拠が蓄積してきた。[2]そのため,衣服から両方の環境に放出されるマイクロファイバーを調査するために,この一連の実験を設計することにした。[3]これは主にその発生源である生地そのものを対象として取り組むべき種類の汚染であるが,我々は,異なる布地が放出に与える影響について調べた。[4]結果は,きつく織り込まれた布地は空気と水の両方へのマイクロファイバーの放出を減らせることを示している。」

語句

fellow	名	フェロー［大学の特別研究員］
evidence	名	証拠
accumulate	動	蓄積する
presence	名	存在
synthetic	形	合成の
design	動	設計する,立案する

pollution	名	汚染,公害
tackle	動	取り組む,立ち向かう
investigate	動	調査する
textile	名	織物,布地
tightly	副	きつく,しっかりと
weave	動	織る,編む

*活用:**weave-wove-woven**

第7段落 文の構造と語句のチェック

[1]<u>The study</u> <u>compared</u> <u>four different garments,</u> 関代↱ which <u>were washed</u> (at 40℃)
    S   V   O   V

(with <u>any released fibers</u> <u>being collected</u>). [2]<u>It</u> <u>showed</u> ⟨ that <u>anywhere between</u>
付帯状況   S′   V′   S V O従接   S

<u>700 and 4,000 individual fibers</u> <u>could be released</u> (per gram of fabric) (during
                                       V

a single wash ⟩⟩.

訳 [1]研究では,4つの異なる衣類を比較した。それらは40℃で洗濯され,放出されたどんな繊維も回収された。[2]その結果,1回の洗濯で生地1グラムあたり700~4,000本の範囲で個々の繊維が放出される可能性があることがわかった。

語句

anywhere between *A* and *B*
                  熟 A から B の範囲で

individual 形 個々の

第8段落　文の構造と語句のチェック

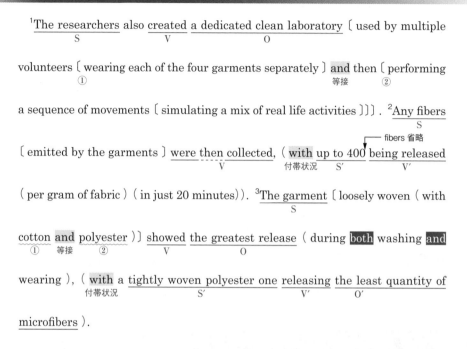

¹The researchers also created a dedicated clean laboratory〔used by multiple
　　S　　　　　　　　V　　　O

volunteers〔wearing each of the four garments separately〕and then〔performing
　　　　　　①　　　　　　　　　　　　　　　　　等接　　　②

a sequence of movements〔simulating a mix of real life activities〕〕〕. ²Any fibers
　　　　　　　　　　　　　　　　　　　　　　　　　　　　　　　S

┌─ fibers 省略

〔emitted by the garments〕were then collected,（with up to 400 being released
　　　　　　　　　　　　　　V　　　　　　　付帯状況　S′　　V′

（per gram of fabric）（in just 20 minutes））. ³The garment〔loosely woven（with
　　　　　　　　　　　　　　　　　　　　　　　　　S

cotton and polyester）〕showed the greatest release（during both washing and
　①　等接　②　　　　　V　　　　O

wearing）,（with a tightly woven polyester one releasing the least quantity of
付帯状況　　　S′　　　　　　　　　V′　　　O′

microfibers）.

訳 ¹さらに，研究者たちは専用の無塵実験室を作り，4つの衣服のそれぞれを別々に着用し，実生活の様々な活動を模擬した一連の動作を行う多数のボランティアがその実験室を使用した。²そして，衣服から放出されたすべての繊維を回収したところ，わずか20分間で生地1グラムあたり最大400本が放出されていた。³綿とポリエステルでゆるく織られた衣服は，洗濯時と着用時の両方で最大の放出量を示し，しっかりと織られたポリエステルの衣服は，マイクロファイバーの放出量が最も少なかった。

語句

dedicated	形	専用の
laboratory	名	実験室，研究所
multiple	形	多数の
volunteer	名	ボランティア
separately	副	別々に

perform	動	行う
a sequence of ~	熟	一連の~
movement	名	動作
simulate	動	模擬する，擬似的に作り出す
loosely	副	ゆるく

[1]However, (based on the overall results), the researchers say 〈 that previous
　　　　　　　　　　　　　　　　　　　　　　S　　　　　　V　O従接　　S

studies 〔 of microplastic pollution 〕 have actually underestimated the disadvantage
　　　　　　　　　　　　　　　　　　　V　　　　　　　　　　　　　　O

〔 of synthetic textiles 〕 (since they did not take (into account) the quantities
　　　　　　　　　　　　　　従接
　　　　　　　　　　　　　　　　　S　　　V　　　　　　　　　　　　O

〔 released directly into the air〕)〉.

> 訳　[1]しかし，全体の結果に基づけば，これまでのマイクロプラスチック汚染に関する研究
> では，空気中に直接放出される量を考慮していなかったため，実際には合成繊維のマイナ
> ス面を過小評価していたことになると研究者たちは述べている。

語句

based on ～	熟 ～に基づいて	underestimate	動 過小評価する
overall	形 全体的な	disadvantage	名 不利な点，不利益
		take ～ into account	熟 ～を考慮する

[1]Professor Richard Thompson, Head of the University of Plymouth's International
　　　　　S　　　　　　　　└─同格─┘

Marine Litter Research Unit, was a senior author 〔 on the current study 〕 and
　　　　　　　　　　　　　　　V　　　C　　　　　　　　　　　　　　等接

gave evidence (to both the British Government's Sustainability of the Fashion
V　　O

Industry inquiry and a recent OECD Forum 〔 in the garment and footwear

sector 〕).

> 訳　[1]プリマス大学国際海洋ごみ研究部門長のリチャード・トンプソン教授は，今回の研究
> の上級著者であり，英国政府によるファッション産業の持続可能性に関する調査と，衣料

品・履物部門における最近の OECD フォーラムの双方に証拠を提供した。

語句

senior	形	地位が高い，上級の
author	名	著者，執筆者
current	形	現在の

inquiry	名	調査，研究
footwear	名	履物
sector	名	部門

第11段落　文の構造と語句のチェック

¹He added: "The key story here is ⟨ that the emission of fibers 〔 while wearing
S　V　　　　　　　　S　　　　V　C従接　　　　　　S　　　　　従接

clothes 〕 is likely 〔 of a similar amount 〕 (as that from washing them ⟩⟩. ²That
　　　　　V　　　　　　　　　　　　　　‖　　　　　　　　　　　S
　　　　　　　　　　　　　　　　　　　　the emission of fibers

　　　　　　①　　　　　　　　　　　　等接 ②
constitutes a non-neglectable and previously unquantified direct release 〔 to the
V　　　　　　　　　　　　　　　O

　　　　　　　　　　　　　　　　　　　┌ 従接 that 省略
environment 〕. ³The results also show ⟨ textile design can strongly influence
　　　　　　　　　　　S　　　　V　O　　S　　　　　　　　V

both release to the air and release due to laundering ⟩; that is a crucial message
　　　　　　　　　　　O　　　　　　　　　　　　　　S　V　　　C

〔 highlighting the importance of sustainable design (for the fashion industry)〕.
　V'　　　　　　O'

⁴Indeed many of the current issues 〔 associated with the environmental impacts
　　　　　S

　　　　　　　　　　　　　　　　　┌─────────────────────┐
of plastic items 〕 stem (from a lack of comprehensive thinking 〔 at the design
　　　　　　　　　V

stage 〕)."

訳 ¹彼は以下のように付け加えた。「ここで重要なのは，衣服を着用する際の繊維の放出量が，おそらく洗濯時と同程度だということだ。²それは無視できない，これまで数量化されていなかった，環境への直接的な放出である。³また，布地のデザインが空気中への放出と洗濯による放出の両方に強く影響を与えることも結果から明らかになった。それは，ファッション産業に向けて持続可能なデザインの重要性を強調する重要なメッセージだ。⁴実

際，プラスチック製品の環境への影響に関連する現在の問題の多くは，デザインの段階で包括的な考えが欠如していることに由来している。」

語句

key	形	重要な
emission	名	放出（量）
likely	副	おそらく
constitute	動	～となる，～に等しい
previously	副	以前に
laundering	名	洗浄，洗濯
crucial	形	重大な，きわめて重要な
highlight	動	強調する
sustainable	形	持続可能な，環境を破壊しない

indeed	副	実際に，本当に
issue	名	問題
(be) associated with ~	熟	～に関連して，～と結びついて
stem from ~	熟	～に由来する，～により生じる
lack	名	欠如，不足
comprehensive	形	包括的な
stage	名	段階

文法事項の整理 ⑨　付帯状況の with

第 7 段落第 1 文の with について見てみよう。

The study compared four different garments, which were washed at 40℃ **with** any released fibers being collected.

　付帯状況の with とは，with のあとに 2 つの要素が続き，〈with＋*A*＋*B*〉で「A が B の状態で」「A を B にしながら」「A が B なので」などの意味を表す用法。A は名詞，B は分詞／形容詞／副詞／前置詞＋名詞。

例　He stood there with his arms folded.
「彼は腕を組んでそこに立っていた」
▶ B の位置に過去分詞（folded）

例　With the boys making noise, it was hard for her to concentrate on her homework.
「男の子たちが騒いでいたので，彼女は宿題に集中するのが難しかった」
▶ B の位置に現在分詞（making）

例 Despite the heavy rain, he continued to walk with <u>his hat</u> <u>on</u>.
「激しい雨にもかかわらず，彼は帽子をかぶったまま歩き続けた」
▶ B の位置に副詞（on）

例 He strolled casually down the street, with <u>his hands</u> <u>in his pockets</u>.
「彼は両手をポケットに突っ込んで，のんびりと街を歩いた」
▶ B の位置に前置詞＋名詞（in his pockets）

ポイントは，〈A ⇒ B〉に〈主語⇒述語〉の関係が成立すること。これを明確にすれば，訳し方は臨機応変に変えて良い。

例 He went for a walk in the park with <u>his dog</u> <u>following him</u>.
「彼は犬が後に付いてくる状態で公園を散歩した」（不自然な和訳）
▶「彼は公園を散歩し，犬が後に付いてきた」（自然な和訳）

（第 7 段落第 1 文）
The study compared four different garments, which were washed at 40℃ with any released fibers being collected.
▶ any released fibers が A，being collected が B の位置。

（第 8 段落第 2 文）
Any fibers emitted by the garments were then collected, with up to 400 being released per gram of fabric in just 20 minutes.
▶ up to 400 が A，being released が B の位置。

（第 8 段落最終文）
The garment loosely woven with cotton and polyester showed the greatest release during both washing and wearing, with a tightly woven polyester one releasing the least quantity of microfibers.
▶ a tightly woven polyester one が A，releasing the least quantity of microfibers が B の位置。※代名詞 one は garment を指す。

確認問題

1. 次の和訳と対応する英語の語句を，頭文字を参考にして書き，空欄を完成させよう。

(各1点×20)

①	c	動	比較する	
②	r	名 動	放出(する)	
③	s	形	重大な，重要な	
④	c	動	結論づける	
⑤	q	名	量	
⑥	e	名	証拠	
⑦	a	動	蓄積する	
⑧	p	名	汚染，公害	
⑨	t	名	織物，布地	
⑩	w	動	織る，編む	
⑪	v	名	ボランティア	
⑫	o	形	全体的な	
⑬	d	名	不利な点，不利益	
⑭	t ～ i a	熟	～を考慮する	
⑮	a	名	著者，執筆者	
⑯	c	形	現在の	
⑰	h	動	強調する	
⑱	s	形	持続可能な，環境を破壊しない	
⑲	s f ～	熟	～に由来する，～により生じる	
⑳	c	形	包括的な	

2. 次の[ ]内の語を並べ替えて，意味の通る英文を完成させよう。(各5点×2)

① In addition, there were [on / how / garments / differences / depending / were / the / significant] made.

128

② This is a type of pollution that should be mainly tackled at its source, the fabric itself, but we investigated [the / the / textiles / release / of / different / influence / on].

3. 次の英文を和訳してみよう。(10点)

Recently, more evidence has been accumulating on the presence of synthetic microfibers not only in the water, but also in the air.

ディクテーションしてみよう！

今回学習した英文に出てきた語句を，音声を聞いて＿＿＿に書き取ろう。

54   In a first-of-its-kind study, some scientists compared four different items of polyester clothing (including one blended with cotton) and how many fibers were released when they were being ❶＿＿＿＿＿＿＿＿＿＿＿＿.

55   The results showed ❷＿＿＿＿＿＿＿＿＿＿＿＿＿ per gram of fabric could be released during a conventional wash, while up to 400 fibers per gram of fabric could be released by items of clothing during just 20 minutes of normal activity.

56   Scaled up, the results indicate that one person could release almost 300 million polyester microfibers per year to the environment by ❸＿＿＿＿＿＿＿ ＿＿＿＿＿＿＿＿＿＿, and more than 900 million to the air by simply wearing the garments.

57   In addition, there were significant differences depending on how the garments were made; the researchers conclude that clothing design and manufacturers ❹＿＿＿＿＿＿＿＿＿＿＿＿ to play in preventing microfibers from being emitted to the environment.

58   The research, published in the journal Environmental Science and Technology, was conducted by scientists at the Institute for Polymers, Composites and Biomaterials of the National Research Council of Italy (IPCB-CNR) and the University of Plymouth. It ❺＿＿＿＿＿＿＿ their

previous studies which showed large quantities of fibers are released during the laundry process.

59   Dr. Francesca De Falco, Research Fellow at IPCB-CNR said: "Recently, more evidence has been accumulating on the presence of synthetic microfibers ❻_____, but also in the air. That is why we decided to design this set of experiments to study microfiber released by garments to both environments. This is a type of pollution that should be mainly ❼_____, the fabric itself, but we investigated the influence of different textiles on the release. Results have shown that tightly woven textiles can release fewer microfibers to both air and water."

60   The study compared four different garments, which were ❽_____ with any released fibers being collected. It showed that anywhere between 700 and 4,000 individual fibers could be released per gram of fabric during a single wash.

61   The researchers also created a dedicated clean laboratory used by multiple volunteers wearing each of the four garments separately and then performing ❾_____ simulating a mix of real life activities. Any fibers emitted by the garments were then collected, with up to 400 being released per gram of fabric in just 20 minutes. The garment loosely woven with cotton and polyester showed the greatest release during both washing and wearing, with a tightly woven polyester one releasing the least quantity of microfibers.

62   However, ❿_____, the researchers say that previous studies of microplastic pollution have actually underestimated the disadvantage of synthetic textiles since they did not ⓫_____ the quantities released directly into the air.

63   Professor Richard Thompson, Head of the University of Plymouth's International Marine Litter Research Unit, was a senior author on the current study and ⓬_____ both the British Government's

130

Sustainability of the Fashion Industry inquiry and a recent OECD Forum in the garment and footwear sector.

64　He added: "The key story here is that the emission of fibers ⓭_____ _____ is likely of a similar amount as that from washing them. That constitutes a non-neglectable and previously unquantified direct release to the environment. The results also show textile design can strongly influence both release to the air and release due to laundering; that is a crucial message highlighting the importance of sustainable design for the fashion industry. Indeed many of the current issues ⓮_____ _____ the environmental impacts of plastic items stem from a lack of comprehensive thinking at the design stage."

確認問題の答

1.　① compare　② release　③ significant　④ conclude　⑤ quantity　⑥ evidence
⑦ accumulate　⑧ pollution　⑨ textile　⑩ weave　⑪ volunteer　⑫ overall
⑬ disadvantage　⑭ take, into account　⑮ author　⑯ current　⑰ highlight　⑱ sustainable
⑲ stem from　⑳ comprehensive
2.　① significant differences depending on how the garments were　（第 4 段落　第 1 文）
　　② the influence of different textiles on the release　（第 6 段落　第 3 文）
3.　最近，合成マイクロファイバーが水中だけでなく空気中にも存在することに関する証拠が蓄積してきた。
　　（第 6 段落　第 1 文）

ディクテーションしてみよう！の答

❶ worn and washed　❷ that up to 4,000 fibers　❸ washing their clothes　❹ have a major role
❺ builds on　❻ not only in the water　❼ tackled at its source　❽ washed at 40℃
❾ a sequence of movements　❿ based on the overall results　⓫ take into account
⓬ gave evidence to　⓭ while wearing clothes　⓮ associated with

アドバイス　❶ worn の /n/ と and の /ə/ が重なり，「ナ」のような音になる（連結）。and は弱形で /(ə)n/ となり，/d/ はほぼ発音されない。結果的に，worn and は「ウォーンアンド」というより「ウォーナン」のように聞こえる。
❷ /t/ や /d/ の音が母音に挟まれるとら行のような音になる（フラッピング）。that up to は「ザットアップトゥ」というより「ザラップトゥ」のように聞こえる。※ら行化するのはアメリカ英語。

10 解答・解説

解答

問1 ③	問2 ②	問3 ④	問4 ②	問5 ③
問6 2nd ③ 5th ⑤		問7 ③	問8 ②	
問9 ③	問10 ③	問11 ②	問12 ②	
問13 A ④ B ① C ④			問14 ②, ④	

解説

問1

contemporary：何かまたは誰かと（　　）時に属する

①次の　　②全体の　　③**同じ**　　④唯一の

▶ contemporary は「同時代の」または「現代の」の意味。直後の第2段落第1文で，過去2世紀にわたって価値観が変動してきたとあるので，ここでは「同時代の」の意味に解釈するのが適切。正解は③。

問2

①保障すべき　　②**恐れられるべき**　　③促進すべき　　④喜ぶべき

▶ 第2段落第2文では技術の進歩に対する optimistic view「楽観的な見方」，続く第3文では，【逆接】の However の後に，技術の進歩に対する pessimistic view「悲観的な見方」について述べている。第4文では This can be seen in ～「これは～に見られる」とあるので，マイナスイメージの内容が続くはず。選択肢の中でマイナスイメージのものは②しかない。

問3

①フィクションと映画　　②熟慮と態度　　③未来と宇宙　　④**希望と絶望**

▶ 直前の文に … in both a negative and positive light とあるので，〈ネガティブ⇔ポジティブ〉の対比になっている選択肢を選ぶ。正解は④。

問4

①科学の向上のおかげで

②**科学の確立された規則や慣行に従って**

③科学の進歩を加速するために

132

④最新の科学的価値を犠牲にして

▶ found *A* on *B* で「B に基づいて A を作る」の意味。受け身形の be founded on ～で「～に基づいて作られる」となる。「基づく」に近い意味のものは，①「～のおかげで」か②「～に従って」であろう。また，principle(s) は「原理，原則」の意味なので，①「向上」は無関係。②「確立された規則や慣行」は「原理，原則」に近い意味と言える。

問5

①描写されて　　②想像されて　　**③影響されて**　　④含まれて

▶ 空欄を含む文の also に注目。also「～も」を見たら，前に似たような形式・内容の表現があると考えて良い。以下の2つの文を比較してみよう。

（第3段落第1文）

Works of science fiction have been influenced by many other literary traditions.

（第3段落第6文）

Creators of science fiction have **also** been （　ウ　） by traditional storytelling techniques.

これで，正解は③だとわかる。

なお，本問は，直後の文（Many works of SF follow storylines that are typical of ancient myths and legends.）からも正解が得られる。ancient myths and legends は「伝統」を具体化しており，「伝統に従う」≒「伝統に影響される」と考えられる。

問6

並べ替えると，found in many ancient myths となる（2番目＝3，5番目＝5）。found は find の過去分詞で，found ～ myths のかたまり（句）が直前の名詞 pattern を修飾している。数量を表す形容詞（many / much / few / little / some / one / two / three … など）は一般の形容詞より前に置かれるので，many ancient myths の語順になる。

問7

This idea of objects ④（1 came　2 come　3 coming　4 has come）to life is quite similar to

前置詞 of には，直前の抽象名詞の内容を具体化する働きがある（【同格】の of）。「…という 抽象名詞 」と訳す。ここでは，idea が抽象名詞で，of 以下で idea「考え」の内容を具体化している。「考え」の内容が objects「物」では意味が通らないので，前置詞 of の目的語はその後の名詞，ここでは動名詞 coming であり，coming の前に 意味上の主語 として objects が付いている，と考える。the idea of objects *doing* で「物が〜するという考え」の意味になる（⇒文法事項の整理⑫（186 ページ）参照）。

問8

①ロボット　　②**魔法**　　③一連の実験　　④技術的発明

In SF, amazing things happen **not** by （　**エ**　）, as in traditional narratives, **but** because of science.

not *A* but *B*「A ではなく B」のパターンに注目する。A を否定，B を肯定する表現であり，A と B が対比される関係。選択肢①，③，④はいずれも science と意味が重なってしまうので，対比の関係にならない。

問9

①電気技師　　②マジシャン　　③**そっくりな物**　　④印刷機

下線部の copy は日本語の「コピー［複製］」のイメージで理解できる。humanity は「人類，人間」。直前の文で … manages to create life itself「生命そのものを創り出すことに成功する」とあるので，人間のコピー，つまり，人間にそっくりな生き物を作ったと解釈する。選択肢③ double には，名詞で「そっくりな物［人］」の意味がある。

例 You are your father's double.「あなたはお父さんにそっくりです」

問10

①故意に　　②事実上　　③**最終的に**　　④必然的に

▶ ultimately は「最終的に，究極的には」の意味。直後の killing its own creator「自分の創造主を殺す」が直前の ends up doing terrible things「最終的には恐ろしいことをする」の具体化である点に注目すれば，推測可能。

問11

①古代の神話に似ている　　②**制御不能になる**

③人類に屈服する　　　　④並行世界に入る

▶ 第6段落第4文が，同第2文の dangers，同第3文の warning を具体化
している点に注目。本問の選択肢の中で，科学技術の危険性を警告する
内容として適切なのは，その創造物が「制御不能になる」であろう。

問12

①もう1つの　　②**他の**　　③他のもの　　④どれも～ない

▶ 直後の times が名詞なので，形容詞を入れる。③と④は代名詞なので不
可。また，another の後は単数形の名詞が続くので，①も不可。

問13

A：④の relate のみ第2音節，他は第1音節に強勢[アクセント]が置かれる。

B：①の horrible のみ第1音節，他は第2音節に強勢[アクセント]が置かれる。

C：④の scientific のみ第3音節，他は第2音節に強勢[アクセント]が置かれる。

問14

① 「フランシス・ベーコンの『ニュー・アトランティス』は，科学技術の恩
恵と切り離せない生活様式を持つ，16世紀の人々を描写している」

▶ 第3段落第2・3文参照。この作品が出版されたのが1627年(= 17世紀)で，
描写されているのは「未来」。よって，誤り。

② **「技術の進歩に対する態度という点で，ジュール・ヴェルヌの小説と
1980年代の多くの SF 映画には違いがある」**

▶ 第2段落第2～4文参照。ジュール・ヴェルヌの小説は技術の進歩に対し
て楽観的，20世紀後半の SF 映画は悲観的な態度を取っている。よって，
正しい。

③ 「ジュール・ヴェルヌ，フランシス・ベーコン，メアリー・シェリーは，
いずれもその作品が古代の神話や伝説に影響を与えた SF 作家である」

▶ 第3段落第1・2文から，フランシス・ベーコンが文学の伝統の影響を受
けていることがわかる(「影響を与えた」のではない)。他の二者について
は，このような記述はない。よって，誤り。

④「読者の中には，技術についての複雑な科学的描写や，まだ来ていない時代についての予言ゆえに，SF をよりいっそう好む人もいる」

▶ 第1段落第2文と一致。

⑤「『スター・ウォーズ』を含む多くの SF 作品の話の筋は，古代の神話や伝説とは共通点がない」

▶ 第3段落第7文参照。多くの SF 作品が，古代の神話や伝説に典型的な話の筋に従っていると述べている。よって，誤り。

⑥「フランケンシュタインの物語は，技術の破壊力を人々に警告するためにフランケンシュタイン博士が自殺せざるを得なかったという意味で悲劇である」

▶ 第5段落最終文参照。博士は「自殺」したのではなく，殺されたのである。よって，誤り。

▼

それでは次に，段落ごとに詳しくみていこう。 65

第1段落 文の構造と語句のチェック

¹The literary genre 〔that is most directly related (to science and technology)〕
S 〔関代〕 V C 〔等接〕

is (of course) science fiction (SF). ²Fans of science fiction love 〈reading the
V C S V O ①

many detailed descriptions 〔of science and technology〕, and the many, often
〔等接〕 〔等接 ②〕

precise, predictions 〔about the future 〕〉. ³Science fiction is also interesting
S V C

(because it shows society's attitudes 〔towards technological development 〕(as
〔従接〕 S V O

well)). ⁴Science fiction is not only a projection 〔into the future 〕, or 〔into
S V C ① 〔等接 ②〕

136

outer space], <u>but</u> <u>it</u> <u>is</u> <u>also</u> <u>a reflection</u> 〔 of contemporary society's cultural

values 〔 towards technology 〕〕.

　　　S　V　　　　C

訳 ¹科学技術と最も直接的な関係がある文学ジャンルは，もちろんサイエンスフィクショ
ン(SF)だ。²SF 愛好者は，科学技術に関する多くの詳細な描写や，未来に関する多くの，
しばしば正確な予言を読むことが大好きだ。³SF はまた，技術の発展に対する社会の態度
をも示すがゆえに興味深い。⁴SF は未来や宇宙についての見通しであるだけではなく，科
学技術に対する同時代の社会の文化的価値観を反映するものでもある。

語 句

literary	形	文学の
genre	名	(芸術作品などの)様式，ジャンル
be related to ~	熟	~と関連して
science fiction	名	サイエンスフィクション(SF)，空想科学小説
fan	名	ファン，愛好者
detailed	形	詳細な
description	名	描写
precise	形	正確な
prediction	名	予測，予言
as well	熟	~も
projection	名	見通し，予測
outer space	名	宇宙
reflection	名	反映
contemporary	形	同時代の，現代の

第 2 段落　文の構造と語句のチェック

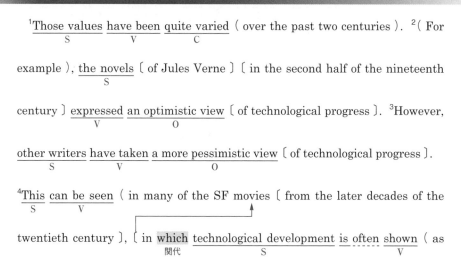

¹<u>Those values</u> <u>have been</u> <u>quite varied</u> (over the past two centuries). ²(For
　　S　　　　　V　　　　C

example), <u>the novels</u> 〔 of Jules Verne 〕 〔 in the second half of the nineteenth
　　　　　S

century 〕 <u>expressed</u> <u>an optimistic view</u> 〔 of technological progress 〕. ³However,
　　　　　V　　　　O

<u>other writers</u> <u>have taken</u> <u>a more pessimistic view</u> 〔 of technological progress 〕.
　　S　　　　V　　　　O

⁴<u>This</u> <u>can be seen</u> (in many of the SF movies 〔 from the later decades of the
　S　　V

twentieth century 〕, 〔 in <u>which</u> <u>technological development</u> <u>is often shown</u> (as
　　　　　　　　　　　関代　　S　　　　　　V

something to be feared))). ⁵The relationship [between technology and culture]
S

is clearly quite complex. ⁶Science fiction has shown technological progress (in
V C   S   V   O

both a negative and positive light). ⁷Stories [about technological progress]
  ① ②   S

often swing (between hope and despair), (between celebration and warning).
  V

⁸Furthermore, these two totally opposite attitudes are also mixed together (in
     S   are   V

works of science fiction).

訳 ¹そうした価値観は過去2世紀にわたってかなり多様であった。²例えば，19世紀後半のジュール・ヴェルヌの小説は，技術の進歩に対する楽観的な見方を表していた。³しかし，他の作家は技術の進歩に対してより悲観的な見方をしてきた。⁴これは20世紀後半数十年間の多くのSF映画に見られ，そこではしばしば技術の発展が恐れられるべきものとして示されている。⁵技術と文化の関係は明らかにかなり複雑だ。⁶SFは技術の進歩を否定的な視点と肯定的な視点の両方で示してきた。⁷技術の進歩に関する物語は，しばしば希望と絶望，祝福と警告の間で揺れ動く。⁸さらに，これら2つの完全に対立する態度は，SFの作品の中で混在することもある。

 第6文 in a ～ light(「～」は形容詞)で「～の観点[視点]で」の意味。

語句

varied	形 多様な		**positive**	形 肯定的な
optimistic	形 楽観的な		**light**	名 観点，視点
view	名 見方，見解		**swing**	動 揺れ動く，移り変わる
progress	名 進歩		**celebration**	名 祝福
pessimistic	形 悲観的な		**warning**	名 警告
negative	形 否定的な		**opposite**	形 反対の，逆の

第3段落 文の構造と語句のチェック

¹Works of science fiction have been influenced (by many other literary
　　S　　　　　　　　　　　V

traditions). ²(For example), Francis Bacon's *New Atlantis*, 〔 published in
　　　　　　　　　　　　　　　　　　　S

1627 〕, was a work 〔 of both fantasy and science fiction 〕. ³The story describes
　　　　　V　C　　　　　　　　　　　　　　　　　　　　　　　S　　　　V

an ideal society in the future 〔 that was founded (on the principles of science)〕.
　　　　O　　　　　　　　　　　　関代　　V

⁴The citizens 〔 of this imagined society 〕 enjoy the benefits 〔 of technological
　　S　　　　　　　　　　　　　　　　　　　V　　　O

inventions 〔 including telephones and flying machines 〕〕. ⁵It is a vision 〔 of
　　　　　　　　　　　①　　　　　等接　②　　　　　　　S　V　C

discovery and knowledge 〕. ⁶Creators of science fiction have also been influenced
　　　等接　　　　　　　　　　　　S　　　　　　　　　V

(by traditional storytelling techniques). ⁷Many works of SF follow storylines
　　　　　　　　　　　　　　　　　　　　　　　　S　　　　V　　　O

〔 that are typical of ancient myths and legends 〕. ⁸(For example), the movie
　関代　V　C　　　　　　　①　　　　等接　②　　　　　　　　　　　　　S

Star Wars follows a traditional "hero's journey" storyline, a pattern 〔 found in
　　　　V　　　　　　　O　　　　　　　　　　　└同格┘

many ancient myths 〕. ⁹Another good example 〔 of ancient stories influencing
　　　　　　　　　　　　　　S　　　　　　　　　　　　S′　　V′

science fiction 〕 is the Jewish legend of the *Golem*. ¹⁰The *Golem* is a clay figure
　　O′　　　V　　　　　　C　　　　　　　　　　S　　V　C

〔 that magically comes (to life)〕. ¹¹This idea 〔 of objects coming (to life)〕 is
　関代　　　V　　　　　　　　　S　　　　　　S′　V′　　　　V

quite similar (to the many human-like robot characters 〔 that often appear (in
　C　　　　　　　　　　　　　　　　　　　　　　　　関代　　V

science fiction books and movies)〕).
　　　　　①　　等接　②
　　　　　　　等接

訳 ¹SF の作品は，他の多くの文学の伝統に影響を受けてきた。²例えば，1627 年に出版されたフランシス・ベーコンの『ニュー・アトランティス』は，ファンタジーと SF 両方の作品だった。³この物語は，科学的な原理に基づいて作られた未来の理想的な社会を描いている。⁴この想像上の社会の市民は，電話や飛行機などの技術的な発明品の恩恵を享受している。⁵それは発見と知識の未来予想図である。⁶SF の創作者たちはまた，伝統的な物語の技法に影響を受けている。⁷多くの SF 作品は，古代の神話や伝説に典型的な話の筋に従っている。⁸例えば，映画『スター・ウォーズ』は，多くの古代の神話に見られるパターンである，伝統的な「英雄の旅」の展開に従っている。⁹古代の物語が SF に影響を与えているもう 1 つの良い例は，『ゴーレム』というユダヤの伝説だ。¹⁰『ゴーレム』は，魔法によって生命を得る粘土の人形だ。¹¹このように物体が生命を宿すという発想は，SF の本や映画にしばしば登場する人間に似た多くのロボットのキャラクターにとても似ている。

語句

fantasy	名	ファンタジー，空想［幻想］小説
ideal	形	理想的な
be founded on ~	熟	~に基づいて（作られて）
principle	名	原理，原則
citizen	名	市民
enjoy	動	享受する
benefit	名	利益，恩恵
invention	名	発明（品）
vision	名	心に描く像，未来（予想）図
creator	名	創作者
storytelling	名	物語（を話すこと）
storyline	名	話の筋（立て），展開

be typical of ~	熟	~に典型的な
myth	名	神話
legend	名	伝説
journey	名	旅，旅行
clay	名	粘土
figure	名	人物の像，人形
magically	副	魔法によって，魔法にかかったように
come to life	熟	生命を宿す，命を吹き込まれる
object	名	物，物体
be similar to ~	熟	~に似て，~と類似して
human-like	形	人間に似た，人間のような

第4段落　文の構造と語句のチェック

¹Science fiction emerged (as a literary genre) (in the nineteenth century
　S　　　　　V

〔 when writers began 〈 creating stories of wonder or horror (in the context of
関副　S　　V　　O　　　　　　①　等接　②

science and technology 〉〉〕). ²(In SF), amazing things happen (not by magic,
①　等接　②　　　　　　　　　S　　　　　V

140

(as in traditional narratives)), (**but** because of science). ³Typically, they are

＊they do 省略

従接 · S V

amazing stories, 〔 set in the future or some parallel world 〕. ⁴Writers create

C ① 等接 ② S V

stories, (making predictions (about the future) (based on scientific and

O ① 等接

technological concepts)). ⁵Science fiction is a genre 〔 that expresses itself

② S V C 関代 V O

(through the language of science))〕.

訳 ¹作家たちが科学技術の文脈で驚異や恐怖の物語を作り始めた 19 世紀に，SF は文学の 1 つのジャンルとして現れた。²SF では，伝統的な物語にあるような魔法によってではなく，科学のせいで驚異的なことが起こる。³それらは通常，未来や並行世界を舞台にした驚異的な物語となる。⁴作家は，科学的・技術的な概念に基づいて未来に関する予測を行いながら物語を創作する。⁵SF は科学の言語を通じて自己表現するジャンルである。

語句

emerge	動	現れる
wonder	名	驚異，不思議
horror	名	恐怖
context	名	文脈
narrative	名	物語，話

typically	副	一般的に，通常は
set	動	(舞台・背景を)設定する
parallel world	名	パラレルワールド，並行世界
(be) based on ～	熟	～に基づいて
concept	名	概念，観念

第 5 段落 文の構造と語句のチェック

¹Mary Shelley's character Dr. Frankenstein is a man 〔 of both ancient and

S └─同格─┘ V C ① 等接

modern science 〕. ²(Through a series of experiments), he discovers the secrets

② S V O

of life, and manages to create life itself. ³His creature is a technological copy of

等接 V O S V C

humanity, 〔 created in a laboratory 〕. ⁴Shelley's story, 〔 written in 1818 〕, is

S S V

thus <u>a journey of scientific discovery</u>. ⁵<u>The experiments</u> 〔 described in the novel 〕
         C   S

<u>were</u> <u>based</u> (on <u>the technologies of the early nineteenth century</u>, <u>and</u> (in
 V   C   ①   等接

particular) <u>the developing technology of electricity</u>). ⁶<u>The story</u> <u>is</u> <u>based</u> (on
                     ②   S V C

the idea 〈 <u>that</u> <u>life itself</u> <u>might somehow be created</u> (using electricity)〉〉. ⁷<u>Yet</u>
       従接(同格) S   V   等接

<u>Shelley's work</u> <u>is</u> <u>a reaction against technology</u>. ⁸<u>It</u> <u>shows</u> <u>technology</u> (in a
     S   V   C   S V   O

negative light). ⁹<u>Dr. Frankenstein's creation</u> <u>is</u> <u>a horrible monster</u> (rather
                     S   V   C

than a perfect model of technology). ¹⁰<u>It</u> <u>is</u> <u>a monster of science</u> 〔 <u>that</u> <u>ends up</u>
                               S V   C   関代 V

┌── by 省略
(doing terrible things), (ultimately killing its own creator)〕.

訳 ¹メアリー・シェリーのキャラクターであるフランケンシュタイン博士は，古代と現代の両方の科学に精通した人物だ。²彼は一連の実験を通して生命の秘密を発見し，生命そのものを創り出すことに成功する。³彼の創造物は，実験室で作られた人類の技術的な複製である。⁴このように，1818 年に書かれたシェリーの物語は，科学的発見の旅である。⁵その小説で描かれた実験は，19 世紀初頭の技術，特に発展途上の電気技術に基づいていた。⁶その物語は，生命そのものが電気を使って何らかの形で生み出されるかもしれないという考えに基づいている。⁷しかし，シェリーの作品は，技術に対する反動である。⁸それは，技術を否定的な観点で示している。⁹フランケンシュタイン博士の創造物は，技術の完璧なモデルというよりむしろ，恐ろしい怪物である。¹⁰それは，最終的には恐ろしいことをする科学の怪物であり，最後に自分の創造主を殺してしまう。

語 句

a series of ~	熟 一連の~	in particular	熟 特に
experiment	名 実験	electricity	名 電気
manage to *do*	熟 どうにか~する，	somehow	副 何らかの方法で，
	物の見事に~する		何らかの形で
creature	名 創造物，発明品，生き物	creation	名 創造物，創作品
humanity	名 人類，人間	end up *doing*	熟 最終的に~する，
laboratory	名 実験室，研究室		結局~する
		ultimately	副 最後に

第6段落　文の構造と語句のチェック

¹The story of Frankenstein shows the dark side 〔 of technological progress 〕.
　　　　　S　　　　　　　　　　V　　　　　O

²It shows its dangers. ³It is a classic story 〔 that carries (with it) a warning 〕.
　S　V　　　O　　　　　S　V　　C　　　　　関代　V　　　　　　　　O

⁴Frankenstein's monster represents technology 〔 that runs out of control 〕,
　　　　　　　　S　　　　　　V　　　　O　　　関代　V

〔 that destroys its human creator 〕. ⁵There are many variations 〔 on this basic
　関代　V　　　O　　　　　　　　　　　　　　V　　　S

pattern 〕, (particularly in the film versions of *Frankenstein*).　⁶(At times)

the scientist is warm-hearted, and we can see his human side. ⁷(At other times),
　　S　　　V　　　C　　　等接　S　V　　　O

he is a man 〔 driven crazy (by his own search for personal power and greatness)〕.
S　V　C　　　　　　　　　　　　　　　　　　　　　　　　①　　　等接　②

⁸His great experiment is cursed (by both bad luck and his search for power).
　　　S　　　　　　V　　　　　　①　　　等接　②

⁹(While Frankenstein's monster is a caring and emotional creature 〔 who only
　従接　　　S　　　　　V　　　　　　　　C　　　　　　　　関代

wants to live and share his life (with others)〕), it is also capable (of great
　V　　等接　　　　O　　　　　　　　　　　　S　V　　　　C

destruction). ¹⁰However, its violence is generally directed (against its creator).
　　　　　　　　　　　S　　　　　　V

¹¹This is an often-seen pattern. ¹²The monster is the result 〔 of a scientific
　S　V　　　C　　　　　　　S　　　V　　C

project 〔 that has gone horribly wrong 〕〕 and it punishes the man 〔 who pushed
　　　関代　V　　C　　　等接　S　V　　　O　　　関代　V

the science (too far)〕. ¹³Shelley's story is still relevant today, (because it
　O　　　　　　　　　　S　　　V　　　C　　　　　従接　S

143

expresses a fear, 〔 as strong today as it was in Shelley's time 〕, 〈 that human
　　　　　　V　　　O　　　　　　　　　　　　　　　　　　　　　　　　　　　　従接(同格)　S

beings cannot always control the consequence 〔 of scientific development 〕〉〉.
　　　　　　　　　　　　V　　　　　　O

> **訳** ¹フランケンシュタインの物語は，技術の進歩の暗黒面を示している。²その危険性を示
> しているのだ。³これは，警告を込めた古典的な物語だ。⁴フランケンシュタインの怪物は，
> 制御不能に陥り，人間の創造主を破壊してしまう技術を象徴している。⁵この基本的なパタ
> ーンには多くのバリエーションがあり，映画版『フランケンシュタイン』では特にそうで
> ある。⁶あるときは，その科学者は心優しく，人間らしい一面を見ることができる。⁷また，
> あるときは，自らが個人的な権力と偉大さを求めるあまり，狂気に駆られた男である。⁸彼
> の偉大な実験は，不運と彼の権力追求の両方によって呪われる。⁹フランケンシュタインの
> 怪物は，ただ他者とともに生き，生活をともにしたいと願う，思いやりと感情のある生き
> 物である一方，大きな破壊も可能である。¹⁰しかし，その暴力は一般に創造主に対して向
> けられるものである。¹¹これはよく見られるパターンである。¹²怪物は科学プロジェクト
> が恐ろしく失敗した結果であり，科学を過度に推し進めた人間を罰するのである。¹³シェ
> リーの物語は今日においてもなお的を射ている。なぜならそれは，人間が科学的発展の結
> 果を必ずしも制御できないという，シェリーの時代と同様に今日でも強い恐怖を表現して
> いるからだ。

語 句

represent	動 表す，象徴する	**emotional**	形 感情的な
run out of control	熟 制御不能になる	**be capable of ~**	熟 ~が可能な，~をする能力のある
destroy	動 破壊する，滅ぼす	**destruction**	名 破壊
variation	名 バリエーション，変形版	**violence**	名 暴力
version	名 ~版，~バージョン	**direct**	動 向ける
warm-hearted	形 心の温かい	**go wrong**	熟 失敗する
drive ~ crazy	熟 ~の気を狂わせる，~を発狂させる	**horribly**	副 恐ろしく，ひどく
curse	動 呪う	push ~ too far	熟 ~をやり過ぎる，~を過度に推し進める
search	名 探求，追求	**relevant**	形 関連がある，的を射ている
caring	形 思いやりのある，気遣いをする	**consequence**	名 結果

144

文法事項の整理 ⑩ 等位相関接続詞

第 1 段落最終文の not only ～ but also ... について見てみよう。

Science fiction is **not only** a projection into the future, or into outer space, **but** it is **also** a reflection of contemporary society's cultural values towards technology.

and, or, but といった等位接続詞（＝前後を対等の関係で結ぶ）が他の語と相関的に用いられる場合がある。いずれも，以下の A と B は文法的に対等の要素が入る。

☐ not *A* but *B*「A ではなくて B」（＝*B*, not *A*）
☐ both *A* and *B*「A と B の両方」（＝at once *A* and *B*）
☐ either *A* or *B*「A か B のどちらか」
☐ neither *A* nor *B*「A も B もどちらも～ない」（＝not ～ either *A* or *B*）
☐ not only *A* but also *B*「A だけでなく B も」（＝*B* as well as *A*）
※「A だけでなく B も」は以下のように様々なパターンがある。

$$\text{not} \left\{ \begin{array}{l} \text{only} \\ \text{just} \\ \text{simply} \\ \text{merely} \\ \text{solely} \end{array} \right\} A \left\{ \begin{array}{l} \text{but also } B \\ \text{but } B \\ \text{but } B \text{ as well} \\ \text{but } B \text{ too} \\ \text{; } B \end{array} \right\}$$

例 He studied both English and French.
          A   R
「彼は英語とフランス語の両方を勉強した」

例 You can either cook it or eat it raw.
                    A   B
「それは調理しても，生で食べても，どちらでもよい」

例 Not only the money but also the jewels were stolen.
                  A   B
「金だけではなく宝石も盗まれた」
（＝The jewels as well as the money were stolen.）

（第1段落最終文）

Science fiction is not only a projection into the future, or into outer space, but it is also a reflection of contemporary society's cultural values towards technology.

▶ not only *A* but also *B* の形。Science fiction is ... a projection ... という文と，it is ... a reflection ... という文が並列されている。

（第2段落第6文）

Science fiction has shown technological progress in both a negative and positive light.

▶ both *A* and *B* の形。形容詞である negative と positive が並列されている（いずれも light を修飾）。

（第3段落第2文）

For example, Francis Bacon's *New Atlantis*, published in 1627, was a work of both fantasy and science fiction.

▶ both *A* and *B* の形。名詞である fantasy と science fiction が並列されている（いずれも前置詞 of の目的語）。

（第4段落第2文）

In SF, amazing things happen not by magic, as in traditional narratives, but because of science.

▶ not *A* but *B* の形。前置詞句である by magic と because of science が並列されている（いずれも副詞句で，動詞 happen を修飾）。

（第6段落第8文）

His great experiment is cursed by both bad luck and his search for power.

▶ both *A* and *B* の形。名詞である bad luck と his search for power が並列されている（いずれも前置詞 by の目的語）。

確認問題

1. 次の和訳と対応する英語の語句を，頭文字を参考にして書き，空欄を完成させよう。

（各1点×20）

①	l	形	文学の
②	p	形	正確な
③	c	形	同時代の，現代の
④	o	形	楽観的な
⑤	p	形	悲観的な
⑥	i	形	理想的な
⑦	p	名	原理，原則
⑧	be t　　o	熟	～に典型的な
⑨	m	名	神話
⑩	l	名	伝説
⑪	c　t　l	熟	生命を宿す，命を吹き込まれる
⑫	be s　　t	熟	～に似て，～と類似して
⑬	c	名	文脈
⑭	c	名	概念，観念
⑮	e	名	実験
⑯	i　p	熟	特に
⑰	r	動	表す，象徴する
⑱	r　o　o　c	熟	制御不能になる
⑲	d	名	破壊
⑳	v	名	暴力

2. 次の[　]内の語句を並べ替えて，意味の通る英文を完成させよう。（各5点×2）

① Science fiction has shown technological [in both / a / negative / light / progress / positive / and].

② The story describes an ideal society in the future [on / that / of / was / principles / the / science / founded].

3. 次の英文を和訳してみよう。(10点)

This idea of objects coming to life is quite similar to the many human-like robot characters that often appear in science fiction books and movies.

ディクテーションしてみよう！

66
71

今回学習した英文に出てきた語句を，音声を聞いて＿＿＿に書き取ろう。

66　The literary genre that is most directly related to science and technology is of course science fiction (SF).　Fans of science fiction love reading the many detailed descriptions of science and technology, and the many, often precise, predictions about the future.　Science fiction is also interesting because it shows society's attitudes towards technological development as well.　Science fiction is not only a ❶＿＿＿＿＿＿＿＿＿＿＿＿＿＿＿＿＿＿＿, or into outer space, but it is also a reflection of contemporary society's cultural values towards technology.

67　Those values have been quite varied over the past two centuries.　For example, the novels of Jules Verne in the second half of the nineteenth century ❷＿＿＿＿＿＿＿＿＿＿＿＿＿＿＿＿＿＿＿＿＿ of technological progress.　However, other writers have taken a more pessimistic view of technological progress.　This can be seen in many of the SF movies from the later decades of the twentieth century, in which technological development is often shown as something to be feared.　The relationship between technology and culture is clearly quite complex.　Science fiction has shown technological progress in both a negative and positive light.　Stories about technological progress often ❸＿＿＿＿＿＿＿＿＿＿＿＿＿＿＿＿＿＿＿＿＿＿, between celebration and warning.　Furthermore, these two totally opposite attitudes are also mixed together in works of science fiction.

68　　Works of science fiction have been influenced by many other
❹_____. For example, Francis Bacon's *New Atlantis*,
published in 1627, was a work of both fantasy and science fiction. The story
describes an ideal society in the future that ❺_____ the
principles of science. The citizens of this imagined society enjoy the benefits
of technological inventions including telephones and flying machines. It is a
vision of discovery and knowledge. Creators of science fiction have also
been influenced by traditional storytelling techniques. Many works of SF
follow storylines ❻_____ ancient myths and legends.
For example, the movie *Star Wars* follows a traditional "hero's journey"
storyline, a pattern found in many ancient myths. Another good example of
ancient stories influencing science fiction is the Jewish legend of the *Golem*.
The *Golem* is a clay figure that magically comes to life. This idea of objects
coming to life is quite similar to the many human-like robot characters that
often appear in science fiction books and movies.

69　　Science fiction emerged as a literary genre in the nineteenth century
when writers began creating stories of ❼_____ in the
context of science and technology. In SF, amazing things happen not by
magic, as in traditional narratives, but because of science. Typically, they
are amazing stories, ❽_____ or some parallel world.
Writers create stories, making predictions about the future based on
scientific and technological concepts. Science fiction is a genre that
expresses itself through the language of science.

70　　Mary Shelley's character Dr. Frankenstein is a man of both ancient
and modern science. Through a series of experiments, he discovers the
secrets of life, and manages to create life itself. His creature is a
technological copy of humanity, created in a laboratory. Shelley's story,
❾_____, is thus a journey of scientific discovery. The
experiments described in the novel were based on the technologies of the
early nineteenth century, and in particular the developing technology of

electricity. The story is based on the idea that life itself might somehow be created using electricity. Yet Shelley's work is a reaction against technology. It shows technology ❿_____. Dr. Frankenstein's creation is a horrible monster rather than a perfect model of technology. It is a monster of science that ends up doing terrible things, ultimately killing its own creator.

71   The story of Frankenstein shows the dark side of technological progress. It shows its dangers. It is a classic story that ⓫_____

_____. Frankenstein's monster represents technology that runs out of control, that destroys its human creator. There are many variations on this basic pattern, particularly in the film versions of *Frankenstein*. At times the scientist is warm-hearted, and we can see his human side. At other times, he is a man ⓬_____ his own search for personal power and greatness. His great experiment is cursed by both bad luck and his search for power. While Frankenstein's monster is a caring and emotional creature who only wants to live and share his life with others, it is also capable of great destruction. However, its violence is generally directed against its creator. This is an often-seen pattern. The monster is the result of a scientific project that ⓭_____

_____ and it punishes the man who pushed the science too far. Shelley's story is still relevant today, because it expresses a fear, as strong today as it was in Shelley's time, that human beings cannot always control the consequence of scientific development.

確認問題の答

1. ① literary　② precise　③ contemporary　④ optimistic　⑤ pessimistic　⑥ ideal
⑦ principle　⑧ typical of　⑨ myth　⑩ legend　⑪ come to life　⑫ similar to　⑬ context
⑭ concept　⑮ experiment　⑯ in particular　⑰ represent　⑱ run out of control
⑲ destruction　⑳ violence

2. ① progress in both a negative and positive light　（第2段落　第6文。negative と positive は逆も可）
② that was founded on the principles of science　（第3段落　第3文）

3. このように物体が生命を宿すという発想は，SF の本や映画にしばしば登場する人間に似た多くのロボットのキャラクターにとても似ている。　（第3段落　最終文）

ディクテーションしてみよう！の答

❶ projection into the future　❷ expressed an optimistic view　❸ swing between hope and despair
❹ literary traditions　❺ was founded on　❻ that are typical of　❼ wonder or horror
❽ set in the future　❾ written in 1818　❿ in a negative light　⓫ carries with it a warning
⓬ driven crazy by　⓭ has gone horribly wrong

アドバイス ❷ an の n の音と，optimistic の /ɑ/ の音がつながり，「ノ」のように聞こえる（⇒連結）。

❾ written の n の音と，in の /ɪ/ の音がつながり，「ニン」のように聞こえる（⇒連結）。また，1818 か 1880 かを区別できるかどうかがポイント。語尾ははっきり発音されないが，eighty は前，eighteen は後ろを強く読むので，アクセントに注意すれば聞き分けられる。

11 解答・解説

解答

問1	④	問2	①	問3	②	問4	④
問5	③	問6	④	問7	①	問8	②

解説

問1

「第2段落で，著者が『笑顔は世界共通の人間の行為である』と述べているのはどういう意味か」

① 「人間はもともと笑顔が得意ではない」

② 「人間は適切に笑顔を作る方法を学習する」

③ 「私たちの全世界が笑顔の人間を必要としている」

④ **「笑顔はすべての人間がするものである」**

▶ universal は「世界共通の，普遍的な」，practice は「行為，行い」の意味。また，although 以下に varies according to culture「文化によって異なる」とあり，これと反対の内容と考えれば推測も可能。正解は④。①「得意ではない」，②「学習する」，③「必要としている」はいずれも含まれない要素。

問2

「なぜポートフィリップでは市役所が路上パーティーを促進するのか」

① **「近所の人と交流する機会を人々に与えるため」**

② 「近隣組織の助言をより良いものにするため」

③ 「地域の人々に食べ物を提供するため」

④ 「地域パーティーの楽しみ方を教えるため」

▶ 路上パーティーの目的については，第4段落第1文に In a related effort to get its residents to know each other, …「住民同士を知り合いにさせるための関連する活動として，…」とある。また，同段落最終文にも，Many people who have lived in the same street for many years meet each other for the first time at a street party.「同じ通りに長年住んでい

る多くの人々が路上パーティーで初めて出会うこともある」とあるので，住民同士の交流が目的であることがわかる。正解は①。

問3

「この記事に基づくと，ポートフィリップ市役所は次のうちどれを住民にして欲しいと望む可能性が高いか」
① 「公共交通機関を使って路上パーティーに行けない場合は，家にいる」
② **「自家用車の所有はできれば避けたいものだと考える」**
③ 「路上パーティーの詳細を市役所に知らせる」
④ 「エネルギー効率の悪い建物には徒歩や自転車で行くのをやめる」

▶ 第6段落第2文(Instead of seeing private car ownership as a sign of prosperity, the city hails a *declining* number of cars — and rising use of public transport — as a sign of progress in reducing greenhouse gas emissions …「自家用車の所有を繁栄のしるしと見るのではなく，市は自動車の数の減少を—そして公共交通機関の利用の増加を—温室効果ガスの排出削減における進歩のしるしとして評価する…」)から，市役所は自家用車所有を否定的に，車の減少・公共交通機関の利用を肯定的に評価していることがわかる。正解は②。①については，路上パーティーに行く交通手段についての記述がないので誤り。③については，詳細は地元の人々に任せている(第4段落第2文参照)ので誤り。④については，確かにエネルギー効率の良い建物は求められているものの(第6段落最終文)，そこに行くための交通手段については言及していない。

問4

「この記事によると，地域住民の生活の質に影響を与えるのはどれか」
① 「路上パーティーがどれほど長時間続くか」
② 「ボランティアにどれだけの納税者の金が支払われているか」
③ 「"G'day" などの標準的な挨拶がどれくらいの頻度で使われるか」
④ **「住民がそこで生活することをどれほど安全だと思っているか」**

▶ 第3段落最終文参照。笑顔がもたらす安心感や犯罪の減少が生活の質において重要な要素だとしているので，正解は④。①と②は本文中に記述

なし。③については，市が標識を設置した目的として，笑顔と挨拶が並列的に挙げられているが，その頻度が生活の質に影響を与えるとまでは言えない。

問5

「ポートフィリップで顔を上げて心を開いた表情で歩いていると，おそらくあなたは…と思われるだろう」

　①「繊細で，新しい人に会うことにショックを受けている」

　②「決断力があり，人から評価されようと心に決めている」

　③「**親しみやすく，他の人に賛同する**」

　④「目立っていて，見知らぬ人と議論する準備ができている」

　▶ 第1・2段落の内容から，本文では「顔を上げて心を開いた表情で歩く」ことは「笑顔」と同等の行為として挙げられていることがわかる。「笑顔」は人とのつながりを感じさせるとあるので(第3段落最終文)，正解は③。approachable は「(人が)気さくな，付き合いやすい」，approve of ～は「～を承認する，～に賛成する」の意味。

問6

「ポートフィリップ警察が『1時間あたり10回の笑顔ゾーン』で笑顔のない歩行者に罰金を与えたり，逮捕したりできないのは，…という理由からだと理解されている」

　①「1時間にそれだけの笑顔を見せることはまったく不可能だ」

　②「すべての歩行者が本当に笑顔かどうかを警察が確認するのは難しすぎる」

　③「警察は近隣の路上パーティーに参加することは許されない」

　④「**その歩行者は何ら法律を犯しているわけではない**」

　▶ 罰金や逮捕などに関する記述はないので，常識的に考える必要がある問題。第3段落によれば，「笑顔ゾーン」の標識を設置した目的は，to encourage people to smile or say "G'day"(笑顔を向けるよう，または「G'day」と声をかけるよう，人々に奨励する)である。「奨励」であって「強制」ではないのだから，守らなくても罰せられないと解される。よっ

て，正解は④。

問7

「アイゼンとレヴィンが行った研究では，電話ボックスの中でお金を見つけることは…を表すよう意図されている」

① 「ポジティブな経験」
② 「無作為な選択」
③ 「窃盗行為」
④ 「友情を育む機会」

▶ この研究については第9段落第2文以降に書かれているが，その目的は第9段落第1文にあるように，ポジティブな経験が人に与える影響を調査することである。正解は①。

問8

「ポートフィリップ市役所による市の生活の質を変えるプログラムは，そこに住む人々が…ので，おそらく機能しているだろう」

① 「善意によって明るく輝いている」
② 「現在は以前より笑顔が増えたことがわかっている」
③ 「毎年の笑顔の成功率を計算している」
④ 「硬貨を見つけるたびに，以前よりも進んで宛先の書かれた手紙を投函（とうかん）するようになった」

▶ 最終段落で，「成功の目安」として「笑顔の増加」を挙げているので，正解は②。

▼

それでは次に，段落ごとに詳しくみていこう。

第1段落　文の構造と語句のチェック

¹(If <u>you</u> <u>were to walk</u> (along the streets of your neighborhood) (with
　　　S　　　　V

your face up and an open expression)), how many 〔 of those 〔 who passed you 〕〕
①   等接 ②   S   関代   V   O

would smile, or greet you (in some way)?
V①   等接 V②   O

> **訳** ¹仮にあなたが近所の通りを顔を上げて心を開いた表情で歩いてみると，通り過ぎる人々の中で，どれくらいの人が微笑んだり，何らかの方法であなたに挨拶をしてくれたりするだろうか？

> **語 句**
> neighborhood 名 近所　　　expression 名 表情

第 2 段落 　文の構造と語句のチェック

¹Smiling is a universal human practice, (although readiness to smile at
S   V   C   従接   S

strangers varies (according to culture)). ²(In Australia, 〔 where 〈 being open
        V   関副   S

and friendly to strangers 〉 is not unusual 〕), the city of Port Phillip, an area
                            V   C   S   └─同格─┘

〔 covering some of the bayside suburbs of Melbourne 〕, has been using volunteers
                                              V   O

(to find out 〈 how often people smile at those 〔 who pass them (in the street)〕〉).
              疑   S   V   関代   V   O

³It then put up signs 〔 that look like speed limits, but tell pedestrians 〈 that
S   V   O   関代   V   等接   V   O₁   O₂ 従接

they are (in, for example, a "10 Smiles Per Hour Zone)〉〕."
S   V

> **訳** ¹笑顔は世界共通の人間の行為である。とはいえ，見知らぬ人に対して進んで笑顔を向けるかどうかは文化によって異なるが。²オーストラリアでは，見知らぬ人に対して心を開き親しくすることは珍しくなく，メルボルンの湾岸沿いの郊外の一部にわたる地域であるポートフィリップ市では，ボランティアを使って，人々がどれくらいの頻度で通行人に笑顔を向けるかを調査している。³さらに，見たところ速度制限のようだが，例えば「1 時間あたり 10 回の笑顔ゾーン」に入ったことを歩行者に伝える標識を設置した。

156

語句

universal	形	世界共通の，普遍的な
practice	名	行為，行い
readiness	名	進んで～すること，喜んで～すること
stranger	名	見知らぬ人
vary	動	異なる

according to ～	熟	～に応じて
bayside	形	湾岸近くの
suburb	名	郊外
volunteer	名	ボランティア
put up	熟	取り付ける，掲げる
sign	名	標識，看板
pedestrian	名	歩行者

第3段落 文の構造と語句のチェック

¹Frivolous nonsense? ²A waste of taxpayers' money? ³Mayor Janet Bolitho
S

says 〈 that 〈 putting up the signs 〉 is an attempt 〔 to encourage people to smile
V　O従接　S　　　　　　　　　　V　C　　　　V′　　　O′　　C′

or say "G'day" — the standard Australian greeting — (to both neighbors and
等接

strangers) (as they stroll (down the street)))〕〉. ⁴Smiling, (she adds),
　　　　　　従接　S　V　　　　　　　　　　　　　　S　　主節の挿入

encourages people 〈 to feel more connected with each other and safer 〉, so it
V　　　O　　C　　　①　　　　　　　　　等接　②　　等接 S

reduces fear of crime — an important element in the quality of life of many
V　　O

neighborhoods.

訳 ¹ふざけたことであろうか？ ²納税者の金の無駄遣いだろうか？ ³ジャネット・ボリソ市長は，標識の設置は，道を散歩しているときに，近所の人にも見知らぬ人にも笑顔を向けるよう，または「G'day」（オーストラリアの一般的な挨拶）と声をかけるよう，人々に奨励する試みだと言う。⁴笑顔は人々により強いお互いのつながりを感じさせ，安心感を与えるので，犯罪の恐怖を減らすことになるが，これは多くの近隣地域の生活の質において重要な要素であると市長は付け加えている。

第4段落 文の構造と語句のチェック

[1](In a related effort [to get its residents to know each other]), the city
government also facilitates street parties. [2]It leaves the details (to the locals),
but offers organizational advice, lends out barbecues and sun umbrellas, and
covers the public liability insurance. [3]Many people [who have lived (in the
same street) (for many years)] meet each other (for the first time) (at a
street party).

> **訳** [1]住民同士を知り合いにさせるための関連する活動として，市役所は路上パーティーも促進している。[2]詳細は地元の人々に任せているが，組織運営上の助言を提供したり，バーベキューの道具や日傘を貸し出したり，公的な賠償責任保険の費用を出したりしている。[3]同じ通りに長年住んでいる多くの人々が路上パーティーで初めて出会うこともある。

語句

related	形	関連した
effort	名	努力，活動
resident	名	住民
facilitate	動	促進する，助長する
leave *A* to *B*	熟	A を B に任せる
detail	名	詳細
local	名	地元の人々
organizational	形	組織的な
barbecue	名	バーベキューの道具
sun umbrella	名	日傘
cover	動	（費用を）まかなう

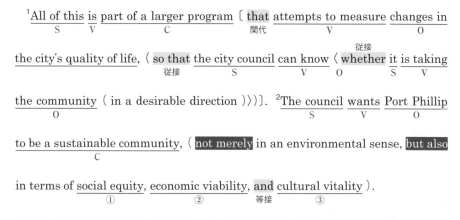

第5段落 文の構造と語句のチェック

[1]All of this is part of a larger program [that attempts to measure changes in
 S   V   C   関代   V   O

the city's quality of life, (so that the city council can know 〈 whether it is taking
     O   従接   S   V   O   従接   S V

the community (in a desirable direction)〉)]. [2]The council wants Port Phillip
     O   S   V   O

to be a sustainable community, (not merely in an environmental sense, but also
          C

in terms of social equity, economic viability, and cultural vitality).
            ①   ②   等接   ③

訳 [1]これはすべて，市議会が地域社会を望ましい方向に進めているかどうかを知るために，市の生活の質の変化を評価しようと試みる大きなプログラムの一部だ。[2]市議会はポートフィリップを持続可能なコミュニティにしたいと考えている。それは自然環境的な意味だけでなく，社会的公正，経済的実現可能性，文化的活力の面においてもだ。

語句

measure	動 評価する，査定する	environmental	形 (自然)環境の，環境(保護)的な
council	名 (地方自治体の)議会	sense	名 意味
community	名 地域社会(の人々)	equity	名 公平，公正
desirable	形 望ましい	viability	名 実現可能性，実行可能性
direction	名 方向(性)	vitality	名 活力
sustainable	形 持続可能な		

第6段落 文の構造と語句のチェック

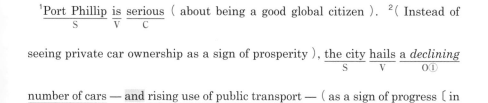

[1]Port Phillip is serious (about being a good global citizen). [2](Instead of
 S   V   C

seeing private car ownership as a sign of prosperity), the city hails a *declining*
                                                        S   V   O①

number of cars — and rising use of public transport — (as a sign of progress [in
     O   等接   O②

reducing greenhouse gas emissions (while encouraging a healthier lifestyle 〔 in
　V′　　　　　　　　O′　　　　　　　　　　　　　　V′　　　　　　　O′

which people are more inclined to walk or ride a bike 〕))). ³The city is also
関代　S　　　　　V　　　　　　①　　　②　　O　　　　　　　S　　V
　　　　　　　　　　　　　　　　　　　　等接 V

seeking designs 〔 for new buildings 〕〔 that are more energy efficient 〕.
　　O　　　　　　　　　　　　　　　　関代　V　　　　　C

訳 ¹ポートフィリップは，良い世界市民であることに真剣である。²自家用車の所有を繁栄のしるしと見るのではなく，市は自動車の数の減少を—そして公共交通機関の利用の増加を—温室効果ガスの排出削減における進歩のしるしとして評価する。その一方で，人々がもっと歩いたり自転車に乗ったりしたい気持ちになるようなより健康的なライフスタイルを奨励する。³また，市はよりエネルギー効率の良い新しい建物のデザインを探し求めている。

語句

see *A* as *B*	熟	AをBとみなす，AがBだと考える
private	形	個人の
ownership	名	所有
sign	名	しるし，証拠
prosperity	名	繁栄
hail	動	(好意的に)評価する
decline	動	減少する，低下する
public transport	名	公共交通機関
progress	名	前進，進歩
reduce	動	削減する，減らす
greenhouse gas	名	温室効果ガス
emission	名	排出
be inclined to *do*	熟	～したいと思って
seek	動	探し求める
energy efficient	形	エネルギー効率の高い

第7段落　文の構造と語句のチェック

¹Some local governments see their role as being to provide basic services 〔 like
　　　S　　　　　　　V　　O　　 　　　　　　　　　　　　　　　　　　　　　　　　　

①
〈 collecting the trash 〉 and 〈 maintaining the roads 〉 — and (of course),
　　　　　　　　　　　　等接　②　　　　　　　　　　等接
　　　　　　　　　　　　　　　　　　　　C

③
〈 collecting the taxes to pay for this 〉〕. ²Others promote the area's economy, (by
　　　　　　　　　　　　　　　　　　　　　　S　　V　　　　O

①　　等接　②
encouraging industry to move to the area, (thus increasing jobs and the local
　V′　　　　O′　　　　　C′　　　　　　　　　　　　　V′　　　O′

tax base)). ³The Port Phillip city government takes a broader and longer-term
　　　　　　　　　　　　S　　　　　　　　　　　　V　　　O

160

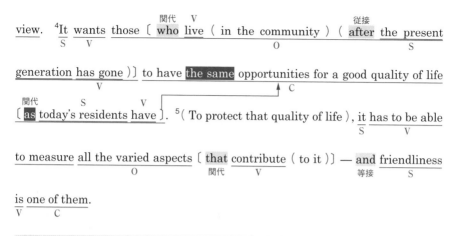

view. ⁴It wants those 〔 who live (in the community) (after the present generation has gone)〕 to have the same opportunities for a good quality of life 〔 as today's residents have 〕. ⁵(To protect that quality of life), it has to be able to measure all the varied aspects 〔 that contribute (to it)〕 — and friendliness is one of them.

訳 ¹一部の地方政府は，自らの役割を，ごみ収集や道路維持などの基本的なサービスを提供すること，そしてもちろん，その費用のために税金を集めることだと考えている。²他の地方政府は，産業を地域に誘致し，雇用と地方税収基盤を増やすことによって地域経済を振興している。³ポートフィリップ市役所は，より広く，より長期的な展望を持っている。⁴現在の世代が去った後の地域住民が，今日の住民が持つのと同じ良質な生活の機会を持てるようにしたいと考えているのだ。⁵その生活の質を守るためには，それに寄与するさまざまな側面をすべて評価できる必要がある。そして親睦はその一つなのだ。

語句

trash	名	ごみ
maintain	動	維持する
tax	名	税金
promote	動	促進する，振興する
tax base	名	税収基盤，課税基盤

long-term	形	長期的な
varied	形	さまざまな
aspect	名	局面，側面
contribute to ~	熟	～に貢献する，～に寄与する
friendliness	名	親善，親睦

第8段落 文の構造と語句のチェック

¹(For many governments, (both national and local)), 〈 preventing crime 〉 is a far higher priority (than encouraging friendship and cooperation). ²But, (as Professor Richard Layard 〔 of the London School of Economics 〕 has argued (in

his recent book *Happiness: Lessons from a New Science*)), 〈 promoting friendship 〉
　　　　　　　　　　　　　　　　　　　　　　　　　　　　　　　　　　　　S

is often easy and cheap, and can have big payoffs 〔 in making people happier 〕.
V① 　　　　 C 　　 等接 　V② 　　　 O 　　　　　　 V′ 　　 O′ 　　 C′
　　　　　等接

³So why shouldn't that be a focus of public policy?
等接　　　 (V) 　　 S　 V 　　　　 C

> **訳** ¹多くの国家および地方の政府にとって，犯罪の防止は親睦や協力を奨励することより
> もはるかに優先順位が高い。²しかし，ロンドン・スクール・オブ・エコノミクスのリチャ
> ード・レイアード教授が最近の著書『幸福：新しい科学からの教訓』で主張しているよう
> に，親睦を促進することはしばしば簡単で安上がりであり，人々をより幸福にする点で大
> きな見返りを得ることができる。³だから，それが公共政策の中心となるべきではないだろ
> うか？

語句

crime	名 犯罪		cooperation	名 協力
priority	名 優先事項		payoff	名 報酬，見返り
			focus	名 中心，焦点

第9段落　文の構造と語句のチェック

¹Very small positive experiences can make people not only feel better about
　　　　　　　　　　S　　　　　　　　　 V 　　 O 　　　　　　　 C

themselves, but also be more helpful to others. ²(In the 1970s), American
　　　　　　　　　　　　　　　　　　　　　　　　　　　　　　　　　　 S

psychologists Alice Isen and Paula Levin conducted an experiment 〔 in which
　　　　　　　└─同格─┘ 等接 　　　　　　 V 　　　　 O 　　　 関代

some randomly selected people 〔 making a phone call 〕 found a ten-cent coin
　　　　　　 S 　　　　　　　　　　　　　　　　　　　 V 　　　 O

　　　　　　　　　　　　　　　　　　　　　　　┌─ find it 省略
〔 left behind by a previous caller 〕, and others did not 〕. ³All subjects were then
　　　　　　　　　　　　　　　　　 等接　 S 　 V 　　　　　　　 S

　　　　　　　　　　　　　　　　　　　　　　　　　　　┌─ 関代 which 省略
given an opportunity 〔 to help a woman pick up a folder of papers 〔 she dropped
 V 　　　 O 　　　　　 V′ 　 O′ 　　　 C′ 　　　　　　　　　　 S 　 V

(in front of them) 〕 〕 〕.

162

訳 ¹とても小さなポジティブな経験により，人々は自己についてより良い気分になるだけでなく，他人に対してもより進んで手助けするようになる場合がある。²1970年代，アメリカの心理学者アリス・アイゼン氏とポーラ・レヴィン氏は，電話をかけている人々を無作為に選び，その一部は前の利用者が残した10セントの硬貨を見つけ，他の人々はそれを見つけない，という実験を行った。³その後，すべての被験者には，女性が彼らの目の前で落とした書類のフォルダーを拾うのを手伝う機会が与えられた。

語句

psychologist	名	心理学者
conduct	動	（実験，調査などを）行う，実施する
randomly	副	無作為に
make a phone call	熟	電話をかける
leave ~ behind	熟	～を忘れていく，～を置き忘れる
previous	形	前の，以前の
caller	名	電話をかける人
subject	名	被験者
folder	名	フォルダー（書類を挟んで運ぶための物）

第10段落 文の構造と語句のチェック

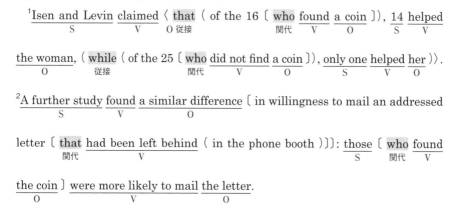

訳 ¹アイゼン氏とレヴィン氏の主張によれば，硬貨を見つけた16人のうち14人が女性を助けた一方で，硬貨を見つけなかった25人のうちわずか1人しか女性を助けなかった。²さらなる研究では，電話ボックスに忘れられた宛名の書かれた手紙を進んで投函するかどうかにおいて，同様の違いが見られた。つまり，硬貨を見つけた人々の方が手紙を投函する可能性が高かったのだ。

第11段落 文の構造と語句のチェック

¹(Although later research has cast doubt (on the existence of such dramatic
従接　　S　　　　V　　O

differences)), there is little doubt ⟨ that ⟨ being in a good mood ⟩ makes people
　　　　　　V　S　　従接(同格)　　　S　　　　　V　　O

feel better about themselves and more likely to help others ⟩. ²Psychologists
C①　　　　　　　　　　等接　　　C②　　　　　　　　S

refer to it as the "glow of goodwill." ³Why shouldn't ⟨ taking small steps [that
V　　O　C　　　　　　　　　　　　　　(V)　S　　　　　関代

may produce such a glow ⟩⟩ be part of the role of government?
V　　O　　　　V　　C

訳 ¹後の研究でそのような劇的な違いの存在に疑問が投げかけられたものの, 上機嫌であることで人々が自己についてより良い気持ちになり, 他人を助ける可能性が高まることにはほぼ疑いがない。²心理学者はこれを「善意の輝き」と呼んでいる。³そのような輝きを生む可能性のある小さな手段を講じることが, 政府の役割の一部となるべきではないだろうか?

第12段落　文の構造と語句のチェック

[1]Here <u>is</u> <u>one measure of success</u>: (over the past year and a half), <u>the</u>
　　　V　　S　　　　　　　　　　　　　　　　　　　　　　　　　　　　　　S

<u>proportion of people</u> 〔 <u>who</u> <u>smile</u> (at you) (in Port Phillip)〕 <u>has risen</u>, (from
　　　　　　　　　　　　　関代　V　　　　　　　　　　　　　　　　　V

8 percent to 10 percent).

訳 [1]以下は成功の一つの目安である：過去1年半で，ポートフィリップで笑顔を向ける人々の割合が8%から10%に上昇した。

語句

measure 　名 基準，尺度，目安

proportion 名 比率，割合

文法事項の整理 ⑪　仮定法未来

条件節（仮定を行う if 節）に〈should ＋原形〉または〈were to ＋原形〉を用いて，未来または現在の起こる可能性が極めて低いこと・起こりえないことを仮定する表現を「仮定法未来」という。

例　If I should win the lottery, I will [would] travel around the world.
「万が一宝くじに当たったら，世界中を旅行するでしょう」

例　If you should meet him by chance, give him my best regards.
「万が一彼に偶然会うことがあれば，よろしく伝えてくれ」

例　If he were to become president, he would implement major reforms.
「もし彼が大統領になったら，大規模な改革を実施するでしょう」

〈should ＋原形〉は極めて可能性が低い場合に用いる。主節は助動詞を過去形にしてもしなくてもよく，命令文になることもある。

〈were to ＋原形〉は可能性を考慮しない場合に用いる。可能性ゼロでも良い。主節は助動詞を過去形にする。

パターンを整理すると以下のようになる。
※ will の部分は can / may / shall，would の部分は could / might / should も可。

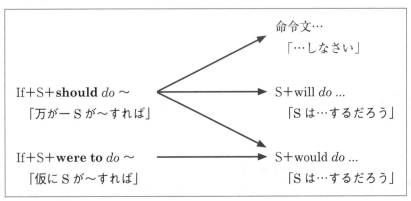

If＋S＋**should** *do* 〜
「万が一 S が〜すれば」

命令文…
　「…しなさい」

S＋will *do* ...
「S は…するだろう」

If＋S＋**were to** *do* 〜
「仮に S が〜すれば」

S＋would *do* ...
「S は…するだろう」

（第 1 段落第 1 文）

If you were to walk along the streets of your neighborhood with your face up and an open expression, how many of those who passed you would smile, or greet you in some way?

▶ 条件節で〈were to＋原形〉，主節で〈would＋原形〉を用いており，可能性を考慮しない（または可能性ゼロ）仮定法未来のパターンになっている。

確認問題

1. 次の和訳と対応する英語の語句を，頭文字を参考にして書き，空欄を完成させよう。

/40点

(各1点×20)

① n ［名］ 近所

② e ［名］ 表情

③ u ［形］ 世界共通の，普遍的な

④ p ［名］ 歩行者

⑤ e ［動］ 奨励する，促進する

⑥ g ［名］ 挨拶

⑦ r ［名］ 住民

⑧ l 　 *A* t *B* ［熟］ A を B に任せる

⑨ m ［動］ 評価する，査定する

⑩ d ［形］ 望ましい

⑪ s ［形］ 持続可能な

⑫ o ［名］ 所有

⑬ p ［名］ 繁栄

⑭ e ［名］ 排出

⑮ m ［動］ 維持する

⑯ a ［名］ 局面，側面

⑰ c 　 t ～ ［熟］ ～に貢献する，～に寄与する

⑱ c ［名］ 犯罪

⑲ s ［名］ 被験者

⑳ c 　 d 　 o ～ ［熟］ ～に疑問［疑念］を投げかける

2. 次の［ ］内の語を並べ替えて，意味の通る英文を完成させよう。（各5点×2）

① Many people who have lived in the same street for many years [each / first / meet / time / at / other / for / the] a street party.

② For many governments, both national and local, preventing crime is [far / priority / a / encouraging / higher / than] friendship and cooperation.

3. 次の英文を和訳してみよう。(10点)

If you were to walk along the streets of your neighborhood with your face up and an open expression, how many of those who passed you would smile, or greet you in some way?

ディクテーションしてみよう！

今回学習した英文に出てきた語句を，音声を聞いて＿＿＿に書き取ろう。

73 If you were to walk along the streets of your neighborhood ❶＿＿＿＿＿＿
＿＿＿＿＿＿＿＿＿＿＿＿＿＿＿＿＿＿＿＿＿＿＿＿, how many of those who passed you would smile, or greet you in some way?

74 Smiling is a universal human practice, although readiness to smile at strangers varies according to culture. In Australia, where being open and friendly to strangers ❷＿＿＿＿＿＿＿＿＿＿, the city of Port Phillip, an area covering some of the bayside suburbs of Melbourne, has been using volunteers to find out how often people smile at those who pass them in the street. It then ❸＿＿＿＿＿＿＿＿＿ that look like speed limits, but tell pedestrians that they are in, for example, a "10 Smiles Per Hour Zone."

75 Frivolous nonsense? A waste of taxpayers' money? Mayor Janet Bolitho says that putting up the signs is ❹＿＿＿＿＿＿＿＿＿ encourage people to smile or say "G'day"— the standard Australian greeting — to both neighbors and strangers as they stroll down the street. Smiling, she adds, encourages people to feel more connected with each other and safer, so it reduces ❺＿＿＿＿＿＿＿＿ — an important element in the quality of life of many neighborhoods.

76 ❻＿＿＿＿＿＿＿＿＿＿＿ to get its residents to know each other, the city government also facilitates street parties. It leaves the details to the locals, but offers organizational advice, lends out barbecues and sun umbrellas, and covers the public liability insurance. Many people who have lived in the same street for many years meet each other for the first time at a street party.

77 All of this is part of a larger program that attempts to measure changes in the city's quality of life, so that the city council can know whether it is taking the community **❼**_____. The council wants Port Phillip to be a sustainable community, not merely in an environmental sense, but also in terms of social equity, economic viability, and cultural vitality.

78 Port Phillip is serious about being a good global citizen. Instead of seeing private car ownership as a sign of prosperity, the city hails a *declining* number of cars — and rising use of public transport — as a sign of progress in reducing greenhouse gas emissions while encouraging a healthier lifestyle in which people are more inclined to walk or ride a bike. The city is also seeking designs for new buildings **❽**_____ _____.

79 Some local governments see their role as being to provide basic services like collecting the trash and maintaining the roads — and of course, collecting the taxes to pay for this. Others promote the area's economy, by encouraging industry to move to the area, thus increasing jobs and the local tax base. The Port Phillip city government takes a broader and longer-term view. It wants those who live in the community after the present generation has gone to have the same opportunities for a good quality of life as today's residents have. To protect that quality of life, it has to be able to measure all the varied aspects that **❾**_____ — and friendliness is one of them.

80 For many governments, both national and local, preventing crime is a far higher priority than encouraging friendship and cooperation. But, as Professor Richard Layard of the London School of Economics has argued in his recent book *Happiness: Lessons from a New Science*, promoting friendship is often easy and cheap, and ❿_____ in making people happier. So why shouldn't that be a focus of public policy?

81   Very small positive experiences can make people not only feel better about themselves, but also be more helpful to others. In the 1970s, American psychologists Alice Isen and Paula Levin conducted an experiment in which some randomly selected people making a phone call found a ten-cent coin left behind by a previous caller, and others did not. All subjects were then ⓫_____ to help a woman pick up a folder of papers she dropped in front of them.

82   Isen and Levin claimed that of the 16 who found a coin, 14 helped the woman, while of the 25 who did not find a coin, only one helped her. A further study found a similar difference in willingness to ⓬_____ _____ that had been left behind in the phone booth: those who found the coin were more likely to mail the letter.

83   Although later research has ⓭_____ the existence of such dramatic differences, there is little doubt that being in a good mood makes people feel better about themselves and more likely to help others. Psychologists refer to it as the "glow of goodwill." Why shouldn't taking small steps that may produce such a glow be part of the role of government?

84   Here is one measure of success: over the past year and a half, the proportion of people who smile at you in Port Phillip has risen, from 8 percent to 10 percent.

確認問題の答

1. ① neighborhood　② expression　③ universal　④ pedestrian　⑤ encourage　⑥ greeting
　 ⑦ resident　⑧ leave, to　⑨ measure　⑩ desirable　⑪ sustainable　⑫ ownership
　 ⑬ prosperity　⑭ emission　⑮ maintain　⑯ aspect　⑰ contribute to　⑱ crime
　 ⑲ subject　⑳ cast doubt on

2. ① meet each other for the first time at　（第4段落　第3文）
　 ② a far higher priority than encouraging　（第8段落　第1文）

3. 仮にあなたが近所の通りを顔を上げて心を開いた表情で歩いてみると，通り過ぎる人々の中で，どれくらいの人が微笑んだり，何らかの方法であなたに挨拶をしてくれたりするだろうか？　（第1段落　第1文）

ディクテーションしてみよう！の答

❶ with your face up and an open expression　❷ is not unusual　❸ put up signs
❹ an attempt to　❺ fear of crime　❻ In a related effort　❼ in a desirable direction
❽ that are more energy efficient　❾ contribute to it　❿ can have big payoffs
⓫ given an opportunity　⓬ mail an addressed letter　⓭ cast doubt on

アドバイス　❶ an の n の音と，open の「オウ」の音がつながり，「アノウ」のように聞こえる（⇒連結）。

❸ put up は t が "ら行化" するため，「プラ」のように聞こえる。一般に，/t/ や /d/ の音が母音に挟まれるとら行のような音に変化する（⇒フラッピング［ら行化］）。

❾ contribute の語尾と to の語頭はいずれも /t/ の音だが，これを2回発音するのは面倒なので，1回だけ発音される（⇒脱落）。

⓭ cast の語尾の /t/ と，doubt の語頭の /d/ は，発音の仕方が近いので，前の子音である /t/ がほとんど発音されない（⇒脱落）。

解 答

| 問1 | (a) | dying | (b) | survival | 問2 | (ア) ② | (イ) ④ | (ウ) ① |

| 問3 | 1. ④ | 2. ② | 3. ① | 4. ② |

問4 ラジャマヌは辺鄙な場所にあり，住民は国の強制移住策を当初は拒否したが結局受け入れて自治を開始した経緯もあり，新言語がこの地域出身のアイデンティティのしるしになったこと。(84字)

問5 全訳参照(p.185 訳 第1・2文)

解 説

問1

(a) be 動詞 are の後なので，考えられるのは，be dead「死んでいる」か，be dying「死につつある，死にかけている」のどちらか。gradually「徐々に」という副詞があるので，変化の過程にあることがわかる。そこで，正解は dying となる。なお，この文では主語が languages なので，die は「死ぬ」というより「消滅する，途絶える」といった意味だろう。

die のような瞬間的な動作を表す動詞を進行形にすると，「～している」ではなく，「～しつつある，～しそうになっている」の意味。

例 The train is leaving.

× 「電車は出発している」

○ 「電車は出発しようとしている」

(b) the の後なので名詞形にする。survive「生き残る」の名詞形は survival「生存，生き残り」。

問2

(ア) resigned themselves to「～を甘んじて受け入れる，～にやむを得ず従う」

① happily accepted「～を喜んで受け入れた」

② **unhappily accepted「～を不満ながら受け入れた」**

③ unwillingly left their jobs for「気が進まずに～のために仕事を辞めた」

④ willingly left their jobs for「自発的に～のために仕事を辞めた」

172

　resign については，「辞職する，辞任する」の意味は必ず知っておくべきだが，resign *oneself* to はやや細かい知識だろう。本問は文脈を押さえることで正解を選べる。

　第5段落の内容はおおまかに以下のようになる。

❶政府が先住民を強制的に移住させる

　　↓

❷先住民は歩いて故郷に戻る

　　↓

❸連れ戻される

　　↓

❹？？？？？？？

　　↓

❺地方自治体として評議会を設置

　選択肢③と④の「仕事を辞めた」はここでは無関係。①と②の違いは受け入れる態度だが，上記❷⇒❸(しかも繰り返されている)から，不満を抱きながらも仕方なく受け入れたと考えられる。以上により，正解は②となる。

(イ) engage in「～に携わる，～に参加する」

　① attract attention with「～で注目を集める」

　② have arguments with「～と議論をする」

　③ jointly anticipate「～を一緒に予想する」

　④ **participate in「～に参加する」**

　engage in ～は「～に携わる，～に参加する」の意味。be engaged in ～とほぼ同じ。実際には「する」「行う」などと訳すことが多い。

　文脈からも推測可能。直前の第6段落で，学者が村に滞在して村人の言語を調査するとの記述があるので，第7段落は村人の言語活動についての説明となるはず。そこで，「コードスイッチング」(言語を混ぜたり切り替えること)を会話中に話し相手とともに「行う」と考えると自然な流れになる。これに最も意味が近いのは，④「～に参加する」。

（ウ） radical

　　① **major「大きな」**　　　　② realistic「現実的な」

　　③ sensitive「敏感な」　　　　④ unusual「異常な」

　　radical は「根本的な，大幅な」「急進的な，過激な」「斬新な」などの意味を持つ。ここでは，changes を修飾しているので，「根本的な，大幅な」の意味で解釈する。

　　文脈からも確認しよう。この段落は，文章全体の主題でもある「ライト・ワルピリ語」の説明をしているが，この言語については，第7段落第4文で，These young people have developed something entirely new.（これらの若者たちは完全に新しいものを開発した）とあり，さらに第8段落最終文で，This is a way of talking so different from either "strong" Warlpiri or Kriol that it constitutes a new language.（これは，「強い」ワルピリ語やクリオール語とは大きく異なる話し方なので，新しい言語となっている）とある。つまり，元の言語から大幅な変化を経たことが読み取れる。以上により，正解は①となる。

問3

1. 「なぜオシャネシー博士のライト・ワルピリ語に関する研究は重要なのか」

　　① 「ライト・ワルピリ語はオーストラリア北部で広く使われている」

　　② 「多くの人がこの言語に関する情報を持っている」

　　③ 「1948 年以降，新しい先住民の言語は発見されていない」

　　④ **「彼女は，この言語が誕生して間もなく，この言語を研究することができている」**

　　▶ 第2段落最終文(Mary Laughren, another linguist, values Dr. O'Shannessy's research ... because "she has been able to record and document a 'new' language in the very early period of its existence." 「別の言語学者であるメアリー・ラフレンは，…『彼女が「新しい」言語を生まれて間もない段階で記録し文書化できている』という理由でオシャネシー博士の研究を評価している」)とあることから，④が正解。

2. 「ライト・ワルピリ語に関する以下の記述のうち，正しいものはどれか」

   ① 「子供たちは，その言語を家で話したがらない」

   ② 「その単語の多くは英語かクリオール語に語源を持つ」

   ③ 「その言語はクリオール語の一種に分類される」

   ④ 「その言語は約 700 人に話されている」

   ▶ 第 7 段落第 2 文(And many words in Light Warlpiri are derived from English or Kriol.「そして，ライト・ワルピリ語の多くの単語は英語やクリオール語に由来している)より，②が正解。

3. 「ライト・ワルピリ語の文法は，他の現地で話されている言語と何が違うのか」

   ① 「『現在または過去で未来ではない』時制がある」

   ② 「赤ちゃん言葉でしばしば見られるような単純化された文法を持つ」

   ③ 「"si" で始まる単語が多い」

   ④ 「『強い』ワルピリ語の語尾がない」

   ▶ 第 8 段落はライト・ワルピリ語について例文を挙げて説明しており，その後半部分で，… indicates that the event is either happening now or has already happened, a "present or past but not future" tense that does not exist in English or "strong" Warlpiri.(…出来事が今起こっているか既に起こったことを示しており，英語にも「強い」ワルピリ語にも存在しない「現在または過去だが未来ではない」時制である)とある。よって，①が正解となる。

4. 「オシャネシー博士によると，ラジャマヌではライト・ワルピリ語は『かなり強い』。この文章によると，その強さを生じているのは次のどの要因か」

   ① 「子供が親に話す『赤ちゃん言葉』が土台になっている」

   ② 「ライト・ワルピリ語話者はその言語を話すことで，アイデンティティの意識を得られる」

   ③ 「現在，『強い』ワルピリ語を話す人は，ライト・ワルピリ語を話す人より少ない」

   ④ 「村人は，自分が知っている他の言語を話す機会がない」

▶ ライト・ワルピリ語が「強い」という記述は最終段落の最後にある。オシャネシー博士によって，この要因として挙げられているのは，第10段落後半の「アイデンティティ」。正解は②となる。

問4

要因として挙げられているのは，

① ラジャマヌが辺鄙な場所であること（第4段落）

② 政府によって強制的に移住させられ，当初は拒否したが，最終的にはこれを受け入れ，自治を開始したこと（第5段落）

③ ライト・ワルピリ語がアイデンティティのしるしになったこと（第10段落）

の3点なので，これをまとめればよい。

問5

Why a new language developed at this time and in this place is not entirely clear. It was not a case of people needing to communicate when they have no common language, a situation that can give rise to a creole.

前半のポイント

☑ Why a new language developed at this time and in this place が S，is not が V，entirely clear が C。

☑ Why は疑問詞で「なぜ…か」と訳す。または，先行詞（The reason）が省略された関係副詞と考え，「…の理由」と訳すことも可。

☑ not entirely は「完全に〜わけではない」という【部分否定】。

後半のポイント

☑ It が S，was not が V，a case が C，of 以下は case を修飾。It は直前の文の「新しい言語が発達したこと」を指す。

☑ people needing to 〜の部分は，needing が動名詞で，people は意味上の主語と考える（needing が現在分詞で，people を修飾するという解釈は文法的には可能だが，「〜する必要のある人々の事例」となり，意味的に不自然）。case of の of は【同格】の用法で，case の具体的な内容を説明する。case は「事例」「場合」「事態」などの訳であれば可。「人々が〜する必要があるという事例」となる（⇒文法事項の整理⑫（186ページ）参照）。

☑ a case of people needing to communicate when they have no common language と a situation that can give rise to a creole が同格になっている。「～，つまり，～」のように訳出すると良いだろう。

☑ situation の後の that は関係代名詞。give rise to ～は「～を生じさせる，～を引き起こす」の意味。

▼

それでは次に，段落ごとに詳しくみていこう。

第1段落　文の構造と語句のチェック

language 省略

¹Many languages〔in the world〕are gradually dying, but at least one has
　S　　　　　　　　　　　　　　　　　　V　　　　　等接　　S

recently been born,（created by children〔living in a remote village in northern
　　　　　V

Australia〕）. ²A linguist〔called Dr. O'Shannessy〕has been studying the young
　　　　　　　　　S　　　　　　　　　　　　　　　　V　　　　　　　　　O

people's speech〔in that area〕（for more than a decade）and has recently
　　　　　　　　　　　　　　　　　　　　　　　　　　　　　等接

concluded〈that they speak neither a dialect nor the mixture of languages〔called
　V　　　　O従接　S　　V　　　　　　　　　　　　　　O①

a creole〕, but a new language〔with unique grammatical rules〕〉.
　　　　　　　O②

> 訳　¹世界中の多くの言語が徐々に消滅しつつあるが，最近になって少なくとも１つの言語が生まれた。それは，オーストラリア北部の辺鄙な村に住む子供たちによって作られた言語だ。²オシャネシー博士という言語学者が，その地域の若者たちの話し言葉を10年以上にわたって研究し，最近になって彼らが方言でもクレオール言語と呼ばれる言語の混合でもなく，独自の文法ルールを持つ新しい言語を話していると結論付けた。

第2段落　文の構造と語句のチェック

[1]This new language, 〔 known as Light Warlpiri 〕, is spoken (only by people
　　S　　　　　　　　　　　　　　　　　　　　　　　　　V

〔 under 35 〕) (in a village of about 700 people in Australia, 〔 called Lajamanu 〕).

[2](In all), about 350 people speak the language (as their native tongue).
　　　　　　　　　S　　　　　V　　　O

[3]Mary Laughren, another linguist, values Dr. O'Shannessy's research (because
　S　　└─同格─┘　　　V　　　O　　　① 従接

"many of the first speakers of this language are still alive)," and (because "she
　　　　　S　　　　　V　　C　等接 ② 従接 S
　　　　　　　　　　①　　　　　②

has been able to record and document a 'new' language (in the very early period
　　V　　等接　　　　　O

of its existence))."

178

第3段落　文の構造と語句のチェック

¹Everyone 〔 in the village 〕 also speaks "strong" Warlpiri, an aboriginal
　　　S　　　　　　　　　　　　　V　　　　O　　└─同格─┘

language 〔 unrelated to English 〕 and 〔 shared with about 4,000 people (in
　　　　①　　　　　　　　　　　等接　②

several Australian villages)〕. ²Many also speak Kriol, an English-based creole
　　　　　　　　　　　　　　　　　　S　　　 V　　 O└─同格─┘

〔 developed in the late 19th century 〕 and 〔 widely spoken in northern Australia
①　　　　　　　　　　　　　　　　等接　②

(among aboriginal people 〔 with many different native languages 〕)〕. ³The
　　　　　　　　　　　　　　　　　　　　　　　　　　　　　　　　　　　　　 S

villagers are happy to have their children learn English (for use in the wider
　　　　　 V　　　　　　　 O　　　　　 learn English　　C

world), but they are also eager to preserve "strong" Warlpiri (as the language
　　　 等接 S　　　　　　 V　　　　　　　　 O

of their culture).

> **訳** ¹村の人々はみな，「強い」ワルピリ語という，英語と無関係の，オーストラリアの複数の村で約4,000人の人々に共有されている先住民言語も話す。²多くの人々はまた，19世紀末に発展し，多種多様な母語を持つ先住民族の人々の間でオーストラリア北部において広く話されている，英語ベースのクレオール言語であるクリオール語も話す。³村の人々は，子供たちに広い世界で使える英語を学ばせていることを喜んでいるが，彼らはまた，「強い」ワルピリ語を自分たちの文化の言語として保護することを熱望している。

語句

(be) unrelated to ～ 熟 ～と関係がない
be eager to *do* 熟 ～することを熱望して

preserve 動 保存する，保護する

第4段落　文の構造と語句のチェック

¹The village's remoteness may have something to do with the creation 〔 of a
　　　　　　 S　　　　　　　　 V　　　　　　　　　　　　　　　　 O

new way of speaking 〕. ²Lajamanu is (about 550 miles south of Darwin), and
                  S   V   等接

the nearest commercial center is Katherine, (about 340 miles north). ³An airplane
                    S   V   C   S

lands (on the village's dirt landing field) (twice a week) (carrying mail from
V

Katherine), and (once a week) a truck brings food and supplies 〔 that are sold
          等接   S   V   等接   関代   V
                                                     O
                                 ① 等接   ②
(in the village's only store)〕. ⁴Oil and solar energy supply electricity.
                                          S   V   O

> **訳** ¹その村が辺鄙であることは，新しい話し方の創造と何か関係があるかもしれない。²ラ
> ジャマヌはダーウィンから約550マイル南に位置し，最寄りの商業中心地は約340マイ
> ル北のキャサリンだ。³飛行機は週に2回，キャサリンから郵便物を運んで村の未舗装の
> 滑走路に着陸し，週に1回，トラックが村の唯一の商店で売られる食品と生活物資を運ん
> でくる。⁴電力は石油と太陽光エネルギーが供給している。

語 句

remoteness	名	辺鄙，人里離れていること	dirt 名 土砂，砂利	
have something to do with ~			landing field 名 滑走路	
	熟	~と何か関係がある	**supply** 名 （複数形で）生活物資，必需品	
creation	名	創造，創出	動 供給する	
commercial	形	商業の	**solar energy** 名 太陽光エネルギー	
			electricity 名 電気，電力	

第5段落　文の構造と語句のチェック

¹Lajamanu was established (by the Australian government) (in 1948), (without
 S   V

the consent of the people 〔 who would inhabit it 〕). ²The native affairs branch 〔 of
                       関代   S
                           S   V   O

the federal government 〕, (concerned about an excess of people and a lack of rain
                                                     等接
                                            ①   ②

〔 in one area 〕), removed 550 people (from there) (by force) (to the place 〔 where
                  V   O   関副

the village is now]). ³(At least twice), the group walked (all the way back to
                                 S   V

┌── the place 省略

⟨where they used to live ⟩), (only to be transported back (when they arrived)).
関副 S   V   従接 S   V

⁴(By the 1970s), villagers had resigned themselves to their new home, and
                     S   V   O   等接

a new council had been set up (as a self-governing community authority).
    S   V

> **訳** ¹ラジャマヌは 1948 年に，そこに住むことになる人々の同意なしに，オーストラリア政府によって設立された。²連邦政府の先住民問題担当部局は，ある地域の人口過剰と雨不足に懸念を抱き，550 人を無理やりそこから現在の村の場所に移動させた。³少なくとも 2 回，その集団は昔住んでいた場所まではるばる歩いて帰ったが，到着すると結局は再び運び戻された。⁴1970 年代までに，村人たちは新しい本拠地を甘んじて受け入れ，自治権を持った地方自治体として新しい評議会が設立された。

語句

establish	動 設立する	by force	熟 力ずくで，無理やり
consent	名 同意	all the way	熟 はるばる，わざわざ
inhabit	動 住む	transport	動 輸送する，運ぶ
affair	名 問題，事柄	resign *oneself* to ~	
branch	名 部局，支局		熟 ~を甘んじて受け入れる，~にやむを得ず従う
federal	形 連邦(政府)の	council	名 議会，評議会
(be) concerned about ~	熟 ~を心配して	set up	熟 設立する
excess	名 過剰，過多	self-governing	形 自己統治の
remove	動 移動させる	community authority	名 地方自治体

第6段落　文の構造と語句のチェック

¹Dr. O'Shannessy, [who started ⟨ investigating the language ⟩ (in 2002)],
     S   関代 V   O

spends three to eight weeks a year (in the village). ²She speaks and understands
 V   O   S   等接

both "strong" Warlpiri and Light Warlpiri, but is not fluent (in either of them).
            O   等接 V   C

> **訳** ¹2002 年にその言語を調査し始めたオシャネシー博士は，1 年に 3〜8 週間を村で過ごしている。²彼女は「強い」ワルピリ語とライト・ワルピリ語の両方を話し理解することができるが，どちらの言語も流暢ではない。

語句

investigate 動 調査する

fluent 形 流暢な

第7段落 文の構造と語句のチェック

¹People in the village often engage in 〈 what linguists call code-switching, mixing
　　　　S　　　　　　　　　V　　　　O 関代　S　　V　　　　C　└─同格─┘

languages together or switching from one to another (as they speak)〉. ²And
　　　　　　　　　等接　　　　　　　　　　　　　　　　従接　　　　　　等接

many words in Light Warlpiri are derived (from English or Kriol). ³But Light
　　　　S　　　　　　　　　　　V　　　　　　　　　　　　　　　等接　S

Warlpiri is not simply a combination of words 〔 from different languages 〕.
　　　V　　　　　　　　　　　　　C

⁴Peter Bakker, a professor of language development, observes 〈 that "These
　　S　　　└─同格─┘　　　　　　　　　　　　　　　V　　O 従接　S

young people have developed something entirely new. ⁵Light Warlpiri is clearly
　　　　　V　　　　　　　　O　　　　　　　　　S　　　　V

a mother tongue 〉."
　　　C

> **訳** ¹村人たちは，言語学者が「コードスイッチング」と呼ぶ，話しながら言語を混ぜ合わせたり，別の言語に切り替えたりすることをよくやっている。²そして，ライト・ワルピリ語の多くの単語は英語やクリオール語に由来している。³しかし，ライト・ワルピリ語は単に異なる言語の単語の組み合わせではない。⁴言語発達学の教授であるピーター・バッカー氏は，「これらの若者たちは完全に新しいものを開発した。⁵ライト・ワルピリ語は明らかに母語である」と述べている。

語句

engage in 〜 熟 〜に携わる，〜に参加する

be derived from 〜 熟 〜に由来する

combination 名 組み合わせ

observe 動 述べる

entirely 副 完全に，まったく

182

第8段落　文の構造と語句のチェック

[1]Dr. O'Shannessy <u>offers</u> <u>this example</u>, 〔 spoken by a 4-year-old 〕 (an English
　　S　　　　　　 V　　 O

translation is given below the example):

Nganimpa-ng gen wi-m si-m worm mai aus-ria. (Light Warlpiri)

[2]We also saw worms at my house. (English)

　　　　　　　　　　　　　 真S
[3]<u>It</u> <u>is</u> <u>easy enough</u> 〈 to see several words derived from English 〉. [4]<u>But</u> <u>the *-ria*</u>
　仮S V　　 C　　　　　　　　　　　　　　　　　　　　 等接　　 S

<u>ending</u> 〔 on *aus* (house) 〕 <u>means</u> <u>"in" or "at,"</u> <u>and</u> <u>it</u> <u>comes</u> 〈 from "strong"
　　　　　　　　　　　　　 V　　　 O　　　 等接　S　　 V

Warlpiri 〉. [5]<u>The *-m* ending</u> 〔 on the verb *si* (see) 〕 <u>indicates</u> 〈 <u>that</u> <u>the event</u> <u>is</u>
　　　　　　　　 S　　　　　　　　　　　　　　　　 V　　 O　 従接　　 S

<u>either</u> <u>happening now</u> <u>or</u> <u>has already happened</u>, a "present or past but not
　　　 V①　　　　　　　 V②　└同格┘

　　　　　　　　 関代　　　　　　　　　　　 等接
future" tense 〔 <u>that</u> <u>does not exist</u> (in English or "strong" Warlpiri)〕〉. [6]<u>This</u> <u>is</u>
　　　　　　　　　　　 V　　　　　　　　　　　　　　　　　　　　　　　 S　 V

　　　　　　　　　　　　　　　　　　　　　　　　　　　　　 従接
<u>a way of talking</u> 〔 <u>so</u> different from <u>either</u> "strong" Warlpiri <u>or</u> Kriol 〕 (<u>that</u> <u>it</u>
　　　 C　　　　　　　　　　　　　　　　　　　　　　　　　　　　　　　 S

<u>constitutes</u> <u>a new language</u>).
　　V　　　　　 O

訳 [1]オシャネシー博士は，4歳の子供が話す以下の例を示している（英語訳は例の下にある）：
　　Nganimpa-ng gen wi-m si-m worm mai aus-ria.（ライト・ワルピリ語）
　　[2]We also saw worms at my house.（私たちは私の家でミミズも見ました。）（英語）
　　[3]いくつかの単語が英語由来なのは十分容易に見て取れる。[4]しかし，*aus*（家）の「*-ria*」と
　いう語尾は，「in」や「at」という意味であり，それは「強い」ワルピリ語に由来する。
　　[5]動詞 *si*（見る）の「*-m*」という語尾は，出来事が今起こっているか既に起こったことを示
　しており，これは英語にも「強い」ワルピリ語にも存在しない「現在または過去で未来で
　はない」時制である。[6]これは，「強い」ワルピリ語やクリオール語とは大きく異なる話し

方なので，新しい言語となっている。

語句

translation	名	翻訳	verb	名	動詞
worm	名	(ミミズなどの)虫，幼虫	indicate	動	示す
ending	名	語尾	tense	名	時制
come from ~	熟	~に由来する	constitute	動	~になる，~に等しい

第9段落 文の構造と語句のチェック

主節の挿入
[1]The development of the language, (Dr. O'Shannessy says), was a two-step
　　　　　　　S　　　　　　　　　　　　　　S　　　　　　V　　　　V　　　　C

process. [2]It began (with parents using baby talk (with their children) (in a
　　　　　　　S　　V　　付帯状況　S′　　V′　　O′

combination of the three languages)). [3]But then the children took that language
　　　　　　　　　　　　　　　　　　　　　　　　等接　　　　S　　　　V　　　O

as their native tongue (by adding radical changes to the grammar, [especially
C

　　　　　　　　　　　　　　　　　　　　　　関代
in the use of verb structures [that are not present (in any of the source
　　　　　　　　　　　　　　　　　　　　　　　　　V　　　C

languages)]]]).

> **訳** [1]オシャネシー博士が言うには，その言語の発達は2段階の過程を経た。[2]それは，親が3つの言語の組み合わせで子供たちと赤ちゃん言葉で話すことで始まった。[3]しかしその後，子供たちは文法，特に，元になる言語のどれにも存在しない動詞の構造の使い方に大幅な変化を加えることで，その言語を自分たちの母語とみなした。

語句

take *A* as *B*	熟	A を B とみなす	structure	名	構造
radical	形	根本的な，大幅な	present	形	存在して
grammar	名	文法	source	名	源，起源

第10段落 文の構造と語句のチェック

¹⟨ Why a new language developed (at this time) and (in this place)⟩ is not
　S 疑　　 S　　　　 V　　　　　　①　　　　等接　　　②　　　　V

entirely clear. ²It was not a case 〔 of people needing to communicate (when
　　　 C　　 S　 V　 C　　　 S′　　　 V′　　　 従接

they have no common language)〕, a situation 〔 that can give rise to a creole 〕.
　 S　 V　　　 O　　　└同格┘　　 関代　 V　　　 O

³New languages are discovered (from time to time), but (until now) no one
　　 S　　　　 V　　　　　　　　　等接　　　　　　 S

has been there (at the beginning) (to see a language develop (from children's
　 V　　　　　　　　　　　　　　 V′　 O′　　 C′

speech)). ⁴Dr. O'Shannessy suggests ⟨ that subtle forces may be at work ⟩. ⁵"I
　　　　　　 S　　　　 V　 O従接　 S　　 V　 C　　 S

think ⟨ that identity plays a role ⟩," she said. ⁶"(After children created the new
 V　 O従接　 S　　 V　 O　　 S　 V　　　 従接　　 S　　 V　　 O

system), it became a mark 〔 of their identity 〔 as being young Warlpiri 〔 from
　　　　 S　 V　 C

the Lajamanu community 〕〕〕."

> 訳 ¹なぜこの時期にこの場所で新しい言語が発達したのかは完全には明らかになっていない。²それは，共通の言語がないときに人々がコミュニケーションをする必要があるという事例，つまりクレオール言語を発生させ得る状況ではなかった。³新しい言語は時折発見されるが，子供たちの話し言葉から言語が発達する様子を見られる初期段階に立ち会ったことのある人は今まで誰もいなかった。⁴オシャネシー博士は，微妙な力が働いているかもしれないと示唆している。⁵「アイデンティティが何らかの役割を果たしていると思います」と彼女は言う。⁶「子供たちが新しい言語体系を作り出した後，それはラジャマヌの共同体出身の若いワルピリ語人であるというアイデンティティのしるしとなりました。」

 語句

give rise to ~	熟	~を生じさせる，~を引き起こす
from time to time	熟	時々
suggest	動	示唆する
subtle	形	微妙な
at work	熟	（力が）作用して，働いて
mark	名	しるし，現れ

¹The language is now **so** well established (among young people) ([that] there
S   V   C   従接

is some question 〔 about the survival of "strong" Warlpiri 〕). ²〈 "**How** long the kids
V   S   O 疑   S

will keep their ability 〔 to speak two or more languages 〕〉, I don't know,"
V   O   S   V

Dr. O'Shannessy said. ³"The elders would like to preserve "strong" Warlpiri, but
S   V   S   V   O   等接

I'm not sure 〈 it will happen 〉. ⁴Light Warlpiri seems quite strong."
S V   C   S   V   S   V   C
           └── 従接 that 省略

訳 ¹今や若者の間でこの言語がとても確立されているため，「強い」ワルピリ語が生き残っ
ていけるのかという疑問が生じている。²「子供たちが２つ以上の言語を話す能力をどれ
くらい長く維持するのかはわかりません」とオシャネシー博士は言う。³「年長者たちは
『強い』ワルピリ語を保護したいと思っていますが，そのようになる確信はありません。
⁴ライト・ワルピリ語はかなり強いものに思われます。」

語 句

established 形 確立した	**survival** 名 生存，残存
	elder 名 長老，年長者

文法事項の整理 ⑫　名詞＋doing

第10段落第２文の people needing について見てみよう。

It was not a case of **people needing** to communicate when they
have no common language, a situation that can give rise to a creole.

　名詞＋doing には，主に以下の４つの可能性がある。特に①と②の区別
が重要。②なのに①で解釈してしまうというミスが多い。

① doing は現在分詞で，前の名詞を修飾している⇒「～している名詞」

例 The professor scolded the student 〔sleeping in class〕.

「教授は授業中に寝ている学生を叱った」

② *doing* は動名詞で，前の名詞は意味上の主語⇒「名詞が〜すること」

例 The professor objected to 〈 the student studying abroad〉.
　　　　　　　　　　　　　　　　　　S′　　　　V′

「教授はその学生が留学することに反対した」

③ *doing* は現在分詞で，分詞構文となっており，名詞は意味上の主語（独立分詞構文）⇒「名詞が〜するので／〜しながら／〜するときに」

例 (The student sleeping in class), the professor got angry.
　　　　　　S′　　　　V′

「その学生が授業中に寝ていたので，教授は怒った」

④ S＋V＋O＋C の C に現在分詞⇒「O が〜しているのを V する」

例 The professor caught the student cheating on the exam.
　　　　　　S　　　　V　　　　O　　　　　C

「教授はその学生が試験でカンニングしているのを見つけた」

（第 1 段落第 1 文）

Many languages in the world are gradually dying, but at least one has recently been born, created by children living in a remote village in northern Australia.

▶ children living の部分は，上記①のパターン。

（第 9 段落第 2 文）

It began with parents using baby talk with their children in a combination of the three languages.

▶ parents using の部分は，上記②のパターン。

（第 10 段落第 2 文）

It was not a case of people needing to communicate when they have no common language, a situation that can give rise to a creole.

▶ people needing の部分は，上記②のパターン。

1. 次の和訳と対応する英語の語句を，頭文字を参考にして書き，空欄を完成させよう。

(各1点×20)

①	d	名	方言
②	n	t	名	母語，母国語
③	e	名	存在
④	p	動	保存する，保護する
⑤	c	形	商業の
⑥	s	e	名	太陽光エネルギー
⑦	e	名	電気，電力
⑧	i	動	住む
⑨	s	u	熟	設立する
⑩	f	形	流暢な
⑪ be	d	f	～	熟	～に由来する
⑫	t	名	翻訳
⑬	i	動	示す
⑭	r	形	根本的な，大幅な
⑮	g	名	文法
⑯	s	名	構造
⑰	g	r	t	～	熟	～を生じさせる，引き起こす
⑱	f	t	to	t	熟	時々
⑲	s	形	微妙な
⑳	s	名	生存，残存

2. 次の［　］内の語を並べ替えて，意味の通る英文を完成させよう。(各5点×2)

① The village's remoteness may [to / creation / do / have / the / of / something / with] a new way of speaking.

188

② At least twice, the group walked all [live / to / to / the / they / back / used / way / where], only to be transported back when they arrived.

3. 次の英文の下線部を和訳してみよう。(10 点)

A linguist called Dr. O'Shannessy has been studying the young people's speech in that area for more than a decade and has recently concluded that <u>they speak neither a dialect nor the mixture of languages called a creole, but a new language with unique grammatical rules.</u>

＊creole(名詞)：クレオール言語[ヨーロッパ言語と現地語との混成語]

ディクテーションしてみよう！

今回学習した英文に出てきた語句を，音声を聞いて＿＿＿に書き取ろう。

86　Many languages in the world are gradually dying, but at least one has recently been born, created by children living in a remote village in northern Australia.　A linguist called Dr. O'Shannessy has been studying the young people's speech in that area ❶＿＿＿＿＿＿＿＿＿＿＿ and has recently concluded that they speak neither a dialect nor the mixture of languages called a creole, but a new language with unique grammatical rules.

87　This new language, known as Light Warlpiri, is spoken only by people under 35 in a village of about 700 people in Australia, called Lajamanu.　❷＿＿＿＿＿, about 350 people speak the language as their native tongue.　Mary Laughren, another linguist, values Dr. O'Shannessy's research because "many of the first speakers of this language are still alive," and because "she ❸＿＿＿＿＿＿＿＿＿＿＿＿＿ and document a 'new' language in the very early period of its existence."

88　Everyone in the village also speaks "strong" Warlpiri, an aboriginal language unrelated to English and shared with about 4,000 people in several Australian villages.　Many also speak Kriol, an English-based creole developed in the late 19th century and widely spoken in northern Australia among aboriginal people with many different native languages. The villagers are happy to have their children learn English ❹_____ _____, but they are also eager to preserve "strong" Warlpiri as the language of their culture.

89   The village's remoteness may have something to do with the creation of a new way of speaking. Lajamanu is about 550 miles south of Darwin, and the nearest commercial center is Katherine, about 340 miles north. ❺_____ the village's dirt landing field twice a week carrying mail from Katherine, and once a week a truck brings food and supplies that are sold in the village's only store. Oil and solar energy supply electricity.

90   Lajamanu was established by the Australian government in 1948, without the consent of the people who ❻_____. The native affairs branch of the federal government, concerned about an excess of people and a lack of rain in one area, removed 550 people from there by force to the place where the village is now. At least twice, the group walked all the way back to where they used to live, only to be transported back when they arrived. By the 1970s, villagers had resigned themselves to their new home, and a new council had been ❼_____ a self-governing community authority.

91   Dr. O'Shannessy, who started investigating the language in 2002, spends three to eight weeks a year in the village. She speaks and understands both "strong" Warlpiri and Light Warlpiri, but is not fluent ❽_____ them.

92   People in the village often engage in what linguists call code-switching, mixing languages together or switching from one to another as they speak. And many words in Light Warlpiri ❾_____ English or Kriol. But Light Warlpiri is not simply a combination of words from different languages.   Peter Bakker, a professor of language development, observes that "These young people have developed something entirely new. Light Warlpiri is clearly ❿_____."

93   Dr. O'Shannessy offers this example, spoken by a 4-year-old (an English translation is given below the example):

Nganimpa-ng gen wi-m si-m worm mai aus-ria. (Light Warlpiri)

We also saw worms at my house. (English)

It is easy enough to see several words derived from English. But the *-ria* ending on *aus* (house) means "in" or "at," and it comes from "strong" Warlpiri. The *-m* ending on the verb *si* (see) indicates that the event is either happening now or has already happened, a "present or past but not future" tense that does not exist in English or "strong" Warlpiri. This is a way of talking so different from either "strong" Warlpiri or Kriol ⓫_____ _____ a new language.

94   The development of the language, Dr. O'Shannessy says, was a two-step process. It began with parents using baby talk with their children ⓬_____ the three languages. But then the children took that language as their native tongue by adding radical changes to the grammar, especially in the use of verb structures ⓭_____ _____ in any of the source languages.

95   Why a new language developed at this time and in this place is not entirely clear. It was not a case of people needing to communicate when they have no common language, a situation that can give rise to a creole. New languages are discovered from time to time, but until now no one has been there at the beginning to see a language develop from children's speech. Dr. O'Shannessy suggests that ⓮_____ may be at work. "I think that identity plays a role," she said. "After children created the new system, it became a mark of their identity as being young Warlpiri from the Lajamanu community."

96   The language is now ⓯_____ among young people that there is some question about the survival of "strong" Warlpiri.

"How long the kids will keep their ability to speak two or more languages, I don't know," Dr. O'Shannessy said. "The elders would like to preserve "strong" Warlpiri, but I'm not sure it will happen. Light Warlpiri seems quite strong."

確認問題の答

1. ① dialect　② native tongue　③ existence　④ preserve　⑤ commercial
　⑥ solar energy　⑦ electricity　⑧ inhabit　⑨ set up　⑩ fluent　⑪ derived from
　⑫ translation　⑬ indicate　⑭ radical　⑮ grammar　⑯ structure　⑰ give rise to
　⑱ from time, time　⑲ subtle　⑳ survival
2. ① have something to do with the creation of　(第4段落　第1文)
　② the way back to where they used to live　(第5段落　第3文)
3. 彼らは方言でもクレオール言語と呼ばれる言語の混合でもなく，独自の文法ルールを持つ新しい言語を話している　(第1段落　第2文　抜粋)

ディクテーションしてみよう！の答

❶ for more than a decade　❷ In all　❸ has been able to record　❹ for use in the wider world
❺ An airplane lands on　❻ would inhabit it　❼ set up as　❽ in either of　❾ are derived from
❿ a mother tongue　⓫ that it constitutes　⓬ in a combination of　⓭ that are not present
⓮ subtle forces　⓯ so well established

アドバイス　❷ In の n の音と，all の「オー」の音がつながり，「イノー」のように聞こえる（⇒連結）。

　❼ set up は t が "ら行化" するため，「セラ」のように聞こえる。一般に，/t/ や /d/ の音が母音に挟まれるとら行のような音に変化する（⇒フラッピング［ら行化］）。

　⓮ subtle の b は発音されない。bt のつづりの場合，b は発音されない点に注意（例　debt, doubt）。

出典一覧：
英文1：Economic aspects and the summer Olympics by Evangelia Kasimati, 03 November 2003, International Journal of Tourism Research.　英文2：Republished with permission of Wiley, from Be the Solution: How Entrepreneurs and Conscious Capitalists Can Solve All the World's Problems, Michael Strong, 2009; permission conveyed through Copyright Clearance Center, Inc.　英文3：南山大学　英文4："Getting Started: Know Your Impact" from GO GREEN, LIVE RICH: 50 SIMPLE WAYS TO SAVE THE EARTH AND GET RICH TRYING by David Bach, copyright © 2008 by David Bach. Used by permission of Broadway Books, an imprint of Random House, a division of Penguin Random House LLC. All rights reserved.　英文5：DATESMAN, MARYANNE KEARNY; CRANDALL, JOANN; KEARNY, EDWARD N., DATESMAN: AMERICAN WAYS AMER CULT_P3, 3rd Ed., © 2005. Reprinted by permission of Pearson Education, Inc., New York.　英文6："Everywhere and nowhere" © 2010 Daniel O'Leary, The Tablet. The Tablet: The International Catholic News Weekly. Reproduced with permission of the Publisher. http://www.thetablet.co.uk　英文7：Retreating Himalayan Icefields Threatening Drought in Bangladesh © 2007 Justin Huggler, The Independent.　英文8：The Bright, Shiny Distraction of Self-Driving Cars © 2018 Vikas Bajaj, The New York Times.　英文10：Culture and Technology © 2003.1.15 Andrew Murphie, John Potts, Red Globe Press, an imprint of Bloomsbury Publishing Plc.　英文11：No Smile Limit © Peter Singer, z-kai Solutions Inc.　英文12：LINGUIST FINDS A LANGUAGE IN ITS INFANCY-NICHOLAS BAKALAR